Academic Freedom and the Transnational Production of Knowledge

Public debates on academic freedom have become increasingly contentious, and understandings of what it is and its purposes are contested within the academy by policymakers and amongst the general public. Drawing on rich empirical interview data, this book critically examines the understudied relationship between academic freedom and its role in knowledge production across four country contexts – Lebanon, the UAE, the United Kingdom, and the United States – through the lived experiences of academics conducting 'controversial' research. It provides an empirically informed transnational theory of academic freedom, contesting the predominantly national constructions of academic freedom and knowledge production and the methodological nationalism of the field. It is essential reading for academics and students of the sociology of education, as well as anyone interested in this topic of global public concern. This title is part of the 'Flip It Open Programme' and may also be available as Open Access. Check our website Cambridge Core for details.

Dina Kiwan is a comparative sociologist of education at the University of Birmingham, UK, educated at the University of Oxford, Harvard University, and University College London. She was previously the Centre for Lebanese Studies Fellow at St. Antony's College, University of Oxford, and Associate Professor in Sociology at the American University of Beirut, Lebanon.

'This is a powerful book by a distinguished scholar who has assembled a remarkable collection of compelling reflections on academic freedom and its relationship to the production of knowledge, and to (de-)legitimized and forbidden knowledge. Unlike Western-centric educational studies, this book uncovers many examples not only from the US and UK but also from Lebanon and the UAE of the violation of academic freedom that challenge us all to think through what it would mean for politics, culture and economy in academia.'

Sari Hanafi, Professor of Sociology, American University of Beirut and President, International Sociological Association

'In this brave book Kiwan courageously lifts the lid on the seething cauldron of academic freedom. Armed with her weapons of searing clarity and academic rigour she exposes the political machinations of not only the left and right, but uniquely the gulf between the Global North and South. A much-needed compass in these times of "woke" culture wars on our campuses.'

Heidi Safia Mirza, Emeritus Professor UCL University of London, Author of *Race, Gender and Educational Desire*

'Breaking new ground by deconstructing the methodological nationalism inherent in debates about academic freedom, this text offers fresh insights and new research which de-exceptionalizes the presumed sites of liberal expression. Dina Kiwan has produced a masterfully synthesized account of how knowledge, and those who produce it, are continually under constraint, politically, materially, and institutionally.'

Jasbir K Puar, Author of *The Right to Maim: Debility, Capacity, and Disability*

Academic Freedom and the Transnational Production of Knowledge

Dina Kiwan
University of Birmingham

Shaftesbury Road, Cambridge CB2 8EA, United Kingdom

One Liberty Plaza, 20th Floor, New York, NY 10006, USA

477 Williamstown Road, Port Melbourne, VIC 3207, Australia

314–321, 3rd Floor, Plot 3, Splendor Forum, Jasola District Centre, New Delhi – 110025, India

103 Penang Road, #05-06/07, Visioncrest Commercial, Singapore 238467

Cambridge University Press is part of Cambridge University Press & Assessment, a department of the University of Cambridge.

We share the University's mission to contribute to society through the pursuit of education, learning and research at the highest international levels of excellence.

www.cambridge.org
Information on this title: www.cambridge.org/9781108490283

DOI: 10.1017/9781108780629

© Dina Kiwan 2024

This work is in copyright. It is subject to statutory exceptions and to the provisions of relevant licensing agreements; with the exception of the Creative Commons version the link for which is provided below, no reproduction of any part of this work may take place without the written permission of Cambridge University Press.

First published 2024

A catalogue record for this publication is available from the British Library

Library of Congress Cataloging-in-Publication Data
NAMES: Kiwan, Dina, 1970- author.
TITLE: Academic freedom and the transnational production of knowledge / Dina Kiwan, University of Birmingham.
DESCRIPTION: 1 Edition. | New York, NY : Cambridge University Press, [2023] | Includes bibliographical references and index.
IDENTIFIERS: LCCN 2023029675 (print) | LCCN 2023029676 (ebook) | ISBN 9781108490283 (hardback) | ISBN 9781108748360 (paperback) | ISBN 9781108780629 (ebook)
SUBJECTS: LCSH: Educational sociology.
CLASSIFICATION: LCC LC191 .K559 2023 (print) | LCC LC191 (ebook) | DDC 306.43–dc23/eng/20230814
LC record available at https://lccn.loc.gov/2023029675
LC ebook record available at https://lccn.loc.gov/2023029676

ISBN 978-1-108-49028-3 Hardback

Cambridge University Press & Assessment has no responsibility for the persistence or accuracy of URLs for external or third-party internet websites referred to in this publication and does not guarantee that any content on such websites is, or will remain, accurate or appropriate.

To my parents Angela and Mageed Kiwan

CONTENTS

Foreword by Ahmad Dallal		viii
Preface		xi
Acknowledgements		xiii
1	Introduction	1
2	Constructions of Academic Freedom: Freedom versus Inclusion?	15
3	Constructions of Knowledge	40
4	Producing Knowledge: The Role of the University	64
5	Challenging Knowledge: Internal and External Restrictions	91
6	'Forbidden' Knowledge	112
7	'Legitimate' Knowledge	135
8	Conclusion	159
	References	179
	Index	193

FOREWORD

Academic Freedom and Transnational Production of Knowledge

Ahmad Dallal

The freedom to teach, pursue research and produce knowledge, and communicate the findings of this research is a value we take for granted as a prerequisite for academic excellence and for the creative production of knowledge within the university space. The integrity of academic institutions is usually assessed in terms of their ability to uphold these values. Moreover, in contrast to free speech, freedom in the context of the academy is often coupled with the expectation of responsible, reasonably justifiable academic expression, within the boundaries of the self-regulating norms of disciplinary communities.

These basic verities notwithstanding, the question of academic freedom remains of interest today as it has been in previous years, and continues to be a subject of probing inquiry. In the last three decades, the intensified investment in knowledge economies and the attendant increase in the number of universities globally have renewed the interest in exploring the boundaries of academic freedom within evolving regional and global contexts. Questions of academic freedom are often amplified by reports of threats to academics. Needless to say, there can be no meaningful academic freedom without functioning academic institutions, and as such academic freedom is premised on the safety and mobility of academics and their ability to exchange academic knowledge, just as much as it depends on the absence of internal and external conditions that inhibit the exercise of academic freedom, from university closures to underfunding and job security.

But physical safety is not the only prism through which academic freedom can be assessed. In this timely work, Dina Kiwan provides a compelling argument for a contextualized understanding of academic freedom and, considering the conditions under which it is exercised, further makes a case for an understanding of academic freedom that accommodates the often-assumed conflicting principles of diversity and inclusion. Kiwan's book approaches the topic of academic freedom from four perspectives:

1) Academic freedom within university space: By examining competing conceptions of the mission of a university, as a producer of 'true knowledge'; a contributor to the economic growth of the nation; or an agent of social change, Kiwan questions the notion that the university is a separate autonomous space in which objective knowledge is produced, independent of social contexts and constraints. She also underscores the role of the university in contextualizing academic freedom.

2) Academic freedom and the production of knowledge: Kiwan shifts the focus from a simple consideration of academic freedom as an unfettered form of free speech to an examination of the conditions for the production of knowledge in socially and institutionally diverse national, regional, and international contexts. She interrogates the conditions under which certain kinds of knowledge are legitimized and others are considered forbidden, and argues that legitimate knowledge is not an absolute value but is itself negotiated. And in turn, she maintains, academic freedom is constrained or enabled by these varying constructions of knowledge.

3) Academic freedom and inclusivity: One of the most compelling parts of Kiwan's book is her interrogation of the presumed irreconcilability between principles of academic freedom and principles of diversity and inclusion. By contextualizing academic freedom in relation to other rights, including the right to not be dehumanized, she argues that the complementarity of the principles of academic freedom and those of justice and inclusion is a 'necessary requisite' for the inclusive production of knowledge.

4) Academic freedom in an international context: Most work on academic freedom focuses on the United States and United Kingdom, and discussion of academic freedom in a global context often frames the approach in binary terms, 'contrasting the Global North as a haven for academic

freedom with the Global South as a context that punitively infringes on academic freedom.' In contrast to this one-dimensional narrative, Kiwan takes into account the complexities of globalization and underscores the agency of countries from the Global South in the drive to internationalize higher education. She examines ways in which academics in a global context experience academic freedom, and how this experience affects their lives and impacts their research and knowledge production.

Dr. Kiwan is personally invested in issues of academic freedom in an international context. She builds upon her earlier research and publications on inclusion and citizenship, and draws on her rich experience studying and working in institutions of higher education in the United Kingdom and the Middle East, and on original empirical data from Lebanon, the UAE, the United Kingdom, and the United States, to outline a transnational theory of academic freedom and the production of knowledge, and to offer compelling and original insights on this crucial topic.

PREFACE

I have wanted to write this book for some time. Intellectually, I conceive of it as growing out of my interests in inclusion and citizenship that I have been engaged with over the years, starting with my doctoral research that led to the publication of my first book *Education for Inclusive Citizenship* (Routledge, 2008). On a personal and professional level, having studied and worked in higher education contexts in the United States, the United Kingdom, and the Middle East, I have been struck by how discourses of academic freedom are shaped by the sociopolitical, geographical, historical, and broader geopolitical contexts. Issues deemed to be 'controversial' and broaching the limits of academic freedom in one context are championed in another, challenging discourses as well as quantitative indices of academic freedom that tell a story contrasting the Global North as a haven for academic freedom with the Global South as a context that punitively infringes on academic freedom.

This book aims to problematise this binary, illustrating the range of complex positionalities that arise and, fundamentally, how this links to the production of knowledge . . . or not: what knowledge is legitimised and what knowledge is 'forbidden'. It also recognises academic freedom and the production of knowledge as transnational – crossing national boundaries and contextualised in relation to the globalisation of higher education, our societies, and our mobilities across borders as students and faculty. As I started to engage with the academic literature as well as policy and media publications on the topic of academic freedom, four issues struck me. First, the majority of literature is centred on the United States and the United Kingdom, with a dearth of work on academic freedom in the Global South. Second, there is little empirical literature, and where there is, it is predominantly data collected in the form of surveys, rather than more in-depth sociologically informed ethnographic approaches that are able to engage with the sociopolitical, geographical, and historical contexts informing the nature and state of academic freedom and academics' lived experiences of academic freedom in relation to their research and knowledge production. Third, much of the preoccupation with academic freedom is elided with freedom of speech and related ideological debates between the political Left and Right as to the purposes academic freedom should serve, pitting freedom of speech against respect for diversity. Finally, the link between academic freedom and the politics of the production of knowledge is under-researched and is not typically addressed within a transnational frame.

So I have been driven to challenge the methodological nationalism prevalent in the academic literature and to take the empirical approach of ethnographic interviewing in order to hear the contextualised stories from academics working across a range of 'controversial' fields in the social sciences, humanities, and sciences in a range of country contexts – Lebanon, the UAE, the United Kingdom, and the United States. A number of these academics had worked in more than one of the four countries and/or had experience in conducting research in one of the other country contexts. The choice of these four countries was both intellectually and personally driven: I have been a student in both the United Kingdom and the United States, an academic in the United Kingdom and Lebanon, and my current university has a branch campus in Dubai, and I grew up in the Gulf from 1971 to 1990.

I started this research in 2019, when I collected all the empirical data and then produced a first draft by March 2020. It was at this point that the global COVID-19 pandemic hit, and long COVID, ill health, and homeschooling in lockdown put paid to my plans to submit the manuscript as I had planned in May 2020. It has taken me two years to find the time and intellectual strength to return to this manuscript. Paradoxically, I have also reflected on whether it is the right time for me to write this book on the topic of academic freedom or whether I should wait until I retire, given the range of contentious views and controversial topics addressed throughout the interviews. However, it is not the purpose of the book to engage in the granular arguments within the different controversial topics discussed, but rather the commitment is to interrogate processes of knowledge production that underpin this work; this overrides my anxieties about the potentially polemical engagements with this work. Please read it in this spirit.

ACKNOWLEDGEMENTS

I would like to thank a number of people and organisations who have supported and encouraged me through this research process. Firstly, I would like to thank the interview participants who so generously gave of their time and trusted me to share the often challenging experiences they have had with their research – this book could not have been written without them. I would also like to thank Professors Dave Gillborn and Kalwant Bhopal, Directors of the Centre for Research on Race in Education, at the University of Birmingham, who kindly gave research support in 2019 and 2022, respectively. I am also indebted to Peter Dorman, the former President of the American University of Beirut (AUB), Lebanon, for the opportunity of spending a formative period of my career at AUB from 2012 to 2017, and his wife, Kathy Dorman, for kindly welcoming me and the family to the AUB community. I also thank the then Provost Ahmad Dallal, former Dean of the Faculty of Arts; Sciences Professor Patrick McGreevy; Head of the Department of Sociology, Anthropology, and Media Studies Professor Sari Hanafi; and Professor Samir Kalaf for leading the dynamic intellectual atmosphere AUB is known for during this period and for their intellectual generosity and friendship.

I am grateful to Rebecca Taylor and Isabel Collins, commissioning editors at Cambridge University Press, who have provided empathetic support and guidance throughout the writing process and have been generous in granting two extensions during the COVID-19 pandemic. Thanks also to Rosie Wood who has worked on the index of the book.

Finally, I would not have been sustained throughout this period without the love of my family and friends. I cannot thank my mother and father enough for a lifetime of love and support, the encouragement of my dear friend Soumaya Al-Hajj, and the love and joy my sons Hibou and Magdi bring me.

1 Introduction

1.1 BACKGROUND

Understandings of what academic freedom pertains to and the purposes it serves are contested within the academy, by policymakers and also amongst the general public. There is a dominant discourse that maintains that the principles of academic freedom sit in tension with and are not reconcilable with principles of diversity and inclusion. This leads to the polarised 'either/or' position that either 'freedom' is prioritised or 'diversity'/'inclusion' is prioritised. Traditional libertarian approaches typically place primacy on unfettered academic freedom and free speech, in contrast to approaches emphasising notions of 'responsible' knowledge production and speech, contextualising academic freedom sociopolitically and historically, thereby recognising power dynamics inherent in the production of knowledge. These debates are reflected in the media; for example, in the UK, there are frequent polemical media reports relating to the banning of controversial speakers; the notion of 'safe spaces', 'trigger warnings', and 'wokeness' of those engaged in social justice work relating to racism, sexism, and other forms of difference, heightened particularly in the post-Brexit and Trump/post-Trump contexts; and the rise of right-wing politics in Europe.

Discourses of academic freedom under threat globally are dominant in the media and in policy. The outgoing Vice-Chancellor of the University of Oxford in October 2022 identified academic freedom and freedom of speech as one of 'four key challenges' for the future, stating that she has 'been shaken by the level of threat and harassment experienced in recent years by some of our academics, especially female academics, and especially via social media'

(Christian Institute, 2022). In addition, various UK reports have been published claiming the decline of academic freedom (Policy Exchange, 2019; University and College Union (UCU), 2022). A study conducted in 2020 based on a survey of 1,500 academics reports that two-thirds (67 percent) of UK social scientists state that they perceive their academic freedom to be under threat (Prelec et al., 2022) – although it should be noted that the response rate was only 6 percent. In the United States, it has been reported that academic freedom has declined by 60 percent over the last decade (University Business, 2022). Declines in academic freedom have also been reported in the Middle East, most notably after the initial promise of the 'Arab Spring' that started in 2011, followed by increased crackdowns on campuses since 2013 (Saliba, 2018). Restrictions of academic freedom can range from self-censorship to institutional measures (e.g. ethics committees), denial of work permits or visas for academic visits (Hanafi, 2022), loss of employment, prison sentences, and even death sentences (Saliba, 2018).

The COVID-19 pandemic has had a significant effect globally on the higher education sector in a number of ways, including the closing of universities, delivery of programmes shifting predominantly online, restrictions on mobility, surveillance of academics and students, and constraints over what knowledge could actually be produced and published about the pandemic itself in the context of a global emergency. For example, intellectual rights become an issue with online teaching on Zoom, which is a private company, and issues of regulation of social media, dissemination, and copyright arise (Popovic et al., 2022). The mass shift to online teaching has led to 'enhanced surveillance of academic labour', increased performance management, and widespread loss of academics' jobs (Nehring, 2021). Furthermore, in emergency contexts, dissent is less tolerated, leading to the 'monopolisation of scientific debate' as evidenced during the COVID-19 pandemic (Aperio Bella, 2021).

In this context of a heightened global awareness of academic freedom, there have been various initiatives, ranging from calls to appoint 'free speech champions' in the UK university context (Times Higher Education, 2022) to US scholars launching an 'Academic Freedom Alliance' emerging from scholars at Princeton across the political spectrum (The Guardian, 2022), as well as the grassroots Boycott, Divestment, Sanctions movement, which has increasingly gained support and endorsement from various academic subject associations (Middle East Studies Association (MSEA), 2022), non-governmental organisations (NGOs), student associations, human rights groups, and trade unions. Moreover, the Academic Freedom and Internationalisation Working

Group brings together UK academics and the All-Party Parliamentary Group on Human Rights to strengthen academic freedom in the context of the internationalisation of higher education.

In contrast, however, there is empirical evidence taking a longitudinal historical perspective that tempers discourses of severe declines in academic freedom. A large-scale global study led by the Varieties of Democracy (V-Dem) project systematically operationalised the measure of academic freedom into five quantifiable indicators[1], which were coded by in-country experts from over 180 countries from 1900 to 2019 (Spannagel et al., 2020). The V-Dem project provides a holistic approach to the study of democratisation, based in Sweden, using an innovative methodology collaborating with over 3,500 country experts globally, aggregating judgements on a range of indicators over time; for example, the Academic Freedom Index is a collaborative effort working with 2,000 country experts from around the world (Varieties of Democracy (V-Dem), 2022). They found that globally there was a small decline in academic freedom during the First World War, whilst there was a significant drop during the Second World War. There were some declines in the 1960s and 1970s, associated with restrictions in the Soviet Union, military dictatorships in Latin America, and wider Cold War pressures on academia globally. The 1980s and 1990s showed improvements and stayed at higher levels, associated with democratisation waves until 2013. They have noted slight drops in some variables since 2013, mainly relating to the academic and cultural expression variable, whilst the other four indicators (freedom to research and teach, the freedom of academic exchange and dissemination, the institutional autonomy of universities, and campus integrity) did not show a significant change. These empirical findings support arguments that sensationalist discourses of academic freedom in decline are ahistorical, failing to recognise political and cultural contexts of academic freedom over the last century.

As has been previously noted, there is confusion and misunderstanding about what 'academic freedom' pertains to, how this is distinguished from 'free speech', and what purposes academic freedom might serve, both within the academy and with the general public. As such, it is critically important to understand the difference in these conceptions and for these to be contextualised both historically and geographically. Debates have tended to focus on

---

[1] The five indicators include the freedom to research and teach, the freedom of academic exchange and dissemination, the institutional autonomy of universities, campus integrity, and the freedom of academic and cultural expression.

issues pertaining to free speech, rather than examining academic freedom in relation to the production of knowledge. In the United Kingdom, 'free speech' is defined in the 1998 Human Rights Act as 'freedom to hold opinions and to receive and impart information and ideas without interference by public authority and regardless of frontiers', whilst in the United States, freedom of speech is derived from the First Amendment, which states, 'Congress shall make no law respecting an establishment of religion, or prohibiting the free exercise thereof; or abridging the freedom of speech, or of the press; or the right of the people peaceably to assemble, and to petition the government for a redress of grievances' (Bacevic, 2022). With regard to academic freedom, Bacevic (2022) notes that this was a negative freedom in its original form, in order to stop the Church or government from interfering in teaching and research. Subsequently, in the UK context, academic freedom after the 1988 Education Reform Act came to be constructed in terms of protecting academics from discrimination, given the changes in law removed 'tenure'; in contrast, in the United States, tenure provides that protection to academics. In the Middle East context, academic freedom is defined negatively in terms of 'absence of legal, physical, or structural interference by state or non-state actors in a researcher's personal autonomy, independence and integrity' (Grimm and Saliba, 2017, 47).

The internationalisation of universities poses new challenges to academic freedom and the production of knowledge beyond traditional frameworks of national borders. Internationalisation impacts curricula not only in branch universities but also on 'home' campuses in the context of large numbers of international students; on what can be researched and where; and the different levels of restrictions that can come into play ranging from self-censorship and institutional restrictions to national and transnational mechanisms – including market forces, labour practices, and national and international laws. Beyond the United States and Europe, in post-colonial and post-conflict societies, the role of the university has typically been framed politically in terms of post-colonial independence. Historically, universities have had an important role in shaping a new national identity and the education of local elites. Academics in these societies grapple with their relationship to the academy, their sociopolitical positionality within their societies, and the nature of their contributions to its key debates and challenges, as well as their position in relation to and contesting 'Western knowledge'. Globally, there has been little substantive attention to the changing contexts of internationalisation, massification, and social diversification of higher education in conceptualising and operationalising academic freedom in an increasingly international and transnational higher education context.

This book aims to address this gap and examines three theoretical and interrelated challenges: (i) the presumed dichotomy between freedom and diversity/inclusion, (ii) the relative lack of attention to the role of academic freedom in knowledge production, and (iii) the lack of recognition of the transnational nature of academic freedom. In addressing these challenges, I take an interdisciplinary approach, bringing together theoretical and original empirical work, which often operate in silos in the work on academic freedom. The understanding of academic freedom in a globalised world will be informed by exploring internal (institutional), external (state), and international restrictions imposed on curriculum content, pedagogic practices, and research knowledge production in Western, post-colonial, and branch university contexts.

1.2 METHODOLOGICAL APPROACH

This book draws on research conducted in 2019, which aimed to examine the understudied relationship between academic freedom and the production of knowledge. This project is situated within the context that there is a dearth of integrated theoretical and empirical research on academic freedom and a dearth of scholarship on academic freedom outside the US and UK contexts. Epistemological and methodological issues relating to the politics of disciplinary knowledge and the relationship between inclusivity and academic freedom are also explored. The rationale for the choice of the four countries, namely Lebanon, the UAE, the United Kingdom, and the United States is to explore academic freedom and the transnational production of knowledge in country contexts of varying levels of academic freedom and in contexts outside the usual Global North focus. With original empirical evidence consisting of interviews with academics, supplemented by analyses of relevant institutional, national, and international policy documentation, the book develops a transnational theory of academic freedom, focusing on its role in knowledge production and the ensuing academic and public implications in increasingly internationalised and socially diverse contexts.

A total of thirty-seven Skype interviews were conducted in English with academics or researchers based at or affiliated to higher education institutions in the four countries – Lebanon, the UAE, the United Kingdom, and the United States. Sampling was theoretically driven, with individuals identified through internet searches and networks indicating an interest or engagement with issues pertaining to academic freedom and/or the production of knowledge or first-hand experiences relating to academic freedom challenges. Fields of study spanned the sciences, social sciences, and humanities, including a wide range of disciplines, fields, and topics: bioethics, genetics, psychology, American studies, anthropology, education, gender studies, critical race theory, geography, history, Islamic studies, journalism, law, medical humanities, Middle East studies, philosophy, politics, security studies, sociology, and theology. A number of participants had experiences across different country contexts, either in terms of having worked at various institutions in different countries or in terms of being based at an institution in one country, whilst conducting their research in one or more of the other country contexts. Interview participants were contacted by email, with a letter outlining the project and a request for interview. On reply, the consent form was sent, and a Skype interview was arranged at a date and time of mutual convenience. Signed consent forms were returned by email, and semi-structured interviews typically lasting around forty-five minutes were conducted and, with participants' consent, recorded. Recordings were transcribed, and all data held securely on a password-protected computer. With regard to attribution of the data, participants were offered the choice of one of three levels of anonymity: firstly, the attribution could be partially anonymised, secondly, fully anonymised, or thirdly, with no anonymisation. I have not taken a blanket approach to cite by name those choosing no anonymity for every quote, but rather I have taken the approach of only citing by name if it is relevant, for example, if discussing the individual's work and if they have given such approval.

Participants were asked about their personal experiences, interspersed with questions about their own normative judgements relating to, for example, whether there is some research that should not be conducted. Details of disciplinary background and career history were taken, followed by a discussion about how interviewees understood the notion of 'academic freedom'. Participants were also asked about their own experiences in transnational knowledge partnerships and the politics of knowledge production in transnational perspective.

The data was analysed drawing on constructivist grounded theory (Bryant and Charmaz, 2007), which recognises multiple perspectives and forms of knowledge, and research positionality (Charmaz, 2011). Codes and sub-codes were applied to the data, in part determined by key concepts within the semi-structured interview schedule, and also in terms of emergent codes arising from the interviewees' personal experiences. These codes have informed the structure and chapter contents of the book, which will be outlined in the following section.

This research is located within an 'interpretivist' paradigm (Guba and Lincoln, 1998; Mertens, 1998), where reality is understood in terms of having multiple perspectives and being subjective (Mertens, 1998; Pring, 2000). This ontological stance is reflected by epistemological assumptions underpinning the research and necessarily has implications for the relationship between the researcher and the research participants. Kvale's (1996) metaphor of 'interviewer as traveller' (as opposed to 'interviewer as miner') is apt here, where the interview is construed as a journey taken by two people, rather than as knowledge to be 'discovered'. As such, the interview data enables the interviewer to understand the research participants' contextualised thoughts, feelings, and values.

The value-laden and potentially controversial nature of the topic of academic freedom had implications for research participants' attitudes to confidentiality and anonymity. Perhaps paradoxically, the majority of participants wanted 'partial' or 'full' anonymity, which corresponded to either not making some parts of the interview public or using a level of attribution where they could not be identified (e.g. 'a Lecturer from the United Kingdom').

Given that the sample of research participants came from a range of different national contexts, with different levels of job security, different positionalities with respect to gender and race, or having a high profile within academia, a standard approach of automatically conferring anonymity and confidentiality was not deemed fit for purpose, and therefore anonymity and confidentiality were discussed individually with each participant. This was considered most appropriate, given the potential sensitivity of the interview data and the researchers' ethical responsibility to participants with respect to potential consequences of the interview on participants (Punch, 1994). Two-thirds of participants stated a wish for partial or full anonymity; 20 percent of participants who requested 'full anonymity' were all non-White participants (except one). The majority of those who signed for 'no anonymity' were White males in the United Kingdom and the United States. A small minority of participants asked if they could approve quotations and interpretation of any interview data used. Whilst the researcher has an ethical duty to respect the views of the participants, there is, on the other hand, a danger that data is censored or interpreted by the participants. I took the position that whilst participants have rights with regard to the ethical treatment of the interview data, they do not extend to the interpretation of the data itself (Cookson,

1994). Therefore, I took the approach to always anonymise at the participants' stated level and avoid using any 'off-the-record' comments; however, I did not seek approval from each participant for the use of quotes and my interpretation of this data.

This project aims to integrate theoretical and empirical research in transnational and comparative perspective and the use of qualitative methods to explore contextually rich accounts to complement quantitative approaches to 'measuring' academic freedom. For example, according to the V-Dem index for academic freedom, countries are categorised into five levels based on scores on the various dimensions used to produce quantified measures of academic freedom. According to this approach, the United Kingdom and the United States are in the top level (0.8–1.0), with Lebanon in the second level (0.6–0.8) and the UAE in the bottom level (0.0–0.2) (Education International, 2020). This project enables a rich ethnographic understanding of how varying sociopolitical contexts in global perspective impact constructions and practices of academic freedom and also problematises discourses of academic freedom deficits/lower 'levels' of academic freedom in the Global South as compared to the Global North.

By critically examining academic freedom and its role in knowledge production in four different contexts – Lebanon, the UAE, the United Kingdom, and the United States – this book builds the case for and articulates a transnational theory of academic freedom contesting the predominantly nationally framed literatures on academic freedom and the role of the university in promoting (national) 'citizenship'.

1.3 OUTLINE OF THE BOOK

The book is structured thematically, utilising empirical material from across different contexts, rather than having separate chapters addressing the different national contexts as case examples. This structure reflects the methodological approach, highlighting the transnational nature of knowledge production and the need to interrogate existing models of academic freedom beyond the methodologically nationalist frame.

Chapter 2 addresses a fundamental debate in the field – the presumed irreconcilability of the principles of academic freedom on the one hand and diversity and inclusion on the other. It examines contested conceptions of academic freedom through academics' experiences in Lebanon, the UAE, the United Kingdom, and the United States. This can be understood philosophically in that traditional libertarian approaches typically place primacy on protecting free speech. From this perspective, there is a perceived 'oversensitivity' of those engaged in the disparagingly labelled 'identity politics' and social justice work relating to racism, sexism, and other forms of difference, particularly relevant in the post-Brexit and post-Trump contexts. In contrast, those working in Western democratic societies from marginalised communities have raised concerns that unfettered free speech can be utilised by those traditionally holding power in ways that harm traditionally marginalised communities. In response to such polemical and polarised debates, it has been theorised that the principles of justice and inclusion and the principles of academic freedom are complementary rather than contradictory, in that inclusivity should be conceived as a threshold condition for academic freedom (Ben-Porath, 2017; Callan, 2016). The emphasis on 'dignity safety' (as distinct from 'intellectual safety') is thus presented as a prerequisite for inclusion in the university context and for the practice of academic freedom (Callan, 2016). However, this potential complementarity has not been examined to date in relation to the production of knowledge. This chapter makes the proposition that this complementarity between inclusion and academic freedom is also a requisite in the production of 'inclusive knowledge'.

The relationship between academic freedom and knowledge production is examined in Chapter 3. Various contested constructions of knowledge within and across the different geographical contexts and by discipline are critically interrogated, and the implications of these constructions are considered for pedagogy, research, and understanding of academic freedom. There are different ways of conceiving knowledge. On the one hand, it can be seen as something separate from those who produce it – as something that can be accumulated and that describes reality. On the other hand, it can be conceived in more subjective terms as something that is constructed, negotiated, and embedded in geographical and historical contexts and in relationships of power. The first model would conceive of teaching predominantly in a transmission model, whereas the second model would conceive of a more interrelational and interpretative model. The Humboldtian model of higher education in the early nineteenth century saw teaching as embedded in research. As such, conceptions of knowledge invoke particular conceptions of the value of education and its aims. This is examined in relation to neoliberal discourses of skills, impact and marketability, positionality, and decolonisation of knowledge initiatives. The temporal and geographical positionality of knowledge is critically interrogated, recognising the Western hegemony of knowledge and its production, calling for the need to situate knowledge sociopolitically and historically, and invoking Fricker's (2009) concept of 'testimonial injustice' – a form of 'epistemic injustice' whereby injustice is committed when there is a lack of recognition or credibility as a producer of knowledge. This necessitates the recognition that academic freedom is similarly situated in space and time, with discussions of examples across the four national contexts, as well as the transnational relativity of academic freedom within and between contexts. Debates surrounding the organisation and gatekeeping of knowledge through the disciplines and the rise of interdisciplinarity are also addressed in Chapter 3.

Chapter 4 develops the arguments of Chapter 3, examining discourses of the perceived role of the university and how this relates to constructions of knowledge and its implications for pedagogy, research, and academic freedom. There is an intellectual history of higher education that has typically constructed the university's mission within a national frame, developing informed, critical citizens and promoting democratic societies (Dewey, 1916; Wright Mills, 1959), in the context of the emergence of the modern nation state. The literature on the role of the university in producing critical citizens informs the intellectual history of academic freedom and its contemporary and contested constructions. Yet, it is important to recognise that this theoretical framing assumes a democratic and national context.

Chapter 4 examines the role of the university transnationally going beyond the familiar democratic contexts, taking account of increased globalisation and its sociopolitical implications for academic freedom and the production of knowledge. Internationalisation and massification are trends in higher education globally, where global averages participating in higher education have risen from 19 percent in 2000 and projected to rise to 40 percent by 2030 (Altbach et al., 2009). These populations are more diversified and more mobile. Yet, despite policies aimed at widening participation, there are increasing social and economic inequalities globally, which can also be attributed to the rapid expansion of private higher education. This shift also illustrates shifts in the conception of higher education as a public good to a neoliberal conception of education as a private good. The mission of the university has implications for the nature of the curriculum. University missions illustrate a range of framings in terms of the conceptions of 'truth', 'public good', and 'knowledge economy', and how these conceptions are translated into curricula objectives is explored in Chapter 4.

Many universities in the Arab region developed as public universities, predominantly after the Second World War, when the national university typically became the symbol of new national identity, development, and autonomy in these new post-colonial contexts (Abi-Mershed, 2010). However, in Lebanon, the majority of universities are private as the civil war context (1975–1991) undermined the state's ability to promulgate a state-controlled higher education system (Buckner, 2011). The UAE illustrates the Gulf region's prioritisation of establishing a 'knowledge economy' as illustrated by Dubai's Knowledge Village. Increasingly, Western universities are opening campuses driven by financial interests, including concerns relating to improving rankings through internationalisation. There are a range of forms of internationalisation, including 'offshore/transnational programmes', where a programme is offered in a host institution, typically using curricula from the foreign affiliate institution and taught by its faculty or 'replica campuses' such as New York University Abu Dhabi. There are critiques of such initiatives with debates over whether these represent neo-colonial or imperialist ventures. In contrast, it is argued that the drive for internationalisation comes from within the countries of the Global South, and their policy priorities illustrate their agency in this regard. Other debates relate to the normative implications arising from having branch campuses set in the context of illiberal non-democratic contexts and the implications for the host university's mission.

The university is also a physical space, and it has been argued that higher education is one of the few remaining public spaces where controversial ideas can be explored and students can learn how to challenge authority (Giroux, 2002). In the Arab world, few universities constitute a public sphere for critical debate, although notable exceptions include the American University of Beirut – in particular, before the 1970s, where public intellectuals, reformists, and nationalists engaged with the public on social and political issues of the day (Hanafi, 2011) and have a continued role today (Kiwan, 2017b). The debating of controversial ideas relates to explicitly challenging the notion of 'legitimacy' and links to Chapters 6 and 7, which focus on 'forbidden' knowledge and legitimacy of knowledge, respectively. The perceived demise of the university as a space for controversial debate over recent decades is typically attributed to the marketised logic of neoliberalism not only in the Global North but also in the Global South. However, it is also attributed to perceived tensions in the principles of academic freedom and principles of diversity and inclusion as discussed in Chapter 2.

Chapter 5 considers a range of internal and external restrictions (individual, institutional, national, and international) on the production of knowledge, which is situated in the dominant framing discourse of global neoliberalism. Recognising forms of restrictions on knowledge relates to how academic freedom itself is constructed, invoking the proposition in Chapter 2 that certain prerequisites are necessary for the practice of academic freedom. This requires that we shift the conceptual framework so that rather than thinking in terms of removing restrictions (as something external and separate to academic freedom), we consider certain features of the context necessary in the first instance so that academic freedom can be practiced.

This chapter extends Chapter 4's focus on the university, which considered how university governance and funding mechanisms can constrain academic freedom. Within the university context, it extends its consideration to the role of ethics committees, the bureaucratisation of university procedures, the role of students, and the university environment. The role of self-censorship at the individual level and the notion of scholars' responsibility as well as freedom are critically examined. State-level restrictions, such as the UK's Research Excellence Framework, and US compliance for American universities in the Arab region are considered. The chapter also situates these university-level and state-level restrictions within transnational restrictions, including international law and movement across borders.

Developing Chapter 4's focus on the role of the university in producing knowledge and Chapter 5's focus on internal and external restrictions, Chapter 6 investigates 'forbidden' knowledge, examining the structures and processes that impede the production of knowledge (Kempner et al., 2011). This has also been referred to as 'negative' knowledge, or knowing what knowledge not to produce (Cetina, 1999), as it can threaten powerful interests mediated through institutions and sociopolitical and religious cultures. This can entail both formal and informal processes including self-censorship, peer review, internal university restrictions, and external sociopolitical restrictions. In the Middle East, external limitations on academic freedom imposed by the state are the predominant focus, with examples of news items including state travel bans on professors and students, practices of state appointment of academics, and postponement of student elections in Egypt, jailing of an economist in the UAE for the promotion of democracy and human rights, and monitoring of social media (Fox News, 2018). The question of academic freedom at Western university branch campuses in the Middle East, and of those universities with Western accreditation (Lynch and Ivancheva, 2015), illustrates the importance of examining these issues in transnational perspective. Chapter 6 firstly considers the construct of 'forbidden' knowledge, recognising it not only as gaps in knowledge but also in terms of the structural and sociopolitical processes and consolidating this knowledge as too dangerous or 'taboo' to produce. Drawing on empirical accounts of the daily lived experiences of academics operating within this terrain, four areas of forbidden knowledge – 'bioethics, psychology, and genetics'; 'Palestine'; 'gender and sexuality'; and 'race, religion, security, and extremism' – are explored. In addition, questions of power, agency, positionality, and sociopolitical and historical contexts are critically elucidated.

Chapter 7, the penultimate chapter, turns to the conception of 'legitimate' knowledge, examining constructions of 'legitimacy', drawing on political, sociological, and philosophical conceptions, and in relation to Fricker's (2009) notion of 'epistemic injustice'. The construction of legitimate knowledge in relation to the conceptions of belief, truth, and justification is considered, themselves contested (Goldman, 2002). In addition, debates pertaining to the recent discourses of the democratisation of knowledge, linked to the notion of 'expertise' and 'stakeholders', indigenous knowledge, and decolonising knowledge are discussed. This entails a critical exploration of various types of factors complicit in the formulation of knowledge, including positionality (with respect to class, political interest, gender, race, and so on); university diversity initiatives; disciplinary quality, methodology, and the 'Canon'; skills, employment, and research assessment initiatives; funding and international partnerships; and global legitimating systems such as global university rankings, publication systems, and citation practices. In addition, it is argued that the production of research does not sit outside of these positionalities and the politics of knowledge production. The production of academic knowledge entails social practices of consensus, located within, and validated by an academic community. I propose that 'legitimate' knowledge not only is the opposite of forbidden knowledge but also relates to the dynamics and relationships of power in what knowledge is deemed acceptable and validated. The manner of its dissemination is also considered, with a critical examination of discourses of civility used to discredit critique.

Chapter 8, the final chapter, draws together the findings to argue for a transnational theory of academic freedom and the production of knowledge. Based on original empirical data from Lebanon, the UAE, the United Kingdom, and the United States, I argue for the necessity of taking account of the complexities of globalisation, internationalisation, and the geographical and historical inter-connectivities, as well as the particularities of context. Bringing together Chapter 2 and Chapter 3's examination of the contested constructions of academic freedom and knowledge, I argue that the construct of academic freedom be premised on inclusivity, rather than the principles of academic freedom being construed as in tension with the principles of diversity and inclusion. This argument is developed from the recognition of the positionality of the knowledge producer, thereby positioning knowledge as relational, contextualised, and within the politics of power relations. The elucidation of this context and its dynamics draws on Chapter 4's focus on the university and Chapter 5's consideration of individual, university, state, and international level restrictions and the intersections between this range of restrictions. Chapters 6 and 7 focus on forbidden and legitimate knowledge, respectively. Methodological conclusions drawn from these two chapters further consolidate arguments for a move away from the methodological nationalism underpinning the study of academic freedom and for its transnational framing in theorising the relationship between academic freedom and the production of knowledge.

2 Constructions of Academic Freedom
Freedom versus Inclusion?

> Academic freedom lives in the ethical space between an ideal of the autonomous pursuit of understanding and the specific historical, institutional, and political realities that limit such pursuits.
>
> (Scott, 2019, p. 35)

2.1 INTRODUCTION

This chapter critically examines the constructions and contestations of academic freedom held by academics from a range of academic institutions in Lebanon, the UAE, the United Kingdom, and the United States. As noted in the preceding chapter, in some instances, academics have had a range of experiences working in different academic institutions in more than one of the country contexts, whilst others are based institutionally in one country context but conduct their research and fieldwork in one of the other country contexts. This reflects the transnational reality of contemporary knowledge production and the need to consider academic freedom beyond the dominant methodologically nationalist frame. These constructions of academic freedom are firstly contextualised within a brief intellectual history of discourses of academic freedom and situating key legal and policy documents, including the Statement of Principles on Academic Freedom and Tenure of the 1940 American Association of University Professors (AAUP) within the US context and the University and College Union (UCU) and Academics for Academic Freedom (AFAF) statements in the UK context. These documents are also considered in relation to branch campuses in the Middle East, distinguishing between the different sociocultural contexts of Lebanon and the UAE and the different educational and political histories of their higher education institutions.

As introduced in the opening chapter, a fundamental debate in the field is the presumed irreconcilability of the principles of academic freedom on the one hand and diversity and inclusion on the other. This tension runs through the empirical data of the interviewees' constructions and contestations of academic freedom. Traditional libertarian approaches typically place primacy on protecting free speech; so from this perspective, there is a discourse of perceived 'oversensitivity' of those engaged in social justice work relating to racism, sexism, and other forms of difference, heightened in the context of post-Brexit in the United Kingdom and post-Trump in the United States, as well as the rise of the #BlackLivesMatter movement against racism and the #MeToo movement against sexual abuse, harassment, and rape culture with heightened global public discourses through social media. In contrast to this position, it is argued that free speech has limits, as it can be used by those in power in ways that harm traditionally marginalised communities. In response to these polemical and polarised debates, Ben-Porath (2017) and Callan (2016) have argued that principles of justice and inclusion and the principles of academic freedom are complementary rather than contradictory, where inclusivity should be conceived as a threshold condition for academic freedom. This means that academic freedom requires certain conditions for its operationalisation, with inclusivity being a prerequisite. This inclusion has been conceptualised as 'dignity safety'. The necessary requirement of 'dignity safety' (as distinct from 'intellectual safety') is thus presented as a requisite for inclusion in the university context and for the practice of academic freedom (Callan, 2016). These arguments have primarily been developed in the context of freedom of speech in academic contexts. However, this potential complementarity has not been examined to date in relation to the production of knowledge. This chapter explores this complementarity between inclusion and academic freedom as a prerequisite in the production of 'inclusive' knowledge.

2.2 ACADEMIC FREEDOM: A BRIEF INTELLECTUAL HISTORY

The notion of academic freedom can be traced as far back as Ancient Greece with the account of Socrates defending himself against a charge of 'corrupt[ing] the youth of Athens' (Stone, 2015, p. 1). Yet, it is within the institutional framework of the university that modern constructions of academic freedom are situated. The Latin word 'universitas' refers to 'a number of persons associated into one body, a society, company, community, guild, corporation, etc.'[1]. The earliest degree-granting university in the world is the University of Al Quaraouiyine, in Morocco, founded in 859 AD by an Arab Muslim woman, Fatima al-Fihri. The Al-Azhar University in Cairo, Egypt, is the second oldest university founded as a 'madrasa' (college of law) in 970 AD[2] and is recognised as the first centre of Islamic learning. Madrasas typically consisted of a mosque, boarding house, and a library and maintained by a 'waqf' or charitable endowment. This medieval period from the eighth to the fourteenth centuries is sometimes referred to as the Islamic Golden Age, where scholars from around the world were brought together to gather and translate classical knowledge into Arabic. It was a dynamic period of cultural flourishing of science and mathematics under the caliphates. There was substantial sponsorship of scholars by the patrons of the Islamic empire, with science conducted during this period on a scale larger than at any time in the past or present (Dallal, 2010). According to Makdisi (1981), madrasas enjoyed institutional and professional autonomy, given their establishment based on an Islamic waqf or charitable trust which gave financial security and institutional autonomy. In addition, professors joined guilds which gave them the freedom to teach and pronounce opinions. Whilst scholars enjoyed a certain level of de facto academic freedom, this was not codified in law. The work of hundreds of scholars and scientists in this period is attributed to have had a significant influence on the emergence of science and institutional higher education in medieval Europe.

These universities in Europe were autonomous institutions of power, with their members setting their own rules, yet academic inquiry was limited within the 'truth' of Christianity (Stone, 2015). However, with the rise of science came conflicts with religious authority, and this religious constraint on academic inquiry, also evident in the US context, continued into the nineteenth century (Stone, 2015).

By the nineteenth century, the main restriction to academic freedom was the nation state. In the United Kingdom, academic freedom has historically been taken for granted especially at the oldest elite universities of Oxford and Cambridge. It was not incorporated into law until the 1988 Education Reform Act, which inserted a clause protecting academic freedom. The illusion of a

---

[1] Lewis and Short (1966) [1879].
[2] It gained official university status in 1961 and now also offers secular programmes.

tradition of academic freedom can arguably be attributed to the historical privileges of Oxbridge academics, rather than constructed in terms of de jure academic freedom. Authoring a report on academic freedom in the United Kingdom for the UCU in 2017, Karran and Mallinson describe academic freedom as 'a neglected right in the UK' (2017, p. 2), and they note that there had only been six court cases up until 2002, compared to over 1,000 in the United States. In part, this is attributed to the fact that universities are subject to state law in the United States, whilst in the United Kingdom, most universities were legally protected from any court challenge up until the 1988 Education Reform Act. In addition, there are comparatively minimal de jure protections for academic freedom in the United Kingdom.

The transformation of modern higher education has been strongly influenced by the Humboldtian university, with the idea that the university is premised on upholding academic freedom. Academic freedom entailed both the freedom to teach and the freedom to learn (Dea, 2018). However, the Third Reich erased academic freedom with 45 percent of German professors removed from their positions by 1939. Academic freedom from an authoritarian state influenced conceptions of academic freedom in the 1930s, where, for example, science was under strict state control in the Soviet Union. The role of the state in relation to academic freedom was also exemplified in the US context of McCarthyism in the 1950s and 1960s.

In the United States, the conception of academic freedom is considered to rest on the intersecting foundations of the long European history of intellectual freedom, the notion of an autonomous community of scholars arising from the tradition of universities in the Middle East and Europe, and the freedoms guaranteed by the Bill of Rights of the federal constitution (Fuchs, 1963). Academic freedom has evolved from within the organisational and policy contexts of colleges and universities and contextual challenges over time; initially, this was predominantly in relation to pressures for religious conformity and, subsequently, became more political and economic in nature (Fuchs, 1963).

Moving to the more recent Middle East context, throughout the nineteenth and twentieth centuries, in the context of colonialism, educational reformers worked to develop national educational systems (Abi-Mershed, 2010). Yet, colonial rulers used education as a means of rule, introducing American and European schools and universities in the region. Education has been centrally important in states' nation-building missions, and the national university was often seen as a symbol of new national identity, national development, and autonomy in post-colonial contexts after the Second World War; education has also been seen as representing a vision of equipping youth to construct a new future (Staeheli and Hammett, 2013). Higher educational institutions in the region can be conceived of as sites of 'intersections' between Western (colonial/neo-colonial/post-colonial) and national sociopolitical particularities and discourses on citizenship in the Arab world (Kiwan, 2017b).

In the Arab region, the number of universities has risen sharply since the mid-twentieth century: in 1939, there were a total of ten universities; in 1961, there were twenty universities; in 1975, there were forty-seven universities, and in 2000, there were over 200 universities (Herrera, 2007). In 2013, it was estimated that there were over 600 universities in the Arab world (Abu-Orabi, 2013). 'Imported internationalisation' can be witnessed through the establishment of partnerships with US and UK universities, especially in the Gulf Arab states, as exemplified by Dubai's Knowledge Park and its mission for establishing a 'knowledge economy'. There are eighty universities ranked in the 2023 QS World University Rankings, with twelve universities in the top 500 (Nabeel, 2022). The Arab region has the world's highest international faculty ratios, including the world's top ten in this category; the UAE has nine of these universities and is the country with the world's most international higher education system (Nabeel, 2022). There is a similar demographic for international students with the top five universities located in the Arab region and four of these universities based in the UAE (Nabeel, 2022). Lebanon has four of the region's top universities, with the American University of Beirut (AUB) ranking the highest in the world's top 250–300 (QS World University Rankings 2022).

Lebanon and the UAE illustrate contrasting historical and sociopolitical contexts with respect to higher education and academic freedom. The AUB in Lebanon established by foreign missionaries in the late nineteenth century is equivalent in status to Oxbridge in the region. AUB as a private higher education institution, with its particular history and development as providing an American liberal education, plays a critical role in constructing an educational and social elite. It is based on the US liberal arts model of education and has a US charter and additionally is bound by the AAUP Statement of Principles on Academic Freedom. AUB holds a significant place in the sociopolitical and cultural imagination of Lebanon and the wider region (Kiwan, 2017b). The UAE has both state university and international 'branch' campuses, with one-third of all branch campuses globally located in the Arab region (Miller-Idriss and Banauer, 2011). These branch campuses are complexly positioned between US and UK requirements of academic freedom and local national law.

2.3 KEY LEGAL AND POLICY STATEMENTS

At the international level, the two United Nations (UN) Human Rights Covenants do not explicitly state a protection for academic freedom in 'hard international law', although a range of articles, for example, Article 19 (right to freedom of opinion and expression) of International Covenant on Civil and Political Rights (ICCPR), Article 13 (right to education), and Article 15 (1) (c) (right to freedom indispensable for scientific research) of International Covenant on Economic, Social and Cultural Rights (ICESCR), and General Comments can be drawn upon and have substantial legal weight. Through the European Court of Human Rights, cases relating to free speech in an academic context has resulted in judgements.

In the United States context of faculty being dismissed from universities for perceived infringements against the religious, political, and economic mainstream, as well as it being deemed important to have a national organisation, the AAUP, consisting of leading university and college professors from sixty institutions, was formed in 1915 (Fuchs, 1963). Although the AAUP was predominantly framed as a professional body of broad remit, of note is the 1915 Statement of Principles of Academic Freedom and Tenure, which states that principles of academic freedom in the American context entail freedom to teach, freedom to research, and the freedom of responsibly exercised 'extramural speech'. This 1915 statement emerged in what is referred to as the 'progressive era' in the United States, with the rise of the research university, autonomy of academics, and a distinction between religious and secular frameworks of knowledge (Scott, 2019). The formulation of the statement aimed to protect those perceived to be challenging traditional knowledge and was associated with critical thinking. The case of the dismissal of the economist Professor Andrew Ross at Stanford University in 1900 for promoting – according to the Founder's widow – 'the vilest elements of socialism' when he critiqued business for 'throttling social criticism', in conjunction with seven colleagues resigning in solidarity, is seen to have contributed to a climate of concern for academic freedom setting the scene for the founding of the AAUP (Scott, 2019, p. 43).

The AAUP statement of academic freedom which was codified in the United States in 1915, known as the 1915 'Declaration of Principles', was revised in 1925 to the '1925 Conference Statement on Academic Freedom and Tenure'. A further reworking resulted in the '1940 Statement of Principles on Academic Freedom and Tenure', with further interpretative remarks added in 1970. The AAUP 1915, and subsequently 1940, Statement of Principles on Academic Freedom and Tenure entails the idea that academic freedom is situated between the university and the general public, what Finkin and Post (2009) articulate as the critical role of the university in promoting the 'common good', where 'the common good depends upon the free search for truth and its free exposition' (AAUP, 1940, p. 14).

Reichman[3] (2018) emphasises the distinction between academic freedom and broader speech rights, citing Chemerinsky and Gillman (2017), who distinguish the protection of academic freedom as being 'inextricably linked to professional standards and decorum' from broader speech rights extending beyond into the community. Similarly, Ben-Porath (2017) argues that whilst academic freedom is a core value of the university, this is not the case for free speech. Although the importance of academic freedom is framed in terms of its importance of knowledge for society, which is underpinned by a commitment to scholarly work, freedom of speech is framed in terms of the democratic notion of the freedom to express oneself (Whittington, 2019). Baer (2019) argues that in the university context, rules around speech are not about political correctness but about regulating behaviour, 'just as rules regulate behaviour in any workplace'. According to Baer (2019), trigger warnings, safe spaces, and speech codes are for equitable learning, rather than censorship.

Therefore, the role of the university in protecting the autonomous production of knowledge by academics is presented in terms of promoting the public good, free from infringement from university trustees, which is expressed in the Statement: '... the work of [which] the trustees holds an essential and honourable place, but in which the faculties hold an independent place' (AAUP, 1940, p. 27). Academics in US institutions are considered to be appointees as opposed to employees, invoking the first amendment freedom of speech state protection, tempered by reference to the importance of 'responsibility' for knowledge production and its uses. The role of the trustees is not to reflect public opinion, but rather to protect the university and its scholars from popularist sentiment. Indeed, many social science academics at the turn of the twentieth century were intellectually engaged with socio-economic and political issues of the time, and they came under pressure from university administrators for lacking objectivity. Discourses of 'rationality' and 'objectivity' continue today in contestations of academic freedom and the production of knowledge.

---

[3] First vice president of the AAUP, chair of Committee A on Academic Freedom and Tenure, and chair of the AAUP Foundation.

Academic freedom in the AAUP is presented as essential to 'the advancement of truth' in both research and teaching (p. 14) and is linked with tenure, where 'freedom and economic security, hence tenure, are indispensable to the success of an institution in fulfilling its obligations to its students and to society' (p. 14). The notion of expertise is an important conception invoked in the AAUP statement:

> As scholars and educational officers, they should remember that the public may judge their profession and their institution by their utterances. Hence they should at all times be accurate, should exercise appropriate restraint, should show respect for the opinions of others, and should make every effort to indicate that they are not speaking for the institution. (p. 14)

This statement would seem to be emphasising the importance of the reputation of the institution; yet, the 1970 commentary asserts that the intention of the statement is to underscore expertise, rather than avoid controversial topics.

The AAUP also applies to some American universities outside the United States, such as the AUB in Lebanon. AUB Faculty United is a group of AUB professors who are actively committed to promoting faculty governance of the university and academic freedom. It is an independent, non-political group and is described as 'a Chartered Chapter of the American Association of University Professors (AAUP), a US-based organisation of professors and other academics founded in 1915 to advance academic freedom and shared governance in higher education' (AUB Faculty United, 2017). It has achieved significant success negotiating the reinstatement of tenure and review of contract terms and conditions, and it is also known for its annual Kamal Salibi Award for academic freedom (Kiwan, 2017b).

It should be remembered that the United Kingdom does not have a written constitution with a form of protection for freedom of speech. Historically, academic freedom as de facto rather than de jure has taken precedence. The UCU statement in 2009 on academic freedom invokes the 1988 Education Reform Act as having 'established the legal rights of academic in the United Kingdom to question and test received wisdom and to put forward new ideas and controversial or unpopular opinions without placing themselves in jeopardy of losing their jobs or the privileges they have'. It also draws on the 1997 The United Nations Educational, Scientific and Cultural Organization (UNESCO) recommendation on the status of higher education teaching personnel. This detailed UNESCO statement, which was developed through extensive consultation with academics, legal experts, non-governmental organisations (NGOs), and member states, was issued in 1997, which affirmed that 'the right to education, teaching and research can only be fully enjoyed in an atmosphere of academic freedom ... the open communication of findings, hypotheses and opinions lies at the very heart of higher education and provides the strongest guarantee of the accuracy and objectivity of scholarship and research' (UNESCO, 1997).

The UCU statement asserts that academic freedom is under threat, identifying those threats arising from the 'changing nature of funding in UK research, in particular the dominance of the Research Assessment Exercise' and also the 'introduction of anti-terrorism legislation resulting in self-censorship. The UCU statement (2009) also asserts:

right(s) to:
- freedom in teaching and discussion;

- freedom in carrying out research without commercial or political interference;

- freedom to disseminate and publish one's research findings;

- freedom from institutional censorship, including the right to express one's opinion publicly about the institution or the education system in which one works; and

- freedom to participate in professional and representative academic bodies, including trade unions.

There is reference to the relationship of academic freedom 'being bound up with broader civil liberties and human rights', the 'responsibility to respect democratic rights and freedoms of others', and the development of 'open, democratic and collegial forms of institutional governance ... with staff play[ing] a pre-eminent role in determining the curriculum, assessment standards and research priorities' (The Education Reform Act (ERA), 1988).

With respect to law on academic freedom in the UAE, the UAE is signatory to the UN ICCPR, and ICESCR, yet this must be understood in relation to the sociopolitical and cultural contexts. As previously mentioned, the UAE is home to a large number of branch campuses of UK, US, and other Western universities, and these universities have policies of academic freedom and are obligated under the laws of the United Kingdom, the United States, and other Western countries. Typically, staff handbook advice on academic freedom in UAE universities is framed in terms of personal responsibility and understanding of local cultural expectations and domestic law.

2.4 CONSTRUCTIONS AND CONTESTATIONS OF 'ACADEMIC FREEDOM'

The academic literature on academic freedom is predominantly a US literature, although there is a growing UK academic interest, and it is increasingly of a topic of public contention reported in the UK media and popular press, albeit largely centred on debates of free speech. Reports on infringements on academic freedom globally have also focused on issues of free speech, 'identity politics', and allegations of terrorism. In Turkey, over 5,800 academics have lost their jobs and hundreds have been prosecuted on terrorism charges in relation to the coup attempt in July 2016 (Human Rights Watch, 2018). In addition, academics have reported interference with research especially on Kurdish-related issues, and as a result, a culture of self-censorship is reported. Debates on academic freedom in Hungary have focused on the fate of the Soros-funded Central European University (CEU) in Budapest, Hungary, where the far-right Orbán government forced its closure and, subsequently, the university had to move to Vienna in October 2018. Gender studies came under particular pressure, and CEU was forced to close its Open Learning Initiative, a highly regarded education initiative for refugees and asylum seekers, as well as the Horizon 2020 project on migration policy (Guardian, 2018). In the Arab region, external limitations on academic freedom imposed by the state are the predominant focus, with examples of news items including state travel bans on professors and students, practices of state appointment of academics, postponement of student elections in Egypt (Al Fanar Media, 2017a), and monitoring of social media (Al Fanar Media, 2017b)..

2.4.1 'Free Speech', 'Responsibility', and 'Expertise'

Contested understandings of 'free speech' in relation to academic freedom arise with varying nuances in academics' conceptions of academic freedom: 'I understand academic freedom as allowing academics to express their views on any issue' (Peter Singer, Philosophy of Bioethics, Princeton University, US, p. 1), and 'Academic freedom is a pompous term for free speech' (Dennis Hayes, Professor of Education, University of Derby, UK, and Founder of Academics for Academic Freedom (AFAF) UK, p. 1). In contrast, the notion of 'evidence-based' as a qualifier is introduced in the following conception of academic freedom: 'I can see absolutely no justification for treating the opinions of academics as being in some way more or less sacrosanct than anybody else's opinions, but that's not what I think academic work should be about, and that's why I stressed the evidence-based' (Professor of History, UK, p. 2).

In the US context, academic freedom entails 'responsibly exercised extramural speech' (AAUP). This raises the issue of the interpretation of the notion of 'responsibly exercised', which could allude to the notion of expertise and evidence-based discourse, as well as accepted disciplinary methods:

> Well I think at its most basic, academic freedom is the right to engage in academic scholarship and research and teaching and writing that is protected speech, meaning that if it is politically sensitive, if it's politically unpopular, that it is permissible and that one cannot get fired from their job for challenging the authority of the university, of colleagues, of the state itself. But also recognising that academic freedom is limited to academic scholarship and not to just any crazy opinion, but it needs to conform to academic methods and scholarly methods that are normative within fields of academia that we work in. So it's not that you can – academic freedom does not protect, in my view, hate speech that is not rooted in academic method or in academic argument. It does not protect ... ideas that can be debunked entirely by the academic method. (Professor of American Studies, University of New Mexico, US, p. 2)

The notion of the pursuit of 'truth' is also linked to the rationale for universities, academic freedom, and the co-construction of knowledge in the process of knowledge production: 'Well I think in the context of the university, universities exist for the pursuit of information and the pursuit of truth' (Emeritus Professor of Law, George Washington University, US, p. 2).

The notion of responsibility necessarily introduces subjective judgement and relativity to the concept of academic freedom, where this judgement relates to the notion of 'public good'.

Talking about the US context, academic freedom is distinguished from freedom of speech and linked to notions of the role of the university to promote a public good:

> Well I think one has to distinguish academic freedom from other types of free speech in the United States because I think the university in the United States – it's probably true in other places – but you know I'm here and I know this perspective well. I think academic freedom in the United States, or academic universities exist for the public good. Whereas speech generally does not have to serve a public good. (Emeritus Professor of Law, George Washington University, US, p. 2)

Similarly, the notion of public good is expressed in terms of limits against harm:

> So I understand academic freedom as the right to enquire into research, talk about, explore through one's teaching any, you know a range of different ideas and areas of interest including ones that might be controversial, and that one should have the freedom to do so. Provided of course that one abides by the codes of ethics and so on. So I do not understand academic freedom as being a complete freedom of speech with no limits. I think like all freedoms it's limited by potential harm done ... So I think there are grey areas around it. (Professor of Education, UCL, UK, p. 2)

Responsibility is contrasted with privilege, with a critique of the statement from UK AFAF: '... I think that [the] responsibility is an important component of this. It's obviously omitted from the statement from Academics for Academic Freedom, just passed over completely that notion of responsibility. It's not a privilege but a responsibility' (Professor of History, UK, p. 2).

Privilege as an entitlement given to individuals as academics is constructed as stemming from the historical conception of the university as a privileged space:

> If it's about your freedom as a Cambridge Don to drink your wine and have your dinners and to teach what you want to teach without any recourse to thinking about inclusion and diversity and the other kinds of knowledges that, huge swathes of other kind of knowledges that are completely excluded you know. And you call that academic freedom? (Professor Emeritus, Sociology, UK, p. 5)

Academic freedom is situated in a contextualised space and time – geographically, historically, and sociopolitically – in contrast to normative theoretical approaches constructing an ideal of academic freedom. The contextualisation of the university similarly identified as a privileged space, and one which is embedded in its particular space and time, is discussed in Chapter 4, which focuses on the role of the university.

The idea of 'responsibly exercised' academic freedom is elastic enough to refer to the form of delivery, invoking notions of 'performances' of 'civility', 'reasonableness', or 'rationality'. Understandings of academic freedom also entailed the ability to exercise academic freedom without fear. The affective dimension to academic freedom will be examined in greater depth later in the chapter on the relationship of affect to academic freedom and the production of knowledge.

2.4.2 Power, Knowledge, and Morality

The elucidation of the differential distribution of academic freedom is illustrated through reference to the positionality of the academic within society and in relation to their research. According to Lubin, he reflects on his own positionality to his research in the field of Transnational American Studies, focusing on the social and political history of US foreign relations in the Middle East: 'In my case, what I've experienced, is that being Jewish and being identified as a white male in the United States affords me a level of protection that Palestinian or any Arab or Muslim scholars do not have' (p. 4).

The power of disciplinarity is also identified, where Lubin describes how 'American Studies is often chastised within the United States as "anti-American" studies' (p. 2), as it entails a 'cultural studies critique of government power ... articulated in race and gender and sexuality and class and on and on' (p. 2). Despite intended US foreign policy intentions, the discipline has been transformed in its exportation to the Middle East. At the AUB, for example, Palestine and Edward Said's work on Palestine have significant import, in contrast to being an 'absent present' in US-based American studies programmes (Lubin, 2016, citing Mahmoud Darwish). The role of subject associations is also drawn into disciplinary battles relating to academic freedom, as illustrated when the American Studies Association passed a resolution in support for the Boycott, Divestment, Sanctions (BDS) movement, consolidating the sentiment that the 'field of American Studies once again, as not only anti-American, but somehow I think being anti-Israel or critiquing Israel is in a strange way seen as being anti-American too'. The role of disciplinary subject associations in the global BDS movement, initiated by Palestinian civil society in 2005, also illustrates how disciplines 'at the centre' have been affected with the 'transnational' turn, the American Studies Association, the Association for Asian American Studies, the American Anthropology Association, and the International Sociological Association vocalising support for the BDS movement.

The power and accompanying sense of security and confidence that comes with academic seniority are also invoked as important:

> Well, you know that institutional frameworks are pushing us to publish as fast as we can, right, in as great a quantity as we can. So I mean I guess this is easy for me to say, right, because I have tenure and I've been promoted to full Professor, so I have much more academic freedom than I did before tenure. So that's another thing about academic freedom, that it's very contingent upon one's rank and one's institutional position and privilege, so I've got a lot of institutional privilege and I therefore have the ability to say, for example, I worked on a book proposal for a while with a Tribe in Oregon and after a while the Tribe said 'you know what we'd

really rather publish this ourselves'. And that's, I'm in a position to say 'absolutely, that's your right'. Whereas I've heard stories of junior scholars, even junior Native scholars who have been in a position where they work for 8 years on a dissertation, getting really amazing information and the Elders say 'we do not want you to publish this' and then that scholar is out of a job. (Professor of Women and Gender Studies, US, p. 3)

The moral responsibility that is perceived to come with the privileges of seniority is elaborated in both the US and UK contexts: 'I feel really strongly that as a tenured Professor it's part of my job to speak out about inequities that I see in the institution, that the junior faculty who do not feel as empowered to speak, it's my job to advocate for them and speak out for them' (Professor of Women and Gender Studies, US, p. 4). Similarly: 'I feel I have a responsibility to speak out, so I'm lucky enough to be in a fairly senior position on a permanent contract' (Professor of Education, UCL, UK, p. 8). Yet this positionality and moral responsibility is gendered: 'I see it as a kind of feminist principle as well, because it is mostly women. It's overwhelmingly women who are being targeted.' (Professor of Education, UCL, UK, p. 8)

However, there is frustration at the perceived tokenism of bestowed privilege in a controlled setting arising from positionality as a Black women. In addition, the psychological burden of colluding in maintaining the status quo is conceived of as significant moral compromise. The perceived powerlessness further compounds this burden:

You're a pawn in that game ... I can have a lovely seminar where we are just getting in there, we are talking about using critical race theory and we are talking about institutional racism and how it works and how it affects us and the microaggressions or you know, and we walk out feeling empowered amongst ourselves, but it's just an illusion because we are not empowered and nothing has changed you know. (Professor Emeritus, Sociology, UK, p. 5)

The idea of a 'psychological contract' is proposed as a way of accommodating teaching and research in the UAE context: 'As with the legal contract an employee makes with his employer in the Gulf there are psychological contracts we make as expats. Perhaps complete academic freedom is one of these' (Medical researcher, Dubai, pp. 4–5). Invoked here are two forms of contract – the first between the 'employer' and 'employee'. The use of this language contrasts with the language of the university appointee referred to in the US context in the AAUP Statement. The language of employer/employee, in contrast, does not denote individual autonomy. In addition, the importance of legal status – citizenship – is implicitly invoked as a second form of contract entered at an individual level implying personal responsibility as a non-Emirati or 'expat'. As previously discussed, the notion of personal responsibility in choosing to work in the UAE is commonly referred to in branch campus staff handbooks.

2.4.3 Contextualisation and Preconditions

The role of the university as the context within which academics practice their academic freedom is the focus of Chapter 4. In this section, the university as a cultural context is considered in terms of how inclusivity relates to academic freedom and theories of knowledge production. The history of missions of the university can be conceptualised as being civic/inclusive, research oriented as in the Humboldtian tradition, or as a mentor for 'select elite students' as in the traditional Oxbridge model (MacFarlane, 2007), all of which have varying implications for understanding academic freedom. There is a history of higher education being conceived as playing a role in the promotion of democratic societies (e.g. Dewey and C. Wright Mills), emphasising the importance of informed and critical citizens, in relation to the emergence of the modern nation state, and now evident in discourses on global citizenship (Kiwan and Evans, 2015). In some discourses on the 'civic university', a liberal education is seen as central in the production of 'a particular kind of critical citizen', whilst other discourses call for a more radical 'transformation of higher education itself' (Biesta 2007, p. 470). It has been argued that higher education is one of the few remaining public spaces where unpopular ideas can be explored, and students can learn how to challenge authority (Giroux, 2002).

In the university context, Callan (2016) and Ben-Porath (2016, 2017) have proposed that inclusivity or access is a threshold condition for academic freedom. Callan (2016) proposes the concept of 'dignity safety' (as distinct from 'intellectual safety'), a necessary condition for inclusion in the university context. Unless the condition of dignity safety is reasonably upheld, there is a threat of dehumanisation that undermines inclusive and equitable participation in the intellectual life of the university, necessary for the proper practice academic freedom. Ben-Porath (2017) proposes that the principles of justice and inclusion and the principles of academic freedom are complementary rather than contradictory. Whilst Ben-Porath and Callan are focusing on the student-learning experience and free speech, a normative argument can be made for what I call 'inclusive knowledge' – both in terms of principles of equality and inclusion and in terms of the search for knowledge. As such, an inclusive context in which an academic conducts their research can be seen as a necessary precondition for the inclusive production of knowledge, as well as the rationale for decolonising the curriculum, which will be critically examined in Chapter 3.

Discussing the relationship between principles of academic freedom and principles of diversity and inclusion, it is argued that academic freedom is being 'weaponised': 'This whole debate about academic inclusion and diversity, you know, was an attack on academic freedom, it's just like, it's a huge mirage where they just want to do what they want to do and they do not want to do what you, you know, they do not want to be more inclusive. And that's it you know' (Professor Emeritus, Sociology, UK, p. 5). The perception is that there is a disingenuous use of academic freedom by a 'beleaguered old guard' (Professor of History, UK, p. 7) reacting to a sense of 'Whiteness under threat' (Professor Emeritus, Sociology, UK, p. 11), at odds with the spirit of 'the theory of academic freedom as it was articulated by Progressives' (Scott, 2019, p. 47). Scott argues that academic freedom as propagated by the Right is conceived in terms of 'the absence of any restraint' (p. 116) where 'free speech is the mantra of the Right, their weapon in the new culture war' (p. 114).

However, whether an inclusive context is actually possible given the institutional history of the university as a 'White male patriarchy' is a frustration expressed, in relation to race and gender:

> I've been a brown body allowed into mega-ly white institutions here and that crashing sense in which you have to conform to get on, and all that you give up for that ... You've got to comply. And the system is bigger than us and we are just, like I said, these little fleas running around you know, allowed to spout out whatever we want but you know we are not changing it. I mean one of the things that I think – and I've seen this amongst so many of my female doctoral students – I mean the system is so against women having kids ... You get out of the system for a couple of years to bring up your children you will not get Chair, you cannot you know. So you can let women into the system but we cannot, when they reach thirty five and they are like either I have a child or I do not have a child, you know I cannot have a child and have this job. The pressure is too much. But I think it's an interesting thing that the structures remain so, they are so solidified, so invisible, because the bodies are changing, not the structures. (Professor Emeritus, Sociology, UK, p. 8)

The notion of a hierarchy of rights, where academic freedom is contextualised in relation to other rights, is advocated in support of creating an inclusive environment for the inclusive production of knowledge: 'I think that academic freedom exists in a hierarchy of various rights, and it's not at the top' (Professor of American Studies, New Mexico, US). Echoing the logic of Callan (2016) and Ben-Porath (2017)'s notion of 'dignity safety', the rights of those not to be dehumanised is prioritised as an essential precondition for the exercise of academic freedom.

A related conception to the idea of the hierarchy of rights is raised in the challenge to the emphasis on constructing freedom in terms of 'freedom to'. In contrast to conceiving academic freedom in terms of 'freedom to', the conception of 'freedom from' emphasises freedom from harassment, assault, and dehumanisation. Whilst scholars may conceive of academic freedom in terms of freedom to publish their research, in the field of US indigenous history, the indigenous community may take the view that 'There may be stories that are sacred, that are not supposed to be shared outside the community' (Professor of Women's and Gender Studies, University of New Hampshire, US, p. 2). In this context, academic freedom can be conceived as the collaborative process with the community being researched and 'to be guided by them in what is appropriate for distribution, rather than conceiving this as an infringement on academic freedom' (Professor of Women's Studies and Gender Studies, University of New Hampshire, US, p. 2).

In much of the literature, the state is typically invoked as the legal framework for academic freedom. This dominant national methodological lens can also be seen in terms of the missions of universities historically in both the Global North and the Global South, where the university aims to inculcate a particular type of predominantly *national* citizen[4]. Academic freedom has also been dominantly studied at the level of the national state, with some comparative studies between nations. 'Your responsibility is to deal with academic freedom where you live' (Professor of Education, University of Derby, UK, p. 13). This approach does not engage with the internationalisation of higher education, as well as with the transnational nature of academic freedom and the production of knowledge. The nationalistic lens can also obscure how academic freedom is practiced for those in legal precarity, such as refugee scholars and academics working under military occupation, and is also illustrated in contested debates about the BDS

---

[4] The rise of internationalisation in higher education is increasingly linked to discourses on global citizenship, and its implications of academic freedom will be discussed in Chapter 4.

movement. According to a UK researcher in the field of medical anthropology conducting research in the West Bank: 'The "state" was not much involved in the research directly but had considerable impact in other ways. The Israeli occupation hampered the freedom of movement and later they bombed Ramallah police station where statistics were being kept.' Judith Butler (2015) makes the case for certain preconditions to be met for the practice of academic freedom. She argues for a broader notion of academic freedom, where freedom from violence, freedom from hunger, and freedom of movement both internally and across borders are recognised as integral preconditions for academic freedom. The dominant notion of academic freedom implicitly requires legal citizenship as a prerequisite to practice academic freedom – Arendt's 'right to have rights'. This national model of academic freedom does not take account of the transnational realities of the practice of academic freedom and the production of knowledge.

The notion of the necessity of preconditions is similarly invoked for academic freedom in UK and US universities with respect to marginalisation by disability, gender, sexuality, race, and religion. Andrews (2018) and Reay (2018)'s discussion of racism in UK universities invoking Lorde's book, *The Master's Tools Will Never Dismantle the Master's House*, logically suggests that academic freedom under such conditions cannot be met. Similar arguments framed in terms of infringement of human rights are also raised in relation to UK and US branch campuses in the Gulf. According to a UCU Branch President: 'It tends to be academics who bring that [LGBTQ rights] up because they are thinking really about their teaching' (p. 3).

2.4.4 Individualisation and Psychologisation

The banning of controversial speakers, the concept of 'safe spaces' (*Independent*, 30 June 2017[5]), and 'trigger warnings' (*Telegraph*, 11 May 2016[6]) have been perceived to infantilise students and taken as indicative of a wider 'psychologisation' and 'medicalisation' of society (Furedi, 2017). Discourses using terms such as 'snowflake' and 'woke' arose in the context of Brexit and Trump, to denigrate the perceived 'oversensitivity' of the student generation as well as those on the ideological Left working

---

[5] www.independent.co.uk/news/education/education-news/university-safe-spaces-academics-professors-fear-lose-jobs-students-free-speech-political-correct-pc-a7815991.html.
[6] www.telegraph.co.uk/news/2016/05/11/trigger-warnings-at-oxford-would-threaten-academic-freedom-and-i/.

on social justice issues relating to racism, sexism, and other forms of difference (*Guardian*, 28 November 2016[7]). These media discourses and policy responses in the United Kingdom and the United States have intensified in response to the #BlackLives Matter and #MeToo social movements.

It has been argued that there has been a therapeutic turn in higher education in UK and US contexts. This is an analysis understood predominantly at the level of the individual, where it is argued that the university is protecting students from distress. As such, the distress is understood as an individual emotional reaction, constructing an infantilised conception of the student as vulnerable: 'I think we were promoting the idea that there was a diminished concept of human beings being promoted in a seemingly caring way. So to see people as potentially victims and it seems very protective' (Professor of Education, University of Derby, UK, p. 4). Whilst not dismissing the therapeutic turn, in terms of both issues of universities' legal responsibilities and market-driven interests in psychological services, what this does not take account of is the diverse range of contextualised lived experiences and positionalities of students. As introduced in the previous chapter, it has also been argued that taking account of such positionalities with trigger warnings, for example, is about inclusive teaching practice and rules in the workplace rather than censorship (Baer, 2019). As such, conceptions of dignity, both individual and group dignity, also underpin discourses of inclusion, as illustrated in Callan (2016) and Ben-Porath's (2017) call for environments that promote 'dignity safety', as opposed to enabling environments of violence and dehumanisation.

Yet, what does this mean for practice? According to a Professor Emeritus of Law (George Washington University US), safe space discourse is 'not a realistic discourse'. Instead, she argues for:

> the ability to access infrastructure. And what the privileged students have is support from infrastructure. So they are free to say certain things without having an impact, economic impact, social impact, et cetera. And certain things that are said about them have no impact because they have access to infrastructure. So my position is to increase access to infrastructure, so that again, more counter speech can be produced, so that those students also have support, rather than the university saying 'Oh there's certain things you cannot say' you know and the like. (p. 10)

---

[7] www.theguardian.com/science/2016/nov/28/snowflake-insult-disdain-young-people.

The invoking of infrastructure identifies the issue at the level of institutional inequality, counterbalancing the individualising therapeutic discourse that locates responsibility at the level of the individual.

Whilst concerns are expressed with regard to the infantilisation and medicalisation of student lives, students at the same time are criticised for being troublesome consumers, imbued with a power to complain and censor. Sara Ahmed's blog on 'Against Students' is highlighted as an explication of how 'neoliberalism operates to contain dissent from students, so that idea of safe spaces and students are, what the system does, it sees them as complaining or difficult or consumer led and it makes students into the bogeyman if you like' (Professor Emeritus, Sociology, UK). So, here we paradoxically witness both the decontextualised individualisation and the pathologisation of the dissatisfied student or 'difficult' academic by the same critics of the medicalisation of society and university life.

2.4.5 Civility, Affect, and Power

There is an intellectual history and practice of ascribing negative characteristics to 'emotion', set up in contrast to 'rationality'. This is evidenced in Enlightenment theories of natural rights constructed as a logic of denying women human rights based on the premise that women lacked rationality, and, similarly, colonial and orientalist discourses have typically constructed their colonial subjects as lacking rationality and by extension – conceived to be less 'civilised' and less human (Said, 1978). Ahmed (2014) has also discussed how there is a dominant Western conception that emotions are 'primitive', with an implied hierarchy between cognition and emotion. Not only are emotions feminised and othered, but they also are often presented as something undesirable to be controlled, with the expression or 'leakage' of emotion constructed as unintended consequences of this lack of control (Kiwan, 2017a).

A mutually reinforcing relationship between civility and rationality is invoked, where visible affect or perceived lack of civility is constructed as literally being 'uncivilised' – carrying with it the history of colonial discourses and as evidencing irrationality. In an article by Professor of Theology, Nigel Biggar, of the University of Cambridge, United Kingdom, he discusses Cambridge's decision to rescind its offer of a visiting position to Professor Jordan Peterson, a Canadian Professor of Psychology with controversial views on transgender, Islam, and race, and he contrasts it with the reactions to his Economic and Social Research Council–funded project 'Ethics and

Empire' that courted some controversy with its focus on examining the benefits of Empire (Biggar, 2019). Referring to Dr. Priyamvada Gopal's (University of Cambridge) criticism of his research project on Twitter, he expressed surprise that the project was considered contentious, as well as disapproval of the *manner* in which it was expressed:

> This occurred in December 2017, when my 'Ethics and Empire' project attracted three online denunciations, one of them led by Dr. Priyamvada Gopal, Reader in Cambridge's Faculty of English and a Teaching Fellow at Churchill College. Dr. Gopal's earliest tweet thus ran: 'OMG. This is serious shit. We need to SHUT THIS DOWN.' All this in reaction to my **modest** view that 'empire' can mean a variety of things, is capable of good as well as evil, raises ethical questions worth thinking about, and requires sophisticated moral evaluation.
>
> My complaint was about the uncivil manner.
>
> Peter de Bolla, Chairman of the Faculty, kept safely clear of any moral judgement, arguing that such speech is simply conventional for its medium, albeit in tension with 'accepted manners or styles of address' in more traditional contexts. (Biggar, 2019)

Biggar defines Dr. Gopal's response as 'uncivil', where the emotive use of language is disapproved of and contrasted with the perception of his rational and objective view of Empire. The notion of incivility also arises in how academics working on issues of social justice, race, and gender are perceived. According to an Emeritus Professor of Sociology of race in the United Kingdom: 'We're not legitimate, we are difficult and angry people. This whole idea of freedom of speech is dangled like a carrot in front of us. It's the yardstick, the thing we have to live up to, but the game is not an equal level playing field at all' (Professor Emeritus, Sociology, UK, p. 9). The objective rationality of traditional disciplines is also contrasted with the subjective and emotive research and teaching relating to social justice: 'So Women's studies, African American studies, Native American studies, these are all grievance studies' (Professor of Women's and Gender Studies, University of New Hampshire, US, p. 5). The term 'grievance studies' constructs these fields in direct contrast to the perceived traditional, objective, and rational disciplines as subjective, emotional, and ideologically driven, where those conducting this work are 'complainers' and where Sara Ahmed's work on complaint is referred to: 'this is Sara's thing. You say there is a problem. You become the problem' (Professor Emeritus of Sociology, UK, p. 9).

Biggar (2019) goes on to contrast his perception of Cambridge University's position as one of 'serial inactions in the case of Dr. Gopal alongside its precipitate action in the case of Professor Peterson', which he sums up as:

> the University does in fact discriminate on the unjustifiable grounds of race, gender, and above all morals and politics. If you are non-white, female, and aggressively 'woke', then you'll be accorded maximal benefit of doubt, given a pass on official norms of civility. However, if you are white, male, culturally conservative, and given to expressing reasoned doubt about prevailing mores, you'll be given no benefit of doubt at all. And, should you do so much as *appear* to transgress ill-conceived norms of inclusiveness, you'll be summarily and rudely excluded.

The performance of civility is weaponised against inclusivity and equality in this account; whilst the claim that 'ill-conceived norms of inclusiveness' result in exclusion, accusations of 'incivility' are used to 'shut down' critiques of research similarly perceived not only to be 'ill-conceived' but also to be harmful.

Furthermore, 'virtue' is linked to civility when Biggar (2019) argues that Dr. Gopal sets a bad example to students, instead of teaching 'the students the virtues of courage, self-restraint, patience, and critical openness necessary to cope with alien ideas liberally and responsibly'. The discourses of 'civility' and 'virtue' are imbued with a moral weight intended to 'shame' the 'other' to 'be a good sport and play by the rules', invoking the language of privilege of class, gender, race, and empire. Yet, similarly, those championing social justice and inclusion also use a 'virtues' discourse, which is also seen as problematic: 'We have a problem with kind of a fanatical sense of "I know what's right. I'm more virtuous, because of my perceived superior virtue I get to dictate what gets taught, how it gets taught, what gets written and whether something is or is not legitimate research". I think it's dangerous' (Professor of English, University of Arizona, US, p. 7).

The focus on etiquette in the public *performance* of academic debate problematises the expression of emotion, which is conceived as illustrating individual lack of control. Yet, Ahmed (2014, p. 14) argues that it is critical to recognise that emotions are social, political, and cultural practices, rather than thinking primarily in terms of an individual's psychological state; as such, this necessitates the recognition of relations and dynamics of power and the 'public nature of emotion and the emotive nature of publics'. Emotions as a public performance entails how discourses of class, gender, and race intersect with the politics of emotion (Athanasiou et al., 2008): 'You name the problem. So I will name racism then I'm the difficult, angry person' (Professor Emeritus, Sociology, UK, p. 9).

The critique of emotionality is further extended where 'emotive' reactions on issues of inclusion are constructed both as an individual psychological weakness and as a manipulative vulnerability: 'the cry, that's offensive was closing down debate, and also tied to some work I was doing on *The Dangerous Rise of Therapeutic Education*, so the idea of a safe space ... that you must not say anything that emotionally upsets anyone' (Dennis Hayes, Professor of Education, University of Derby, UK, p. 1). However, academics who are the targets of intimidation, death threats, and rape threats, often through the medium of social media, express fear:

> People speaking at those events have been bullied, physically bullied, targeted with threats. Meetings have been shut down. I mean any meeting that I've attempted to go to has had last minute venue changes because of bomb threats to the venue. Quite aggressive people sort of demonstrating outside and shouting targeted abuse and harassment at people. I personally know people who have had death and rape threats on social media, from activists who are aware of the stance they are taking. (Professor of Education, UCL, UK, p. 4)

This visceral experience of fear is also expressed in the accounts of academics in the United States and the UAE as well as the United Kingdom: 'I think we are all kind of terrified, you know, of being kicked out of the country' (Professor of Sociology, UK, formerly UAE academic, p. 11). Similarly, in the US context, a Professor of Women's Studies recounts her experiences having criticised the wearing of monkey suits on campus:

> There were posters put around our campus accompanied by bananas and I think pacifiers ... with my face and some graffiti at the library ... I got death threats and hate mail and threats of particularly gender violence that were frightening and it was just a barrage of frightening stuff. (p. 2)

This gendered nature of the experience of intimidation and insecurity, especially in the United Kingdom and the United States, was noted: 'It's overwhelmingly women who are being targeted' (Professor of Education, UCL, UK, p. 8).

In contrast, legal status was often perceived as the greatest source of insecurity. According to a UK-based European Muslim female academic, formerly an academic based in the UAE, there is a heightened sense of insecurity in the form of job precarity in the United Kingdom relative to the UAE:

> A lot of the people who are working in these places [UAE] do have their lives there and do have their families there, and they do like living there very much. And this is not just like from a Western perspective, just because of the tax-free salary, but a less precarious academic life. A lot of the people have married to people that they have met in these places. They gave birth to their kids in this place so they have a very emotional you know, sense of belonging to the city that is beyond this milking this system from an expat point of view. So, which is why I mean, instead of coming back to Europe and working with year contracts they are very happy to stay there. (pp. 8–9)

Another dimension of insecurity relates to a sense of heightened scrutiny of academics' political positions because of assumptions made about their positionality, as seen in the following excerpt from a Muslim UK-based academic:

> I do not or I cannot be as vocal about certain issues such as military interventions in certain parts of the Middle East and how that is sort of like justified through like orientalist discourses in the West. I always feel that I have to sort of dim it down because they may think that that is because of my sort of imagined common identity with these people that inhabit these areas. So I feel so much more 'surveillanced' somehow. (Lecturer in Migration Studies, UK, p. 10)

In addition, a sense of precarity in academia comes for some based on the contentious issues they work on, described as a 'global trend of, this precarity, increasing precarity in academic work which I think also relates to the issues that you are working on which is academic freedom' (Lecturer in Migration Studies, UK, p. 9). Many of the interviewees expressed fear of losing their jobs in the United Kingdom, and this fear was also expressed by non-tenured academics in the US context.

This contextualised precarity and its relationship to the emotive experience of academic freedom have not been experienced and are not recognised by those whose positionality carries with it a sense of safety and power as is more likely the case for White male academics, who then take this as universal. For example, referring to the issue of consent and level of attribution for this book project, one UK-based White male professor expressed the following:

> But any academic who wants to keep their views anonymous is part of the problem. How cowardly is that? Academics, they are not actually under threat, they can speak up but they just will not and I think it pays off in the sort of cosy contentiousness and basically do not challenge the institution and the institution does not challenge you. (Dennis Hayes, Professor of Education, University of Derby, UK, p. 4)

2.5 CONCLUDING THOUGHTS

This chapter has critically interrogated contested conceptions of academic freedom through academics' experiences in Lebanon, the UAE, the United Kingdom, and the United States. Tensions between discourses of academic freedom and of inclusion and diversity run through the empirical data of the interviewees' constructions and contestations of academic freedom. Differential understandings of academic freedom arise in the perceptions of the relationship between academic freedom and free speech, which is linked to positioning the role of academic 'expertise'. The issue of 'expertise' is critically examined in the following chapter in relationship to constructions of knowledge and debates relating to disciplinarity, interdisciplinarity, the canon, and notions of 'truth'. The transnational production of knowledge will also be examined, where geographical location plays a critical and complex role.

There is also contestation with regard to whether academic freedom is a universalised and decontextualised absolute position, in contrast to the notion of a hierarchy of rights where academic freedom is contextualised in relation to other rights and is advocated in support of creating an inclusive environment for the inclusive production of knowledge. Similarly, 'freedom from' is contrasted with 'freedom to', with the former emphasising freedom from harassment, assault, and dehumanisation, and where publication is not seen as the exclusive right of the researcher but arising as a negotiated co-production with the researched population. Finally, individualising and psychologising discourses as well as discourses of civility and affect shape constructions of academic freedom. The implications of these discourses for the production of knowledge are also examined in the following chapter.

3   Constructions of Knowledge

> For the defense of academic freedom, it makes a great difference how knowledge production is metaphorically understood.
>
> (Kivisto and Pihlstrom, 2017, p. 791)

3.1 INTRODUCTION

In the previous chapter, constructions and contestations of academic freedom were examined from a transnational perspective, reflecting the transnational reality of contemporary knowledge production and the need to consider academic freedom beyond the dominant methodologically nationalist frame. Discourses of 'expertise', politics and affect of knowledge production, interdisciplinarity, ethics, and temporal and geographical positionality were elucidated drawing on the empirical data from Lebanon, the UAE, the United Kingdom, and the United States. This chapter examines the various contested constructions of knowledge within and across the different geographical contexts and by discipline, and the implications of these constructions for pedagogy, research, and understanding of academic freedom. There are different ways of conceiving knowledge: on the one hand, it can be seen as something separate from those who produce it – as something that can be accumulated and describing reality. Alternatively, it can be conceived in more subjective terms, as something that is constructed, negotiated, and embedded in geographical and historical contexts, and in relationships of power. The first model would conceive of teaching predominantly in a transmission model, whereas the second model would conceive of a more interrelational and interpretative model, where teachers and students work together in producing knowledge. Drawing on the empirical data, the chapter interrogates how constructions of knowledge, pedagogy, research, and academic freedom are inextricably connected.

3.2 CONSTRUCTIONS OF KNOWLEDGE

Theories of knowledge can be conceived as 'filters' through which we navigate the world and its ideals (Sadiki, 2015). Whilst Kant invokes rationality, Hume links knowledge to 'sensitivity'; in contrast, Muslim conceptions of knowledge can be conceived of as a synthesis between the two, entailing both science and religious belief: 'neither a priori (Kant) or a posteriori (Hume)' (Sadiki, 2015, p. 708). It is increasingly being recognised that there is a plurality of knowledges both within intellectual traditions and across different geographical contexts, with contemporary movements to 'decolonise' and contextualise knowledge.

Contemporary Western constructions of knowledge have been heavily influenced by the Humboldtian tradition, where the Humboldtian model of higher education in the early nineteenth century saw teaching as embedded in research – in effect, that it was, in fact, carried out through research. In this model, teachers and students work together constructing ideas and knowledge, where teaching was conceived as being embedded in research or 'learning in research' – the translation of Humboldt's central idea (Elton, 2005, p. 111). In this model, there is an expectation that students engage with teachers in the joint production of knowledge, with a teaching objective that students actively participate in the inquiry within the discipline (Robertson, 2007). Here, knowledge is viewed more subjectively, as a product of interpretation and negotiation, and influenced by geographical and temporal contexts. In contrast, traditional models of knowledge construe entry into a disciplinary field via a codified body of knowledge and methods. In this model, knowledge is objectively externalised, and hence learners are not conceived of as engaged in the construction of this knowledge. Knowledge is therefore understood as scientific, literal, non-metaphorical, separate, and unrelated to the human mind. In such a model, learners come to conceive of such knowledge as objectively true and corresponding to a description of an existing reality in the world (Brew, 2003), rather than perceiving knowledge to be contested or constructed.

Throughout history, knowledge production has been framed through metaphors (Kivisto and Pihlstrom, 2017). The metaphor of uncertainty can be seen in the Humboldtian model, which also recognises the value-laden nature of knowledge, in contrast to the traditional model where meaning is relatively objective, 'true', and fixed. The Humboldtian model, therefore, constructs the learner as a partner within the academic community, as opposed to an infantilised or second-class citizen. Notions of the 'purposes' of knowledge as a source for social and political change, invoking a metaphor of flux and change; knowledge as discovering the truth, invoking a metaphor of perseveration and stability; and knowledge for instrumental and economic benefits of society in a market perspective, invoking the metaphor of 'capital' and 'knowledge economy', will all be explored later in the chapter relating to contestations with interdisciplinarity. As such, the 'discipline' is an important construct, mediating the research–teaching relationship, and the conception of knowledge itself. Furthermore, metaphors of horizontality and verticality, corresponding to breadth and depth, are invoked in discourses of interdisciplinarity.

3.2.1 The Value of Education

Conceptions of the nature of 'knowledge' necessarily invoke particular notions of who the knowledge is for and what it aims to achieve. The metaphor of capital with respect to knowledge is clearly evident in the following excerpt on the 'value' of education, linked directly to employment outcomes:

> Well, as I'm sure you know, there is a big debate now about the value of education, I mean, **literally the value** ... especially in the US ... And now funding agencies, funders, including parents and students who borrow money to pay for their education, I mean, they are also thinking in terms of, when they think of value and they think of **employability**. (Professor of History, branch campus in Gulf State, p. 1)

Similarly, the concept of 'enterpreneurship', 'marketability', and 'skills' is invoked in the following excerpt of the state of academia in the US context:

> So even students who are majoring in Liberal Arts are encouraged to see themselves as entrepreneurs ... no one cares about having them read Noville or Homer. It's learning how to write on a white board. You know learn how to be a communication facilitator, learn how to use social media, so it's an increased emphasis on alleged skill building that will be marketable, immediately marketable. (Professor of Women's and Gender Studies, University of New Hampshire, US, p. 6)

Knowledge and skills are contrasted in the above account, where skills are in effect a form of capital that can literally be cashed in for a financial return. Whilst academia overall is affected in this regard, humanities and the social sciences are particularly affected, linked again to notions of capital and translating that learning 'capital' to literal capital through employability. Conceptions of the 'knowledge economy' have gained significant prominence in policy planning for the global economy since the 2000s, construed as a factor in production and global competition. In the Gulf States, and specifically the UAE, there is a dominant discourse and policy planning to transition from being oil-dependent states to knowledge-based economies (Hvidt, 2021). There is further impetus for this transition with global efforts to address climate change and shifting to greener sources of energy, reflected by the UAE's hosting of the sixth annual knowledge summit in November 2019, entitled 'Knowledge: The Path to Sustainable Development' (Amin, 2020) and COP28 in 2023. The UAE has also invested in space technologies and has built Masdar City, one of the world's most sustainable Urban communities, built on a philosophy of 'economic, social, and environmental sustainability' (Masdar, 2022). Higher education is presented as key to the strategic vision of achieving a knowledge-based economy that is globally competitive.

Whilst a global trend, the status of humanities and the social sciences in the Arab region is considered particularly bleak. Although the most competitive universities in the Arab region require some general education requirements including social science and humanities courses, 'this is not the case in the vast majority [of universities] of the Arab World', 'with less investment, there is less production ... the numbers are ... quite dismal' (Professor of History, branch campus in Gulf State, p. 2). The emphasis in the Gulf States, as in the Arab World on professional degrees, is reflected in the programme offerings and specialisms of branch campuses in Dubai. Commenting on the course offerings of the University of Birmingham in Dubai: 'That'll be linked to what they perceive as the market demand. I think there's certain subjects that they would not take to Dubai' (UCU branch officer, UK, p. 5).

Discourses of real-world applicability illustrate the contested nature of knowledge and its links to policymaking and business. Peter Singer, Professor in Philosophy, comments on the nature of scholarship in the discipline of Philosophy, positioning himself as

> I was always interested in questions that had some real world significance, you know, there's a lot of intellectual interest in trying to show that I know that I'm not dreaming now but in practical terms it does not make a lot of difference to

most people's lives, although questions in ethics obviously do, especially if you get to applied ethics or practical ethics and that's perhaps why I was interested in that. (p. 1)

Similarly, a critique of research conducted on the Global South by Global North researchers and, in particular, those theorising sociological critiques of development research advocate real-world applicability:

> I feel like there is a lot of this ivory tower research that examines the natives and is critical of development interventions and whatever else that we do and we kind of glibly say, and I just do not feel like that's added a lot of value. By the way that we write that is very theoretically, that is very complex, it's really abstract, does not lend itself well to knowledge that is shared. I have a very low tolerance for that kind of stuff. So I'm a little bit protective of the space and the time and the purpose of the research that we do, as much as I can control. (Director of Arab Institute for Women in Lebanon, p. 9)

This account alludes to the theory/empirical data hierarchy that dominates knowledge production, also raised in the UK context by a Professor of Education, critiquing the state of sociology of race several decades ago as 'theorising was all from an armchair, so some people would argue that it was to do with kind of deficient culture or family structure, some people would argue that it was to do with racism, but there was almost nothing actually inside a school to say "what does this look like inside a school?"' (Professor of Education, University of Birmingham, UK, p. 2). Also invoking the positionality of social class, he reflects that his background was significant in perceptions of his own work: 'He works hard, he's a good ethnographer, but he does not do theory' (p. 5).

Constructs of 'impact', 'concreteness', and 'implementability' are also considered in relation to discussions of real-world impact. Commenting on research in the field of gender and development:

> So are you asking questions that have a direct impact on people's lives? And is it very clear? You know we ask a lot of fluffy questions. Is it clear that these questions are going to give you answers that are concrete, that you can then turn into something that you might implement? (Director of Arab Institute for Women in Lebanon, p. 9)

This conception of external knowledge to be discovered has its value defined in terms of evidence of effect in the relative short term. This reflects contemporary national and global debates on the interrelationship between research, policy, and practice. In the field of education, for example, funding for systematic reviews can be linked to the impact agenda and the Research Excellence Framework (REF) in the UK context, which illustrates the validation of certain forms of research as directly 'useful' for end users – whether policymakers, practitioners, or local populations. Conceptions of knowledge transfer and public engagement also illustrate policy initiatives prioritising the importance of the direct application of research to the various 'publics' and its role in promoting the economy (notion of 'knowledge economy'). In addition, it has also invoked debates relating to methodology and quality of research. In the UK context, the rise in systematic reviews in education arose in the context of critiques from policymakers (as well as some academics' criticisms, e.g. Hargreaves and Tooley[1]) regarding the quality of educational research and its perceived relevance to the concerns of policymakers, practitioners, and so-called end users of education. Concerns were expressed about academics being detached from the everyday realities of educational practice, with a call to make research more relevant and its production more democratic[2]. Systematic reviews in education have drawn on approaches to synthesising research evidence from the field of health promotion. The Cochrane Collaboration was established over two decades ago and is a well-known network of researchers, professionals, and other interested 'end users' who conduct systematic reviews with the aim of gathering evidence to make informed decisions in the field of health promotion. This approach provided a model for developments in education; the Campbell Collaboration is an international education network conducting systematic reviews on the impact of educational interventions.

Proponents of systematic reviews argue that they reduce bias, are replicable, and provide a more reliable evidence base upon which decisions are made in policy or practice (Oakley, 2003). In addition, they can identify gaps in the research. However, there has been considerable criticism of systematic reviews in education. In part, some of these concerns are based on concerns with regard to the methodology. Although systemic reviews (SRs) in education purport to engage with a range of research questions and both qualitative and quantitative methodologies, critics argue that SRs are, nevertheless, underpinned by positivist epistemological assumptions about the nature of

---

[1] Press release for Tooley's 1998 Report 'Majority of Academic Educational Research Is Second-Rate'.
[2] The EPPI-Centre at the Institute of Education, where I worked from 2000 to 2006, was set up in 2000 by the then Department for Education and Skills to lead on methodological developments in systematic reviews in education and to train academic researchers in a range of topics in education to conduct systematic reviews in these areas.

knowledge and research, linked to long-standing debates or 'paradigm wars' between qualitative and quantitative approaches and their epistemological differences. Other institutional/structural concerns have also been raised, for example, by Thomas and Pring (2003), Hammersley (2001), MacLure (2005), and others pertaining to the issue of the relationship between research, policymaking, and practice, with concerns expressed over the central role the government has increasingly played in setting the research agenda. There are very practical implications for research as a consequence of the state's allocation of research funding in education, and by implication for academic freedom. Such initiatives narrow what is considered to be 'acceptable' research (MacLure, 2005), leaving little space for 'blue skies' research and 'thinking the unthinkable'. Further, the emphasis on clarity in the methodological process is arguably not only a technical issue but also a political one, which entails the regulation of practices in less powerful communities (Giroux, 1992).

3.2.2 Positionality, Activism, and Public Knowledge

Western constructions of knowledge have been critiqued for not taking critical account of what 'knowledge' denotes, the politics of knowledge, and the structural conditions within higher education (Weiler, 2009). In Western discourses, rationality is associated with the pursuit of knowledge, which is gendered and raced, deriving from Enlightenment theories of natural rights, where women were seen as irrational and denied rights on that basis; similarly, colonial and orientalist discourses have typically constructed their colonial subjects as lacking rationality and by extension – conceived to be less human (Said, 1978). Similarly, Fricker (2009)'s concept of testimonial injustice is used to describe certain groups having less credibility as producers of knowledge, resulting in them being 'silenced'. Conversely, emotions have been constructed as both 'primitive' and 'feminine', set up in contrast to rationality. As discussed in the previous chapter, emotion can be conceived as a social and political practice, rather than understood solely as an individual psychological response (Ahmed, 2014). Studying social movements provides an illustration of the active production of knowledge beyond the academy, which can include cultural production, social media, and political cartoons, for example (Kiwan, 2017a).

The positionality of knowledge producers is contested in debates on knowledge production in the academy, where knowledge for social change through activism is critiqued by those defending the idea of a traditional canon and disciplines: 'Often public knowledge is discredited because it's not expressed in certain academic terms' (Lecturer in Human Geography, University of Leicester, UK, p. 6). Describing the establishment of Faculty United at the American University of Beirut, Lebanon, a Professor of Psychology reflects on his activist role in the establishment of the body that acts as a union for university faculty and its relationship to his academic work:

> Faculty United came to be in the first place as a reaction by some Faculty, by a number of small group of Faculty towards administrative decisions that were taking place that were unilateral without consultation with Faculty members and did not engage us. And it's tied to my work in discipline because I'm very much interested in group dynamics and conflict and obedience and hierarchy and collective action is also part of what I'm doing. And I'm involved in affairs related to Palestinian issues and so on and so forth. So that kind of activism is part of my personal life, my academic life and my professional life at AUB. (Professor of Psychology, American University of Beirut, p. 2)

Examples of initiatives for public knowledge both within and outside the academy across the different geographic contexts include the US Lesbian 'Herstory', the online, independent e-zine 'Jadaliya' providing critical analysis on the Middle East, the feminist journal 'Kohl' produced in Beirut, Lebanon, and the UK-based centre at University College London on the Study of the Legacies of British Slave-Ownership. The Lesbian Herstory was started in 1974 as part of the gay liberation movement, with the aim to produce an accessible archive of lesbian lives, and is now the largest collection globally. In the Lebanese context, a trilingual (English/Arabic/ French) gender studies journal was established in 2014, which is independent of a higher education institutional setting and works as a transnational feminist collective, funded by the Heinrich Ball Foundation. It is positioned as both academic and activist, with submissions from across the Middle East region and also from those in the Global North whose work relates to the Middle East region. The UK-based research centre on the Study of the Legacies of British Slave-Ownership is characterised as having impact in terms of a contribution to public history. However, the aim is that this would be a contribution to public history through museums and cultural institutions, rather than solely in academic terms. In discussing how this work relates to the reparations movement, the approach is characterised as objectively collecting empirical data, and not becoming involved in seeking reparations. This construction of knowledge also has implications for the understanding of the nature of 'evidence' and history as a discipline, which will be returned to later in the chapter. The issue of positionality is examined in more depth in the following section on the decolonisation of knowledge.

3.3 DECOLONISATION OF KNOWLEDGE

'Decolonisation', although a contested term, can be seen to have two key components: firstly, 'a way of thinking about the world which takes colonialism, empire, and racism as its empirical and discursive objects of study', and secondly, 'to offer alternative ways of thinking' (Bhambra et al., 2018, p. 2). This necessarily brings positionality to the fore, acknowledging the temporal and spatial situatedness of knowledge. There is also an emphasis on change, both with respect to teaching and research. According to Mignolo (2010, p. 342):

> Decolonial theory makes a louder and more radical challenge, linked more directly to protest and direct confrontations with existing practice. Decolonial theory is focused on an epistemic challenge to colonialist thinking, with an emphasis on radical delinking from the sources of ongoing inequalities that have deep historical roots in European imperialism, but that are continually re-staged and re-routed through the continuing and deepening inequalities brought about through neoliberalism, including in the neoliberal university system.

This section interrogates the role of politics, dissent, and affect in knowledge production and its methodologies, whilst the university as a key site of this struggle will be the focus of the following chapter.

The British anthropologist, Mary Douglas, in 1975 is noted for claiming that: 'The colonisation of each other's minds is the price we pay for thought'[3]. Reflecting on growing up in the Caribbean, a UK-based Emeritus Professor of Sociology comments:

> They took away everything else. So this is the idea of the Mimic Man, you have to erase all sense of yourself and then implant the view of the coloniser. You become totally colonised. So it's that – you know the Canon just is not simply white men's books. It's about mind control. (Emeritus Professor of Sociology, UK, p. 12)

---

[3] *The New York Times*, 22 May 2007, front page; quoting the British anthropologist Mary Douglas on the occasion of her death on 16 May 2007.

Some of the more radical theories of 'colonising the mind' (Dascal, 2007) pre-close the notion of an exchange of ideas, tending to construct power as a finite resource positioned from above between the 'powerful' and the 'powerless'. In addition, it assumes a regionally if not methodologically nationalist approach to knowledge production; implicit in such theorisations is a notion of the 'purity' of a culture and its ideas, which does not account for the complexities of knowledge production, transfer, and legitimisation (Kiwan, 2017a). Whilst the Mary Douglas quote could be interpreted as an apologia for the colonisation of knowledge, the production of knowledge can be understood beyond, or through, the polemical binaries of colonial or decolonial knowledges. More radical approaches do not recognise more Foucauldian understandings of power as relational, contested, and contextualised, nor do they recognise different forms of agency in how knowledge is used, produced, and reconstructed (Kiwan, 2017a). Indeed, Connell (2014) notes that in the field of gender, some of the most creative work in the South arises from the 'critical appropriation of Northern ideas, in combination with ideas that come from radically different experiences' (p. 527).

This is not to be ahistorical or ignore differentials in power, but rather to recognise the dynamic elasticity of knowledge, its incrementality, and its relationality; that it is dialogical, plural, and unbounded; and that it is transformed, owned, and embodied in different sites, recognising the agency or those deemed to be the recipients or colonised by such knowledge. This contextualisation can be conceived of as being 'embodied' in that people live it as an experience and in relation to others. This has an unpredictability about it as knowledge is constructed, contested, reconstructed, and transformed. Indeed, Nandy (2014) distinguishes between hegemony and dominance, where hegemony is more dangerous as it is the internalisation of the coloniser's categories. However, he, nevertheless, acknowledges that 'no hegemony is complete unless it can specify, monitor or control the conventions of dissent and resistance to hegemony' (Nandy, 2014, p. 1). This tension between the internalisation of the coloniser's categories and the fluidity unpredictability and dissent in engaging with knowledge is clearly evident in the above account. In a similar vein, Homi Bhabha makes the case that 'liminality' also empowers, enabling a capacity of resistance and re-narration (Bhabha, 1994). The fluidity and relational nature of 'power' is evident, where power relations unfold in all social relations, including the production of knowledge, rather than solely being conceived in terms of a finite resource from above (Foucault, 1991).

This resistance takes a variety of forms, with complaint and early retirement in one account explained as a form of resistance to institutional structures, invoking Ahmed's work on refusal and complaint:

> And the system is somehow neutral and open and yet you have got all these difficult, complaining students who do not know any better, and how they are threats to the sanctity of what real good knowledge is, what real you know, the right kind of knowledge. How dissent is gobbled up and repackaged as now the difficult and complaining students. (Emeritus Professor of Sociology, p. 9)

The institutional setting of the university within which such complaint and refusals are made is explored in the following chapter, which focuses on the university.

Academic freedom is critiqued as a tangential issue: 'So the threat to academic freedom, it's such a boring thing you know. Sorry. Because what's at stake is much, much bigger' (p. 12). Whilst there is a drive for resistance and the production of new knowledge, there is concomitantly the sense of powerlessness and frustration:

> They're kind of toying round the edges when what we are really talking about, entrenchments of structures and systems of thinking and feeling and knowledge, that keep us second rate, make us nobodies you know. The human spirit is so great and our will to survive and to struggle is that we have taken that, that we have been given and turn it into something else for ourselves and have re-appropriated that knowledge and those ideas and made new things out of them. (Emeritus Professor of Sociology, UK, p. 12)

Expressed here is a frustration at a perceived lack of social change. Contested constructions of social change include functionalist approaches which see change as necessary and desirable as long as it is gradual over time, largely in order to preserve the status quo. In contrast, conflict theory conceives of social change as arising from social inequality and that protest is desirable and necessary in order to achieve social change. Social change can be broadly conceived in terms of both the notion of structure, including social, legal, and political institutions, and the ways of living and thinking as reflected in language, beliefs, values, customs, and lived practices (Kiwan, 2017a); my previous research on social movements has highlighted activist constructions of social change as a process, noting the temporal nature as opposed to a more static framing focused on outcome in a moment of time. When social change is viewed as process, it can be seen as 'a way of living', where social change and knowledge production are mutually constitutive of one another as socio-temporal processes.

The process of 're-appropriation' of knowledge and the making of something 'new' are also raised by Baden Offord, Professor of Cultural Studies and Human Rights, Curtin University, Australia, who, referring to the post-colonial scholar, Nandy, describes the production of knowledge as 'being basically a Western template' dictating 'what kind of knowledge, what knowledge is for' (pp. 11–12), and that 'knowledge that's produced through that Western model is very exploitative'. Commenting on the practice of Western scholars researching the 'other' in minority communities, or outside the West, he raises the ethical issue of over-researched communities. In the UK context, a Professor of Education describes his emerging awareness as a Ph.D. student of the ethical issues of White researchers researching Black communities: 'My crisis was the … my interactions with the field, that as a white researcher am I reproducing this pattern of building a career but making no difference to the people that I claim to be wanting to help' (p. 4). The politics of knowledge production where 'actually members of the oppressor class are taken more seriously as witnesses to oppression … where the fact that I'm white has meant that I've been able to say things that I might not have got away with at that time if I was a minoritised scholar' (p. 4), illustrating the 'testimonial injustice' (Fricker, 2009) of greater credibility as a White male academic researching race. This positionality with respect to the production of knowledge is further examined in the following section.

3.4 TEMPORAL AND GEOGRAPHICAL POSITIONALITY

The Western hegemony of knowledge and its production have been increasingly challenged over the last several decades from all over the world as well as from within the Global North (e.g. Bhabha, Bhambra, Dallal, Foucault, Hanafi, Mignolo, Mirza, Nandy, and Spivak). The central idea that temporal and geographical contextualisation is necessary in situating knowledge and its production is a dominant assertion. In addition, Nandy calls for the rejection of a synchronic model, and in its place a diachronic model, challenging the premise of European colonisers that the 'developing world' was moving towards the same destination as the 'developed world' albeit at a slower rate, whereby 'colonialism became a pedagogic mission … with the colonisers bearing the burden of a civilising mission' (Nandy and Darby, 2018, p. 280).

The notion that 'all social imaginaries present blind spots owing to their inherent socio-centrism' (Sadiki, 2015, p. 704) challenges the assumed universalism and abstract neutrality of the 'Western Canon', as well as its forms of knowledge production. Commenting on the use of the term 'orient', Sadiki (2015, p. 717) asserts that this constructed 'other' provides a means to illustrate 'what the "West" is and is not. In such images, the "non-West" is marginal to rationality, peripheral to theory and on the sidelines of knowledge-making'. This section illustrates the temporal and geographical positionality of knowledge production and its transnational nature. This is further developed through an interrogation of discourses of interdisciplinarity in the following section.

Recognising the temporal and geographical situatedness of knowledge logically necessitates that academic freedom is similarly situated in space and time: 'I do think academic freedom exists and you know, it exists at the moment people act it out. It does not exist in a vacuum ... I do think that there are different pressures in different places' (former Professor of History, American University of Beirut, p. 2). Further, the moralising frame of the perceived lack of academic freedom in only some parts of the world is highlighted in several accounts: 'its not like these are bad countries and these are the good countries, but for me that's two sides of the same coin' (Lecturer in Human Geography, University of Leicester, UK, p. 2). The metaphor of the coin implicitly carries with it the notion of mutuality and interconnectedness, an idea developed further in her account on the nature of the contemporary legacy of colonialism effecting knowledge production through institutional mechanisms such as funding. Echoing the concern with a moralising critique of academic freedom outside the West, the role of branch campuses in relation to academic freedom in the Gulf States is contextualised: 'I do not have a moralising sort of answer for you, you know, whether I think that they are good or bad. They're there and they are doing certain things' (Associate Professor of Anthropology, US, pp. 7–8).

The geographical positionality of academic freedom can be clearly witnessed in the accounts, where the production of certain areas of knowledge have differential political and ethical values ascribed to them. Zachary Lockman, Professor of Middle East History, New York University, dryly notes that there was a time in the United States where one would not even mention 'Palestine in polite company' (p. 2), whilst another in the UK context comments that it is 'a taboo area' (Professor of Sociology, UK, p. 10).

Several accounts of those conducting research related to Palestine and the Middle East in the US and UK contexts refer to constraints on their academic freedom and a hostile working environment: 'Within the American Academy when it comes to Israel/Palestine, my resounding answer is, no there is not really academic freedom when it comes to this issue' (Matthew Abraham, Professor of English, University of Arizona, US). Matthew, the author of *Out of Bounds: Academic Freedom and the Question of Palestine*, details how throughout his career he has received warnings and 'even veiled threats to stop writing on these issues, and that I would not get a job or would be denied tenure, or would not be able to get key grants to support my research. I've lost grants before, after they were guaranteed to me in writing under the cover of bureaucratic error' (p. 2). Yet, Abraham reflects on his own positionality, noting that: 'I think I was, kind of immunised in my written work because my last name is Abraham and a name like Matthew Abraham, people assume I'm Jewish when in fact my parents are originally from Kerala in India. But people when they would actually meet me, they would assume I'm Palestinian' (p. 8).

The contrast in researching Palestine in the United States compared to in Beirut, Lebanon, illustrates the geopolitical situatedness of the production of knowledge and its implications for academic freedom. Alex Lubin, Professor in American Studies at the University of New Mexico and former Director of the Centre for American Studies and Research (CASAR), comments on his experience of teaching and researching on the United States and its geopolitical relationship to Israel and Palestine:

> Well I think that it [AUB, Beirut, Lebanon] was a far more open place to study, write about, lecture. In the United States, it was impossible, at least when I went to Beirut in two thousand and eleven, it was still very difficult in the US to engage those conversations without being accused of being antisemitic frankly. And Beirut and AUB was for me – and I specify that it was specifically for me because I know it's not for everybody – it was a very open place to engage in the kinds of research that I was doing. And to think about the question of Palestine in the US in a very different way. (p. 6)

Lubin further contextualises the study of Palestine within the United States: 'I would also say that New Mexico, it's a state with a relatively small Jewish population, and without well organised Israel-supporting Jewish communities. If I were engaged in my work in New York or in parts of California, I think that I would probably come under much more attack' (p. 4).

Furthermore, Lubin also invokes the positionality of the individual researcher, as in Matthew Abraham's account above, with respect to academic freedom in both the US and Lebanese contexts. He also reflects on his academic experience of conducting research on Palestine in the United States compared to others with different positionalities in the academy:

> So for example at the University of New Mexico, another area that I would also mention is that I'm on a list, as many scholars are, that's compiled by Canary Mission which is a secret group. And I have a pretty ugly biography there. And I think that those things have great impact on scholars without tenure. They have great impact on graduate students and junior faculty who are not White and they have greater impact on faculty who are not Jewish, at least in the context of the Israel/Palestine issue. (p. 4)

Whilst in the Lebanese context, he also reflects how the production of his knowledge carried greater credibility:

> Now I think that I was afforded a certain amount of freedom to engage in that scholarship in part because I was a white, Jewish American. The administration saw me as maybe a more legitimate interlocutor on the question than had I been a Palestinian American scholar ... I never felt that they limited my academic freedom in any way. (p. 6)

The relativity of academic freedom in the UK context also refers to the issue of researching or speaking on Palestine/Israel, perceiving this to be the most controversial field. A UK Lecturer identifies the three most challenging areas to conduct research in the United Kingdom as Palestine/Israel, Whiteness, and masculinity and reflects on the nature of the containment of producing knowledge in these fields:

> They're three things that worry me greatly. And I do not hold back from criticising them, I do criticise them, but I am cautious when I do in a way that I'm generally not cautious about other things. So the fear that I may be accused of being anti-Semitic, sexist towards men – as if that even exists – and, you know, racist towards White people – again as if that actually exists. So it's charges of a moral wrong which is in fact the very moral wrong that I am committing my work to challenging. So in all three cases, you know, that's what's going on. So I would always argue that reverse racism and sexism are fictions and so I think that though I worry about being charged with those things, I feel that they aren't real and I can easily argue for that, if need be, not that everybody would come on-board. Whereas anti-Semitism is real, you know, and is a really worrying serious thing. And so I think that would feel particularly difficult as a charge to deal with compared with the other two. There's obviously a huge context around this in the UK at the moment and just in the Western world generally, so yeah. (pp. 5–6)

Researching Palestine/Israel is a highly emotive field, and the containment and sanctions for those researching in this field are similarly through the emotional *practice* of levelling an accusation of committing a 'moral wrong'. This central role of affect in the politics of knowledge production has been overlooked, in terms of both its production and policing or 'governmentality' of its production. There is the moral discourse of policing the boundaries of academic freedom forming the basis of practical sanctions referred to, such as surveillance and threats, loss of livelihood and earnings, loss of intellectual reputation, and even criminal proceedings.

The geopolitical situatedness of academic freedom is also commented on in the context of the UAE. According to a University and College Union branch officer in the United Kingdom discussing course content at branch campuses on Dubai:

> There are certain subjects, particularly in the humanities, in politics, that they know full well if they took them to Dubai they'd just be outraged because they'd have to completely rewrite the syllabus, the staff would be very against it ... I mean if an academic were to go over to Dubai and be on Panopto and start talking about ... you know ... anything that could be illegal, so it's quite serious. (UCU branch officer, UK university, p. 5)

Whilst academics with the experience of teaching in branch and local universities in the UAE state that they have had freedom to develop their own courses which are not screened or censored by local authorities, the above account focuses on possible legal implications, where power is conceptualised in a unitary way as held from above as opposed to relationally. Given the seriousness of possible sanctions, this construction of power is understandable, especially given the role and responsibility of a university union in protecting staff. Yet, there is ambiguity with respect to branch campuses, given that the law of land takes priority, and there is a discourse of responsibility being with the academic to comply with the local law: 'So it's sort of like "Nothing to do with us". The complicating factor is that they also have to comply with UK law and they also have to comply with EU law. One of the things they did not think through is the intersection between those three legal frameworks' (p. 10), illustrating the transnational and intersecting nature of the law and its implications for academic freedom and the production of knowledge, which is ambiguous and unresolved. This legal conundrum is also evident in the Lebanese context where academic freedom is curtailed where academics at the American University of Beirut can no longer conduct research on those who are on the US terrorist list:

And the number of organisations that are put on the terrorist list by the US who happen to be in our region are tremendous – they have Palestinian organisations on the terrorist list, they have Syria's Government on the terrorist list, they have Iran, they have Hezbollah and half the Lebanese population – what am I supposed to do, stop doing research? ... So this is Trump now and his bigotry. What if he says tomorrow 'well Muslims are terrorists and you cannot talk to them' – what are we going to do? (Professor of Psychology, AUB, Lebanon, p. 13)

The comparative and transnational perspective on knowledge production and academic freedom raises the question of whether there is a qualitative difference in academic freedom between the different geographical contexts in the West compared to the Gulf States and the broader Middle East region. A US Professor with experience of teaching in the Gulf asserts that universally, one 'learns the codes of the place', yet 'it becomes censorship in certain contexts, and other contexts, business as usual' (p. 3). It raises the question of whether democracy is a prerequisite for academic freedom, as Sadiki (2015, p. 703) astutely points out that 'the control of knowledge production and practices is one omission in most definitions of authoritarian structures of power'. The accounts from academics in the different geopolitical contexts of Lebanon, the UAE, the United Kingdom, and the United States illustrate the boundedness of academic freedom, indicating a continuum with geopolitical red lines in the different contexts. What differs is the degree of severity of sanctions and the discourses within which these are embedded. In the UK and US contexts, a morally imbued discourse is weaponised to regulate knowledge production coupled with self-censorship and the fear of loss of employment. Morally imbued discourses are also used to regulate knowledge production in the UAE and Lebanon around various topics, which may also be framed in relation to a religious framework, in relation to topics including gender and sexuality, national identity, and security. Rather than a qualitative difference, the different modes of state governance – authoritarian compared to democratic apply quantitatively more severe sanctions, which can include imprisonment or being denied entry to the country.

3.5 INTERDISCIPLINARITY

Throughout the twentieth century, it has largely been taken for granted that the production of knowledge is organised through academic disciplines. The contestation around disciplinarity is underpinned by conceptions of knowledge and 'truth', as discussed earlier in the chapter. Contesting discourses of various disciplines emerge in the interviewee accounts; for example, the discipline of History is constructed as 'relentlessly empirical' (Professor of History, UK) in one account, with confidence in the objectivity of this evidence corresponding to the truth if challenged. Yet, it has been argued that history in effect is a meeting of the past and the future at a moment in time when the archive is read and is understood within the discourses and understandings of the present – challenging the notion that 'history is a slave to the archives and it has no place for human emotions and human subjectivities, as the aim is to exile subjectivity from history' (Nandy and Darby, 2018, p. 284). Another account challenges both the methods of the discipline and its traditionally accepted content. Beth Baron, Professor of History, City College and Graduate Center, CUNY, NY, US, traces her intellectual development in the field of women's history reflecting:

> My first works were on women intellectuals at a time when I actually did not even use the word 'intellectual'. I mean I did not even think that women could be intellectuals or Middle East women could be intellectuals, I mean women anywhere. I mean I just, you know one associated men with intellectuals, women produced journals and wrote and so on. (p. 1)

Not only was there an absence with regard to the history of women, but there was also an absence of the concept of women as producers of knowledge, corresponding to Fricker's (2009) concept of 'hermeneutic injustice', where inequalities in power can constrain certain groups from understanding their own lived experiences. Drawing on Marx, Fricker (2009) comments that those with less power or who are marginalised live in a society structured for those in power, and collective social understandings and identities are influenced accordingly.

In the discipline of Sociology, a Professor of Sociology in the United Kingdom charts the changes in the discipline where it has become more 'applied', arguably a 'hermeneutic injustice' (Fricker, 2009), in response to institutional demands of illustrating 'impact' in the Research Evaluation Framework exercise for university government funding. He also notes the rise in interest in 'behavioural science':

> If you wish to improve pupil performance of pupils from disadvantaged backgrounds, so a standard sociological approach might say well it's a consequence of inequality so you address poverty, you address inequality and that will improve pupil performance, but there is no interest in doing anything about poverty or inequality so it's given inequality, given poverty, how do we improve pupil

performance. And that becomes the behavioural rather than the social structural emphasis. And I think that overall is a disadvantage for sociology. (pp. 4–5)

A review of impact case studies submitted to the 2014 REF in Sociology did not include 'one impact case study in sociology which addressed what conventional sociologists would regard as a critical or social justice topic' (p. 5). With a shift in Sociology towards applied social studies, more sociologists submit to the Social policy REF panel. He suggests that this is linked to interdisciplinarity where 'the nature of the work in that area becomes less sociological, so people start describing themselves as working on a particular applied topic' (p. 5), such as education or health.

3.5.1 'Disciplinary Decadence' and the Rise of Interdisciplinarity

It has been argued that the defense of disciplines results in their reification, and its contents and methods overshadow the production of knowledge so that, in effect, the 'discipline becomes the world' (Gordon, 2014, p. 86). Gordon (2014) refers to this as disciplinary decadence where the 'discipline turns into itself and implodes' (p. 86), and each discipline takes a standpoint of assessing and rejecting all other disciplines. He argues that this also occurs at the level of method. He describes the 'teleological suspensions of disciplines' as 'epistemic decolonial acts' (p. 87) and the response of interdisciplinarity.

In the latter half of the twentieth century, new ways of organising knowledge across disciplinary boundaries – including, for example, gender studies, cultural studies, and post-colonial studies – challenged the assumed 'naturalness' of the disciplines. Yet, arguably, interdisciplinary fields of study themselves have come to replicate features of disciplines in terms of defined institutional homes in higher education and their own methods of policing method and content (Williams, 2016). Those decrying a perceived demise of the disciplines and the accepted Canon argue that interdisciplinarity is a rejection of knowledge, where 'knowledge as intrinsically valuable carries little legitimacy today' (Williams, 2016, p. 120). This view is based on the epistemological position that knowledge is objective, rather than geographically or temporally situated and corresponds to an external truth. As such, Williams (2016) laments the politicisation and instrumentalisation of knowledge, describing this as the 'end of knowledge'. In this logic, to defend the disciplines is a defense of truth and the means to achieve academic freedom. Whilst academic disciplines continue to evolve and are not static, critiques of interdisciplinary approaches to knowledge production argue that the discipline represents an accepted canon of universally recognised work in the field, with validated methods available as a framework from which to evaluate and critique work in the given area. Rational objectivity in empirically knowing the 'truth' is implicated. The unquestioned acceptance of an objective canon is challenged in a number of accounts, explicitly expressed by a Professor of Sociology in the United Kingdom: 'But you know what is the Canon? Who invented the Canon and the roots of that Canon are rotten to the core you know. And the thing is, it's like the Canon it's man-made and it's you know, it's historically rooted in racial thought and ideology and about the power' (p. 12).

Interdisciplinarity is also contested, where there are different forms of interdisciplinarity, a form of 'market interdisciplinarity' promoted by higher education institutions and research councils, in contrast to an 'intellectual interdisciplinarity'. One scholar working in the interdisciplinary field of Native American Studies in the United States wryly comments:

> So Women's studies, African American studies, Native American studies ... in the eyes of the average noble tax payer, not worth our tax dollars because they are not actually teaching students marketable skills, they are only teaching students to complain about the existing political order, which of course is the whole point of an education in the first place. (p. 5)

A Professor of Sociology in the United Kingdom distinguishes between 'critical interdisciplinarity' and 'applied interdisciplinarity', highlighting the marketisation and instrumentalisation of applied interdisciplinarity:

> So critical interdisciplinarity is the kind of engagement that reconstructs disciplines and does so across disciplines. So if I take the example of feminism, say well feminism has an impact upon sociology but it also has an impact upon politics, anthropology and so on. And so you could say that feminism is an interdisciplinary movement that critically reconstructs disciplines. And I think that decolonising the curriculum or decolonising research would be a form of critical interdisciplinarity, performing a similar role to the role that feminism played. However, what people they mean by interdisciplinarity now is some sort of banal notion that oh problems are complex and they need the resources of more than one subject, so they actually become ... so applied interdisciplinarity is actually conservative in its relation to disciplines and it seeks to amalgamate those disciplines to address social problems but, increasingly, those social problems are identified in a hierarchical fashion, so that applied interdisciplinarity becomes a funder's favoured way of funding separated from the interests of wider populations and groups. (pp. 11–12)

3.5.2 Geographical Positionality and Disciplinarity

Contemporary research in mobilities of knowledge emphasises the notion of 'negotiation' and 'translation', rather than the 'unproblematic transplanting of ideas, theories and empirical realities from one nation-state . . . to another' (Waters and Leung, 2017, p. 271). There is the social production of new knowledge (Faulconbridge, 2006), rather than place having no relevance – what Morgan (2004, p. 3) has referred to as the 'exaggerated death of geography'. As argued earlier in the chapter, it is important to recognise the embedded and culturally specific nature of knowledge, as well as recognising Foucauldian understandings of power as relational, contested, and contextualised, thus recognising different forms of agency in how knowledge is used, produced, and reconstructed. The example of the interdisciplinary field of American Studies in Lebanon illustrates the importance of geopolitical place in the construction and contestation of these fields.

3.5.2.1 AUB American Studies

The focus of American studies programmes in the Middle East are somewhat different from how the field is constructed in the United States. Despite intended US foreign policy intentions, the discipline has been transformed in its exportation to the Middle East. At the American University of Beirut, in Lebanon, Palestine and Edward Said's work on Palestine has significant import, in contrast to being an 'absent present' in US-based American studies programmes (Darwish, 2010). Alex Lubin, Professor of American Studies, University of Mexico, and former Director of the CASAR at AUB, Lebanon, traces the intellectual development of the field located within a 'transnational' turn, which entails the study of the sociopolitical history of the United States and its global engagements. Patrick McGreevy, Founding Director of CASAR, situates the establishment of CASAR at a time when American Studies was making its transnational turn: '. . . the Middle East was kind of the biggest thorn in the US's relationship with the world outside in the last few decades. So the US and the Middle East became this sort of crucial thing about how you understand the United States' (p. 8). As a consequence, such an approach engages in critiques of government power 'articulated in race and gender and sexuality' (Alex Lubin, p. 2) and has been 'chastised within the United States as "anti-American Studies"' (Alex Lubin, p. 2). Lubin describes the hosting of events at CASAR at the American University of Beirut:

Our national association, the American Studies Association you know, would have some panels about that in their conference but it really wasn't at the centre. Whereas the conferences that were hosted by CASAR became these huge events and this is – I'll take some criticism personally for this – but it became an event that was maybe even more important for US-based scholars than it was for scholars across the region. And that's because it opened up an avenue for discourse that was difficult in the United States. (pp. 6–7)

Yet, the role of CASAR at AUB has been contested, with an alternative vision of CASAR as a place 'to tell the story of America' (p. 7), with a concern that CASAR had become 'seen as a place just to be critical of the United States and not as a place producing new knowledge or doing the work of teaching the Lebanese about US culture' (p. 7). This concern has developed over time, and with changes in personnel in administration, Lubin recalls conversations between members of the AUB administration saying that 'CASAR had become too focused on the Palestine question' and 'too homosexual' (p. 7). He describes the mission and work of CASAR as having substantially changed since his time under a different leadership at AUB, with Patrick McGreevey, founding CASAR Director, commenting that the work is 'just focusing on the arts and literature without kind of the sort of social side or the political side' (p. 5).

This shift in position was also evident with regard to the appointment of Stephen Salaita as a visiting professor in the academic year 2015–2016, and the events surrounding his subsequent application for the position of Director of CASAR in 2016, which will be discussed in Chapter 5 on 'restrictions'. Salaita became the centre of a high-profile controversy when the University of Illinois rescinded its offer to him following objections to his tweets that were critical of Israel's bombing of Gaza in 2014. According to a member on the Senate:

We had a huge confrontation in the Senate – I do not know if you heard about that. But what happened was that Stephen Salaita, he was chosen by a committee to be the Director of CASAR . . . 'Listen, you cannot appoint this guy. [there is] . . . somebody else in mind and [. . .] wants to appoint somebody different' [we were told]. (p. 3)

Relatedly, the relatively recent role of disciplinary subject associations in the global Boycott, Divestment, Sanctions (BDS) movement, which was initiated by Palestinian civil society in 2005, also illustrates how disciplines 'at the centre' have been affected with the 'transnational' turn, the American Studies Association, the Association for Asian American Studies, the American

Anthropology Association, and the International Sociological Association, vocalising support for the BDS movement (Kiwan, 2017a).

3.6 IMPLICATIONS FOR ACADEMIC FREEDOM

This chapter has interrogated the various contested constructions of knowledge, investigating how such conceptions affect understandings of academic freedom. What are the implications of understanding academic freedom when teaching and research are conceived of as discovering an empirical, verifiable, and external truth? Will this conception of academic freedom differ from a conception of academic freedom when knowledge is conceived as constructed, partial, and relationship, situated within geographical and historical contexts? And further, how is academic freedom impacted by a conception of knowledge as capital, with an emphasis on skills to serve the economy?

In the UK and US contexts, there has been a resurgent discourse of support for academic freedom, in the context of challenges to the Canon and disciplinarity largely aligned to right-wing conservative ideologies, which has been critiqued by the liberal left wing as a disingenuous attempt to weaponise academic freedom to, in effect, challenge and restrict the production of new knowledges that challenge the status quo: 'This whole debate about academic inclusion and diversity, you know, was an attack on academic freedom, it's just like, it's a huge mirage where they just want to do what they want to do and they do not want to be more inclusive. And that's it you know' (Professor of Sociology, UK, p. 5). The construction of knowledge as out there in the world to be discovered, with a denial of the role of values in the production of this knowledge, inevitably leads to the dismissal of knowledge conceived as relational, contextual, and positioned, as this is deemed to be politicised. Commenting on the value-ladenness of science: 'Science is full of values in terms of how we investigate things but also in terms of what we investigate as well' (Lecturer in Medical Ethics and Humanities, UK, p. 10). The quality of scholarship is also invoked at the level of method to discredit new knowledge, engaged in by both liberals and conservatives. This weaponisation of the accepted methods of the disciplines and the perceived 'gold' standard of the Canon could be perceived as a masking of what is tantamount to an infringement of academic freedom for those working in new fields or those challenging the canon: 'the power of who gets to name academic freedom' (Professor of Sociology, UK, p. 5).

In contrast, at a theoretical level, when knowledge is recognised as partial, positioned, and contextualised, a range of perspectives is more easily accommodated, with a broader tolerance for academic freedom. Yet, the question of 'red lines' also remains within this framework of knowledge, expressed in affective and morally imbued discourses of values when challenging research is deemed to be 'racist', 'imperial', or 'sexist', for example: 'Hate does not advance knowledge. It is not expressing a view that is otherwise unknown' (Professor of Gender Studies, p. 7). This attests to a conceptualisation of academic freedom itself as relative rather than as absolute. This relates to the notion of the preconditions for academic freedom as discussed in the previous chapter. However, importantly, these are *a priori* conditions framing academic freedom guided by commitments to social justice and inclusivity, rather than *a posteriori* infringements posed in response to challenges to White supremacy and maintenance of the privileges of the status quo.

4 Producing Knowledge

The Role of the University

> The university's separateness has been a legal and political feature but also a widely shared imaginary that is implicated in questions about university autonomy, academic freedom, and the very goals and possibility of higher education.
>
> (McGreevy, 2018, p. 3)

4.1 INTRODUCTION

This chapter develops the arguments of Chapter 3, examining discourses of the perceived role of the university and how this relates to constructions of knowledge and its implications for pedagogy, research, and academic freedom. The previous chapter elucidated various constructions of knowledge and the ensuing implications for academic freedom. Discourses on the value of education, the temporal and geographical positionality of knowledge, and the institutionalisation of knowledge through the disciplines attest to the need to contextualise the understandings of academic freedom. This chapter institutionally contextualises the understanding of the production of knowledge in relation to the role of the university.

There is an intellectual history of higher education (HE) playing a role in the promotion of democratic societies (Dewey, 1916; Wright Mills, 1959), and the development of informed, critical citizens, in relation to the emergence of the modern nation state, and now evident in discourses on global citizenship (Kiwan and Evans, 2015). In some discourses on the 'civic university', a liberal education is seen as central in the production of 'a particular kind of critical citizen', whilst other discourses call for a more radical 'transformation of higher education itself' (Biesta, 2007, p. 470). It has been argued that HE is one of the few remaining public spaces where unpopular ideas can be explored, and students can learn how to challenge authority (Giroux, 2002). In the Arab world, few universities constitute a public sphere for critical debate, although notable exceptions include the American University of Beirut (AUB), in particular, before the 1970s, where public intellectuals, reformists, and nationalists engaged with the public on social and political issues of the day (Hanafi, 2011) and have a continued role today (Kiwan, 2017b). Historically, in the colonial context, education was a means of rule, and these traditions continue to exist today in post-colonial states. In many Arab countries, there is a tradition of public universities, developed predominantly after the Second World War, when the national university typically became the symbol of new national identity, development, and autonomy (Abi-Mershed, 2010). However, in Lebanon, the majority of universities are private as the civil war context (1975–1991) undermined the state's ability to promulgate a state-controlled HE system (Buckner, 2011). The UAE illustrates the Gulf region's prioritisation of establishing a 'knowledge economy' as evidenced with Dubai's Knowledge Village. Increasingly, Western universities are opening branch campuses driven by financial interests, including concerns relating to improving rankings through internationalisation.

The literature on the role of the university in producing critical citizens informs the intellectual history of academic freedom and its contemporary and contested constructions. Yet, it is important to recognise that this theoretical framing assumes a democratic and national context. There is also an emerging field of critical university studies, developing since the 1990s, interrogating the university as an institution (Bottrell and Manathunga, 2019; Collini, 2012, 2017; Furedi, 2017; Manathunga and Bottrell, 2019; Newfield, 2008, 2016; Noble and Ross, 2019; O'Sullivan, 2016; Thomas, 2018; Williams, 2012, 2016) with its historically embedded processes and structures of inequality, exploitation, and marginalisation, reflected in critical pedagogical movements (e.g. Freire and Giroux).

This chapter interrogates the role of the university transnationally beyond the familiar Western democratic contexts, situated within the post-colonial legacies and nation-building projects in Beirut and Dubai (Abi-Mershed, 2010; Anderson, 2011; Buckner, 2011; Khalaf, 2012; Kiwan, 2017), as well as the global neoliberal initiatives of internationalisation and branch campus projects (Davies and Bansel, 2007; Miller-Idriss and Banauer, 2011; Olds, 2007; Olssen and Peters, 2005; Vora, 2019; Wasserman, 2017; Waters, 2016; Waters and Leung, 2017) and the sociopolitical implications for academic freedom and the production of knowledge. Interviewees identified three key themes linking the role of the university to the production of knowledge and academic freedom: firstly, contestation over the mission of the university and its relationship to its situated context, secondly, the internationalisation of HE, and thirdly, the role of governance and funding.

4.2 MISSION OF THE UNIVERSITY

4.2.1 'Truth' and 'Public Good'

Universities exist for the pursuit of information and the pursuit of truth.
(Emeritus Professor of Law, US, p. 2)

As noted in the introduction, there is an intellectual history of the role of the 'civic university' in society and the nature of its public mission. This continues to be a contested role, ranging from the idea that universities must produce 'true' knowledge to the idea that universities' central mission is constructed in terms of creating economic growth and the idea that the university is a means for change in an increasingly globalised world facing numerous challenges (Bogelund, 2015). These different constructions of the role of the university are underpinned by different constructions of knowledge as discussed in the previous chapter. The construction of the university as a producer of 'pure knowledge' conceives of knowledge production and knowledge as truth as central to this mission, whilst the application of knowledge for social and economic purposes underpins university missions centred around creating economic growth. The third model of the university as a change agent is informed by an emphasis on social and political contextualisation of knowledge. The independence and academic freedom of the university takes the separation of knowledge and power as a premise (Scott, 2019) and, as such, comes the rationale that the university is a protected space for critical thinking.

The notion of 'public' good in particular is raised in relation to whether a university is privately or publicly funded. These distinctions can become blurred due to historical legacy and sociopolitical circumstances, as in the case of the AUB, ranked as one of the top institutions in the region:

> You know in Arabic, university is a 'jamiea': you know, it's something that gathers people together. It is not about having a business enterprise run by business people. And even if we are a private university, this is the oldest one in the Middle East. And I argued with them once in the Senate that AUB has become a

public good. It's not any more a private university. It belongs to the region, it belongs to the graduates, it belongs to everybody who spends time here. They had an argument that they did not want to publish the budget because the government will come and scrutinise their taxes, something very stupid as an argument and I told them you know 'Everything you do in AUB should be public. You're almost a public university. You're not a typical private university'. (Professor of Economics, AUB)

Here, 'public good' trumps private ownership, due to the standing of the institution in the region and its stated educational mission of being of the region and serving the region. 'Jamiea', the word for university, links to the root meaning group or 'cooperative', invoking the idea of shared ownership.

Contestations over the nature of 'truth' and 'knowledge', the focus of the previous chapter, are situated in relation to debates about 'the canon', interdisciplinarity', and positionality with respect to the production of knowledge. Knowledge is recognised as inherently political, and partial, with the university ideally providing a space for enabling inclusive knowledge production. It has been further argued that 'knowledge' and 'truth' in the humanities and social sciences are particularly prone to contestation and, thus, the most in need of the protection of academic freedom (Scott, 2019); therefore, it is the university that is the 'indispensable organ ... to hold an independent place' (American Association of University Professors (AAUP), 1915, p. 27). Institutional support and funding for the humanities and social sciences is globally under pressure, with the associated status of humanities and social sciences particularly low in the context of the Arab world:

> There is a misconception in our part of the world, equating research with 'scientific' research and measuring research outputs and metrics, you know, using metrics that have been developed for the health sciences, so I think there is definitely need for social science and humanities research. If you think about for example the deployment of religion and religious claims that are made, these are areas that should be researched and there should be serious soul searching and thoughtful reflection on these areas, because they are affecting everything, they are affecting the present and the future. (former Professor of History, AUB, Lebanon, p. 12)

The importance of the social sciences and humanities in informing ethical considerations in the fields of science and technology is also raised. Debates relating to epistemologies and methodologies of newer disciplines in the social sciences and humanities attest to this contestation, as well as critiques of new interdisciplinary fields of study, underpinned by activist agendas:

I guess what's different now is this complete divestment from education as a public good and once education becomes as thoroughly privatised as it has in the United States. We're in deep trouble because we are now beholden – you know I teach at a public University which is, in theory, a public good but we get exactly 6% of our budget from the State and the rest comes from students who are now being construed as consumers, not as citizens in the making but as consumers who have the right to say what they do not like to hear or what they'd prefer to hear or what they'd prefer to learn and not prefer to learn and the State for all of its whopping 6% of our budget that they give us is continually trying to pass laws cracking down on, I do not know if this phrase has come up over there, but the phrase over here is now grievance studies. (Professor of Women's and Gender Studies, US, p. 5)

The denigrating term 'grievance studies' attributed to interdisciplinary fields of study of disability, gender, race, and sexuality is a contestation around the educational mission of the university – firstly, in terms of what 'knowledge' is literally of *value* in a skill-oriented and entrepreneurial knowledge economy, and secondly, in terms of debates around the lack of *objective truth* due to the political positionality of activist knowledge producers. The institutionalisation of such fields of study within the university in terms of departments and programmes of study are thus perceived to threaten the objective production of 'true knowledge' and is seen to undermine academic freedom.

4.2.2 Liberal Arts and the 'Knowledge Economy'

A traditional US liberal arts education is typically championed as supporting the university's mission in supporting democracy and producing well-rounded critically informed citizens. The celebration of the liberal arts education, at AUB in Lebanon, is also strongly evident. AUB is a private university, established in 1866 by American missionaries formerly known as the Syrian Protestant College, with a charter from the State of New York; in 1920, it changed its name to AUB. Since the beginning of the twentieth century, AUB has been imagined as a site of 'intersections', where American aims for liberal education have been juxtaposed onto the particularities of sociopolitical events and public discourses on nationhood, citizenship, personhood, and gender in the Middle East (Kiwan, 2017). In 2016, AUB celebrated its 150th anniversary since it was founded, where it has proudly presented itself as 'authentically' embedded in its local communities and the region with a civic mission, a 'liberal' ethos and a commitment to 'liberal education', whilst also of international significance as a knowledge producer with a wide range of international teaching, research, and business partnerships (Khouri, 2016).

However, a liberal education approach is not the dominant approach of university education in the Arab region. According to a former Professor of History at the AUB, Lebanon, a greater value is attached to a liberal education in the United States compared to the Arab region:

> At least in the US there is still some value attached [to a liberal education]. So even if you are pursuing a profession and most, the best universities usually, although there are professional universities, but the best universities, they require a year or two of general education, there is this requirement. And there is also the expectation that the best degrees are produced by such universities which such approach. This is not the case in the vast majority of the Arab world. The vast majority of the Arab world, most have professional degrees and the professional degrees are not based on a liberal education approach. So the situation is much more critical I think in the Arab world. In terms of funding, in terms of the actual structure of institutions and the tendency now is to create more and more professional specialised institutions, not institutions for education, with some exceptions. (p. 2)

In the branch campus universities of the Gulf, a liberal education is branded as a hallmark of a 'high-quality' American education. Yet, whilst there are universities in the region following a liberal arts curriculum with social sciences and humanities course requirements, this is:

> different from having a social science degree and a humanities degree. So in a university like NYU Abu Dhabi, I mean, there are a few ... there are social sciences and humanities of course but it's engineering and science and so on and if you drill and if you look closer, even within the social sciences, the social sciences areas of specialisation I think tend to be safe. (former Professor of History, AUB, Lebanon, p. 3)

This suggests that the humanities and social sciences in the region face two challenges, the first being, as in the UK and US contexts, a tension with the global discourse of meeting the needs of the economy with a focus on professional skills and competencies:

> But the notion of the corporate university is now a very tricky thing because it really does go to the question of what is its purpose and what is the nature of knowledge production at this moment you know. So you have got this very

corporate, you know, shell there that's working quite, like it's on steroids really. And it's an instrumental thing in itself. And the production of knowledge through that is in a sense to extend that wealth production. There's a kind of schizophrenia going on. (Professor of Cultural Studies, Curtin University, p. 6)

In the Arab region, there are high levels of youth alienation and despair, given the poor educational opportunities and high levels of unemployment, with youth unemployment being the highest in the world (on average, 25 percent) (IMF, 2012). It has been argued that the revolts in the region (Arab Spring) were a result of the combination of severe economic conditions under authoritarian regimes, where people have suffered from high unemployment, poor quality of life, and denial of political and civil rights (Teti and Gervasio, 2011). Not only is there high unemployment, but education too does not meet the needs of the economy to which political instability is in part attributed (Campante and Chor, 2013). Whilst there has been public investment in education, in those countries that do not provide for labour market opportunities, there has been political instability (e.g. Egypt, Tunisia, Yemen, Libya, Jordan, and Morocco), in contrast to the more stable Arab Gulf countries of the UAE, Kuwait, and Qatar with their strong economies (Campante and Chor, 2013).

However, the second challenge is that the humanities and social sciences are also seen to be potentially 'dangerous'. Surveying social science courses on offer in the branch campuses in the UAE suggests a concern with 'playing it safe'. Interviewees note that some course names have been changed or 'neutralised', and course offerings are often controlled centrally with a concern not to challenge perceived sensitivities, despite interviewees attesting to the experience of the freedom to teach 'whatever I wanted'. The issue of academic freedom, therefore, is most tested in the domains of the humanities and social sciences as indeed noted by Dewey a century ago, when comparing academic freedom in the sciences with the social sciences (Dewey, 1916).

Yet, the UAE is not exceptional in this regard either:

> I mean, there's no such thing as absolute academic freedom, it's just within particular kinds of constraints everywhere we go, whether they are forthright or whether they are, you know, nationalist, whether they are part of the tenure system, which is incredibly hierarchal. So I feel like people learn the codes of the place that they are at, whether those are corrupt or not and then regulate themselves in particular kinds of ways and then it's interesting to me because it becomes censorship in certain contexts and other contexts it just becomes business as usual, you know. (Associate Professor of Anthropology, US, p. 3)

The perspective that the UAE is not exceptional, and the importance of taking account of comparative positionality, is similarly echoed in this account:

> So I really do not think Dubai is an exception, especially in the way diversity is managed. So I'm very much against like the portrayal of the city as an exception because it very much sort of feeds into the hostile immigration policies of the UK, and that is obviously my experience as a [non-UK] national living in both of these places, UK and in Dubai. And I mean as a [non-UK] national I feel much more precarious here in the UK in terms of my immigration status than in Dubai. I'm also like you know, my research going forward is going to de-exceptionalise this region and its immigration policies too based on my lived experience as a [non-UK] national in the UK. (Lecturer in Migration Studies, UK, p. 4)

Debates in Western contexts over the Canon, new forms of interdisciplinary studies – including gender, race, disability studies – all attest to a concern with a challenge to the status quo and the risk of social transformation through education:

> Between 1999 and 2014, there were internal pressures upon the nature of what we taught. So to get a gender, sexuality and culture unit up was very difficult. I did manage that in the end, but there were also great tensions with the Deputy Vice Chancellor for Academic who objected to a core unit in our Bachelor of Arts which was called 'Unruly Subjects of Citizenship'. It was a Citizenship Unit really but it was a Cultural Studies oriented unit that looked at various issues around power relations, as you might imagine, identity, but they did not like the title 'Unruly' so there was a great deal of pressure to change the title to something much more standard, even though that unit had been going for a long time, and it was a very popular unit. (Professor of Cultural Studies, Curtin University, p. 3)

As such, it is argued that Western critiques of branch campuses are historically decontextualised and lack self-criticality and moral self-awareness:

> I'm very sceptical of the way that the criticisms of these projects have played out, I feel like they are incredibly orientalist and they reproduce this idea that somehow American higher education in America is like this pure space where we are actually achieving the values of liberalism and stuff when it's completely not! (Associate Professor of Anthropology, US, p. 8)

Such decontextualised critiques are positioned outside history and do not recognise the long history of education and scholarship in the Muslim world, with the first university, the University of Al Quaraouiyine, in Morocco, established in 859 AD, and the Al-Azhar University, in Cairo, established in 970 AD, predating the establishment of the European medieval universities of Oxford, Cambridge, and Bologna. The transnational production and circulation of knowledge also long predate contemporary internationalisation initiatives with archived accounts attesting to the fluidity of exchanges and relationships between regions and scholars. Furthermore, such critiques do not acknowledge the role of the university in the West as an institution embedded in histories of slavery, eugenics, and ongoing contemporary institutionalised racism, sexism, and complicity with controversial government policies such as the Prevent policy in the UK context. Campaigns such as Rhodes Must Fall and a number of universities in the United States, and, more recently, the University of Cambridge, United Kingdom, are starting to acknowledge the involvement of these institutions in slavery. According to a UK Professor of History, commenting on the history of a leading university in the United Kingdom: 'The [university] of course has been the repository of a long tradition of eugenics and pseudoscience on race for a long time and is only now beginning I think to come round to rethink and face up to that history and background' (p. 7). Similarly, one interviewee notes the publicised case of Goldsmiths College, University of London, United Kingdom, and the campaign against the 'alleged' 'endemic problem' of sexual harassment which has been 'persistent and consistent over years and years', whilst another US-based professor describes the situation on US campuses, where 'sexual assault is outrageously prevalent on campuses over here and it's true that frequently students have tried to make this known and it's been covered up'. (Professor of Women's and Gender Studies, US, p. 11).

4.2.3 (De-)Constructing the Nation

The intellectual history of the university represents a discourse of a nation's imagined futures. There is a substantive literature on education, citizenship, and nation state formation, examining how the nation state uses educational policies in constructing and propagating a vision of national citizenship through education (Kiwan, 2018). As previously mentioned, the university's mission in the US context has been framed within a discourse of promoting democracy and creating well-informed critical citizens. Yet, this discourse is contested and is in tension with more explicitly instrumental discourses of the 'knowledge economy' and meeting a society's employment needs, increasingly a dominant global discourse. Decolonisation discourses in the US, UK, and African university contexts have taken the form of 'colouring' leadership of these institutions. One UK Professor of Sociology on visiting a South African university observed what she refers to as 'mimicking':

> The institutions there, the buildings, the structures, the apartheid system is already spatially and geographically and architecturally imposed. And now, twenty five years after the liberation of South Africa and the fall of apartheid, we have these incredible black scholars and activists now slotting into those institutions. But those institutions are still white. They are brown bodies in white institutions and they are still, the power – so they might have a black VC or a woman VC or whatever, they are still white male institutions. (p. 8)

The description of a 'white male patriarchy but with brown bodies' (p. 8) is similarly attributed to the UK university as an institution:

> I, as an outsider, I could feel the monolithic-ness. And I think I can feel it because I experience it here every day of my life. I've been a brown body allowed into mega-ly white institutions here and that crashing sense in which you have to conform to get on, and all that you give up for that. (p. 8)

Colonial rulers in the nineteenth and twentieth centuries in the Arab region used education as a means of rule, introducing American and European schools and universities in the region with these competing traditions continuing as a legacy in post-colonial states (Sbaiti, 2010). In the Arab region, education has been centrally important in states' nation-building missions, and the national university is typically seen as a symbol of national identity, national development, and autonomy in post-colonial contexts after the Second World War. In 1939, there were a total of ten universities in the Arab world, increasing to twenty universities in 1961, forty-seven universities in 1975, and over 200 universities in 2000. This 'massification' (as well as privatisation) in HE – a worldwide trend – is evident in the Arab world, with 398 universities in the Arab world by 2011 (Jaramillo and Melonio, 2011).

However, this framing in terms of 'nationalising' projects needs to be historically contextualised to recognise that the production of knowledge and schools in the Arab region have a long history, long predating modernity and the nation state (Kiwan, 2018). As such, schools and higher educational institutions in the region can be conceived of as sites of 'intersections' between Western (colonial/neo-colonial/post-colonial) and national sociopolitical particularities and discourses on citizenship in the Arab world (Kiwan, 2017b).

The AUB in Lebanon has played an important role in educating the Arab elite and middle class of the region, as well as educating teachers and bureaucrats serving under the colonial mandate governments in the region at that time. As an institution, it holds a significant place in the regional imagination, with literatures on its role in the region not only as a highly ranked educational institution with alumni of regional and international significance (AUB, 1979; AUB Centennial Lectures, 1967; Bliss, 1994) but also for its role in Arab nationalism (Anderson, 2011), student politics, and women as citizens and learners in the early twentieth–century Beirut (Cortas, 2009; Makdisi, 2006).

Contestations of education as a nation state bounded project in the region emerge in response to large non-citizen populations – both refugees in the Levant region and 'guest-workers' in the Arabian Gulf region. There is a literature that considers supranational initiatives, and, for example, how 'quasi-state institutions' such as the Palestinian Authority deal with notions of citizenship through education policy. The position of Palestinian and Syrian refugees across the Arab region, notably in Lebanon and Jordan, raises policy dilemmas in the absence of any foreseeable route to legal citizenship in these host countries. The positionality of the everyday lived experiences of non-citizens in the nation-building discourses of the UAE and Qatar also nuance dominant 'ethno-nationalist' models of citizenship (Koch, 2016; Vora, 2019).

4.3 INTERNATIONALISATION OF HIGHER EDUCATION

Over the last half century, we have witnessed changes in HE globally that are as significant as the developments in the nineteenth-century Germany when the research university first emerged. 'Massification' is now seen as inevitable, with global averages of those participating in HE having risen sharply from 19 percent in 2000 to 26 percent in 2007, and it is projected to continue to rise to 40 percent by 2030 (Altbach et al., 2009). It is expected that more women and more diversified student populations (older, part-time, etc.) will feature prominently in debates about access for disadvantaged groups. Sub-Saharan Africa has the lowest participation rates at 5 percent (Altbach et al., 2009) with the Arab region at around 36.42 percent in 2014 (Our World in Data, 2018), 48 percent of 25–34-year-olds in the United States in 2017 (OECD, 2018), and 49.8 percent in the United Kingdom in 2017 (Department for Education, 2018). HE enrolment rates in the Arab world more than doubled between 2000 and 2016 (UNESCO, 2018).

Despite international and national policies to widen participation, there are increasing social and economic inequalities globally. Widening participation is often contested and juxtaposed against a discourse of concerns about quality and lowering of standards. Global neoliberalism is transforming the discourse from social justice to economic development and its associated discourses of quality, competitiveness, and individual 'choice' (Burke, 2013). However, there are inequalities in access, despite a trend of increased numbers entering HE – in effect, an increase in access, rather than a widening of access. The privileged have retained their advantages globally, with socioeconomic status being the greatest predictor of exclusion, given that HE costs are a huge barrier to access. This is the case even when tuition is free because of the hidden costs of transport, living expenses, loss of income, and psychological fear of debt.

Private HE is rapidly expanding, with a shift from HE being seen as a public good to a private good driven by funding shortages (Altbach et al., 2009). HE is increasingly envisioned as a means to provide access to the global economy, leading to increased enrolment. In addition, quality assurance is central to many nations' policy agendas and is also driven by 'consumer' demands for certification, student mobility, and 'outcomes' of education. As such, the global model of the 'successful' university is one that is 'disconnected from the nation state and constituent cities and regions' (Goddard et al., 2016, p. 3), instead focusing on diversifying its sources of funding and being globally competitive (Kiwan, 2017b), with the sought-after brand of the 'global university'.

The Arab region has also seen what Buckner (2011) terms 'imported internationalisation', with the establishment of numerous partnerships with US and UK universities, especially in the Gulf Arab states, keen on establishing a 'knowledge economy': examples include Doha's Education City (Qatar) and Dubai's Knowledge Park (UAE), which house a large concentration of branch campuses of prestigious US and UK universities. There are a range of different models of these partnerships, with over half being 'branch campuses'. One-third of all branch campuses globally are located in the Arab region and have opened since 2000 (Miller-Idriss and Banauer, 2011). These branch campuses typically specialise in a few academic fields, usually professional fields, such as business, accountancy, technology, education, and engineering; hire foreign faculty from the affiliate institution; and grant degrees from this affiliate institution (Miller-Idriss and Banauer, 2011). This is in contrast to institutions established in the late nineteenth and early twentieth centuries, such as AUB and the American University in Cairo, which were established by foreign missionaries, are based on a US liberal arts model of education, and have US charters. Other forms of internationalisation include 'offshore/transnational programmes', where a programme is offered in a host institution, typically using curricula from the foreign affiliate institution and taught by its faculty: 'replica campuses' such as New York University (NYU) Abu Dhabi, which are research universities offering liberal arts and sciences to undergraduate and postgraduate students using curricula from NYU in the United States and typically delivered by its faculty and virtual branch campuses with a limited presence in the host country (Miller-Idriss and Banauer, 2011).

There is a critique of the mission of the university being eroded both by neoliberal pressures and financial interests as well as internationalisation ventures in the form of branch campuses in non-liberal contexts outside the West. Commenting on the Australian branch campus of Curtin University in Dubai:

> What is it about being a global university for Curtin and how does it actually go and have campuses, how does it set up shop in countries in which it is criminal to be an LGBTIQ person? How can we do that? And that was a very challenging and difficult discussion for the Vice Chancellor who prides himself on inclusion and so on. (Professor Baden Offord, Curtin University, p. 7)

In addition, these critiques also take the form of characterising the phenomenon of branch campuses as neo-colonial/imperialist ventures. Commenting on branch campuses in the UAE, one UK UCU Branch officer argues that this amounts to an 'imperial project where we are exploiting slave labour in Dubai and we are extracting a lot of money from Dubai. So it's very similar to some of the historically imperialist companies that operated in the Middle East actually' (p. 9).

Similarly, Professor Andrew Ross of NYU details his concerns with the establishment of NYU Abu Dhabi:

> There was a lot of concern about violations of labour standards and human rights. There's really well documented patterns of exploitations. So we wanted to try to ensure that the building of the campus would be – you know, would be an operation that observes fair labour standards. And we formed a coalition on campus, called the Fair Labour Coalition, which the administration found very hard to adopt labour values. And on paper they did agree to do so – and they are the strongest labour standards in the region as it happens. But implementation is very, very difficult, and a lot of our efforts were focused on trying to get third party monitoring of labour conditions. We were not very successful in doing that, and so there were, you know, repeated accounts of violations. (p. 4)

These positions are presented normatively, justified in terms of human rights abuses. Yet, constructs such as 'imperialist' mischaracterise the relational transnational power dynamics and also efface agency and responsibility of UAE actors. Normative arguments become decontextualised from the socio-political and economic agentic missions of the region. The UAE, and Dubai in particular, is the most important economic centre in the Middle East, with thriving sectors of foreign trade, tourism, and banking. Education is a key priority in the UAE as reflected in their 2017–2021 strategic education plan and the Higher Education Strategy 2030; in addition, the UAE's internationalisation strategy has been successful in transforming it to one of the leading transnational education hubs in the world. It has high outbound student mobility, which increased by 31 percent between 2012 and 2016, with the United Kingdom and the United States being the most popular destinations. However, significantly inbound student mobility is huge and rising exponentially, with the highest rate in the world at 48.6 percent (World Education News and Reviews, 2018). According to the United Nations Educational, Scientific and Cultural Organization (UNESCO) (2023), the UAE, with a population of 9 million, hosted 220,000 international students, proportionally more compared with both the United Kingdom, with its population of 67 million hosting just over half a million international students, and the United States, with a population of 333 million hosting 1 million international students.

Concerns were expressed, however, with the normative implications of the 'illiberal' branch campus, where a biological metaphor of 'embodiment' characterises the relationship of the branch campus as a constituent body part, under the control of the main campus body, such as the limb is under the control of the brain:

> So I've put it very clearly to them that having campuses, embodied campuses, so you know, there's a lot of nuance that has to be had with these discussions because international – a university by itself in some ways ought to be engaging and going through encountering other cultures, and countering different systems of knowing and encountering otherness. So I do not think, that's never an issue for me whatsoever. But when we start to have embodied campuses, that is extensions of our own campus here, in places in which the laws of that place actually apply on the campus – it's not like an embassy for example. An embassy can put a rainbow flag up in Dubai you know, in the Australian Embassy without any punitive problems, but you cannot do that with the campuses. (Professor Baden Offord, Curtin University, p. 7)

The metaphorical image is one of a limb no longer synchronised with the workings of the brain. Rather than conceptualising education in terms of its bodily 'boundedness' and ethical coherence, the more recent interdisciplinary turn in the mobilities literature reconceptualises education and space focusing not only on the *mobilities* of people and educational policies but also on the mobility of academic institutions, such as the growth in transnational education and the growth of branch campuses and the mobility of ideas (Waters, 2016). As such, this enables a recognition of the relationality and *fluidity* of power within the transnational relationships of branch campuses and the main US- or UK-based campuses. This is illustrated in the account below of the positionality of research in the Gulf region at its branch campuses:

> We're thinking already in a self-conscious way of ways in which we can take advantage for our location and sort of ... and develop ways of research interests and also, you know, leverage certain perspectives which are not available to us from Washington or somewhere. People tend naturally towards certain areas because of the location, so for example there's a big focus here on Indian Ocean studies, you know, cultural and political and so on. There is more focus here on developments in the East, you know, whether it's in terms of state formation but also at the cultural level, a critical assessment of regional studies, so there are certain areas. Another area of interest is Islamic bioethics. (Professor of History, Gulf region, p. 5)

Similarly, the university positionality of AUB enables a unique construction of American Studies that is not directed from a US construction of the field, as discussed in Chapter 3. Despite intended US foreign policy intentions, the discipline has been transformed in its exportation to the Middle East. Professor Alex Lubin, former Director of Centre for AUB Beirut's Center for American Studies and Research, contrasts his experience in the different higher educational institutional contexts of the United States and Beirut, Lebanon:

> In the United States it was impossible, at least when I went to Beirut in 2011, it was still very difficult in the US to engage those conversations without being accused of being antisemitic frankly. And Beirut and AUB was for me – and I specify that it was specifically for me because I know it's not for everybody – it was a very open place to engage in the kinds of research that I was doing. (p. 6)

He describes how 'CASAR became an oasis for those of us who are interested in a critique of US empire that focused on US policy in the Middle East. And that's because it opened up an avenue for discourse that was difficult in the United States' (p. 6).

The concern with human rights abuses and difference in values is presented as a result of the dominant neoliberal enterprise:

> But in terms of whether, is Dubai a mistake? Yes I think it is. And I think that in terms of why it's a mistake is because I think that the very basis of going to Dubai was built upon a very corporate idea of what Curtin is. It's a very instrumentally based thing. (Professor Baden Offord, Curtin University, p. 8)

This judgement is based from the perspective of the home institution in Australia; in contrast, a US-based Anthropologist argues that:

> in criticising another place and presuming that that other place is authoritarian, illiberal, you know, like all the tropes that then get smuggled in with saying 'oh, you know, this is a neoliberal enterprise', like, they still rely on these highly racialised ways of thinking about how the world is split up and these moral ideas about who's superior and who's inferior. (p. 9)

4.4 GOVERNANCE AND FUNDING: WHO OWNS THE UNIVERSITY?

We also have this conception, which I'm assuming you do over there as well, we have a conception of faculty governance, right, or we used to have a conception of faculty governance which in theory – I mean this is the poison of New Liberalism right, that it's being taken away from us on a daily basis.
(Professor of Women's and Gender Studies, US, p. 4)

4.4.1 Management and Audit Culture

There is a global discourse of the 'knowledge' economy shaping structures, processes, and practices in HE. In addition, reduced government funding for HE has resulted in the growth of the private university sector, as well as a managerial and accountability discourse with practices of incentives in teaching and research. For example, in the UK context, the introduction of the Research Assessment Exercise in the 1980s and academic appraisals have been described as 'managerial technologies' and have become examples of many such technologies introduced into HE, borrowed from the private sector (Cribb and Gewirtz, 2013). More recent technologies in the UK context include the

Workload Recognition Model, the Research Excellence Framework, and the Teaching Excellence Framework. Increases in student numbers and programme offerings have been framed in terms of meeting the economic needs of the knowledge economy. The rise of initiatives relating to knowledge exchange, quality assurance, and other forms of university management similarly illustrate the changes in organisational culture reflected in language as well as practices:

> I mean, there's some really bullshit management speak, like multiplex delivery needed and stuff like this. And it just sounds like a total auto-satire because, for me, the level of language is so ridiculous and often it's not even managers that are the worst but academics who are striving to be in management and almost trying to outperform management and are actually much worse. (Lecturer in Geography, University of Leicester, UK, p. 8)

Cribb and Gewirtz (2013) characterise the university as the 'hollowed out' university, where the university is a place providing a service as opposed to an academic self-governing community:

> There are no strategies for Departments themselves can determine, you know, they have to have their strategy agreed but, in a sense, the focus of that strategy is defined outside the Department, even to the extent of what the research plans, you know, the focus of the research of the Department should be (Professor of Sociology, UK, p. 4).

The effect of managerial technologies in HE on academic freedom is enabled through the neoliberal culture of the student as customer which is perceived to curb academic freedom:

> There have been so many discussions about people feeling that their censorship is coming from the students because they are now customers and all the rankings and stuff and, at the moment, I'm at a university which is not a Russell Group university and has maybe also an aspiration to join that group, I do not know so much about that here because I've just joined and I do not know basically anything about the politics here other than we have a problematic management with every university. (Lecturer in Geography, University of Leicester, p. 8)

The system of tenure in the US context is also frequently commented on where greater academic freedom is accorded with tenure:

> Well, you know that institutional frameworks are pushing us to publish as fast as we can, right, in as great a quantity as we can. So I mean I guess this is easy for me to say, right, because I have tenure and I've been promoted to full Professor, so I have much more academic freedom than I did before tenure. So that's another

thing about academic freedom, that it's very contingent upon one's rank and one's institutional position and privilege, so I've got a lot of institutional privilege. (Professor of Women's and Gender Studies, US, p. 3)

A number of senior academics with tenure and job security reflected on the sense of responsibility that comes with this towards more vulnerable colleagues:

So I kind of alternate between thinking I cannot take this anymore, I'm not going to say anything else about it, I'm just going to shut up, and thinking the opposite actually. I'm really, really furious about what's going on. And the other thing is that I feel I have a responsibility to speak out, so I'm lucky enough to be in a fairly senior position on a permanent contract. I feel like a lot of more junior colleagues would not take that risk because these things can have really serious consequences. And I understand that and I would not expect everybody to speak out, because people are more vulnerable. So I feel people like me who can afford to take certain risks because of our secure position within our institutions have a duty to speak out in defence of young colleagues. (Professor of Education, UK, p. 8)

The gendered and racialised nature of this vulnerability was commented on:

I see it as a kind of feminist principle as well, because it is mostly women. It's overwhelmingly women who are being targeted and it's also of course, I mean another thing that really upsets me about this is I've done quite a lot of work with critical philosophy of race and I've made efforts within my discipline to bring young researchers, people of colour, you know young researchers, new academics into mainstream and ... publishing and so on. They're really dealing with, there's quite a lot of evidence, of the obstacles that black women face in academia and the UK in terms of promotion and so on. And so they are more likely to be in the more insecure, lower down positions. And so they are also the ones least likely to be able to speak out. So I think there's a way in which it becomes a self-perpetuating thing in which it's the same senior white middle aged women who are always speaking out. (Professor of Education, UK, p. 8)

This positionality with respect to gender and race within the institutional structure of the university is further explicitly noted: 'No, I do not think being white and male has ever been a disadvantage to anyone in a university setting. I do not believe that'. (Professor of Education, University of Birmingham, UK, p. 5)

In addition to the change in university culture and perceived lack of academic community, there is a concomitant discourse of lack of well-being and mental health of both staff and students. Within this sample of interviewees, there was a gendered and racialised pattern to comfort with the level of attribution of data, striking in the context of a study on academic freedom. Interviewees referred to a culture of stress, fear, and powerlessness. Social media is a spatial extension of this space:

> And I'm quite amazed actually at the people I know who are very active on social media who engage in these kind of debates and discussions all the time. I do not know how they deal with, you know they obviously have a very thick skin or nerves of steel, because I do find it emotionally extremely stressful, the bit of exposure I've had. And that's why I've sort of taken a decision not to be on social media. I know that I could not cope with that kind of thing. I'm not emotionally strong enough to deal with it I do not think. And I completely understand that some people just cannot take that level of stress. (Professor of Education, UK, p. 9)

Another interviewee reflects on the conditions leading to the decision to taking early retirement:

> You invest in the system, you invest in the structures, and when you get to the top of the mountain, you look down, you see the lie that it is and you see the way that you have been used in the system and you just feel depressed you know. And it's part of the reason that I took early retirement. (Emeritus Professor of Sociology, UK, p. 10)

This act can be understood not as an individual act of defeat or disempowerment but as a performance of agency and disruption. Emotional responses can be understood not just as an individual psychological reaction to stress but also as a political practice (Ahmed, 2014). Yet, the display of emotion can be used by university managers and university processes to undermine the critique of the institutional status quo:

> Then I'm the difficult, angry person. But they kind of like you to be difficult and angry because that means that they can pathologise you and put you in a box and allow you to spout off in your corner. Like I said at the beginning, the safety valve, our bodies become, and who we are and what we do become the safety valve. (Emeritus Professor of Sociology, UK, p. 4)

Gregg and Seigworth (2010) similarly conceive of theorisation of affect as the 'politically engaged work' of such groups marginalised in terms of gender, sexuality, disability, and those in the Global South. Understanding emotion as a social and political practice thus enables us to explore how affect is utilised in the production or silencing of knowledge:

> You will not get money, no, because of the system. It's an illusion. You'll be allowed to publish but it's off your own back, it's off your own experience. It's emotionally draining. It's exhausting. You're not able to compete with your peers and other scholars who are not doing race work. You know exactly what I'm talking about. (Emeritus Professor of Sociology, UK, p. 7)

The illusion of bringing about change is also referred to with regard to higher education's managerialisation of diversity:

> So you give someone like me a position like that so that I can be the safety valve for the establishment. And I'm aware of that every single day. So I'm allowed to spout off whatever I like. And they do not come, they never come to my sessions but they are happy I'm doing them. 'Oh [Interviewee name] doing that. We've ticked that box, it's fine'. And in fact it's actually worse in some – not worse than you know, losing your life, but it allows the status quo to just be you know. (Emeritus Professor of Sociology, UK, p. 4)

The bodily sense of the emotional burden is further elucidated with reference to the metaphor of 'sin eater':

> And we are invited to speak and to do – that's my agreement really, that we are invited to speak and do and say, because of our bodies. They want our bodies to carry that weight for them. It's like we are this – I saw this movie many years ago called The Sin Eater where this person comes and eats, they can eat all the food when somebody dies and they take on the sins of that person. It's like we take on the – they do not have to deal with racism because we are the vents. We are the depositories of all their sins and they do not have to deal with it and they go their merry way you know. (Emeritus Professor of Sociology, UK, p. 11)

4.4.2 Funding

Scott (2019) traces the origins of academic freedom in the US context over the last century, stating that its aim was to address 'conflicts about the relationships between power and knowledge' (p. 39). The 1915 'Declaration of Principles' of the AAUP in the context of the new research university was aimed at protecting the autonomy of academic faculty from the corporate structures that support it. Yet, embedded in this articulation is an unresolved tension between being independent from the sources of financial power supporting the university and indirectly serving these sources through the production of knowledge over a contested 'public good' (Scott, 2019).

The lack of funding in certain areas, in particular, the field of race, is evident in the funding priorities of research councils:

> If I did randomised control trials of educational innovations in school effectiveness I could make millions of pounds, but the research that I do tends to be, most of my research is not externally funded at all. Every now and again I get external funding for a dedicated project. But it's always when race will have been raised as an issue somewhere else. The State and research funders really aren't that interested in anti-racist research. (Professor of Education, UK)

Institutionalised structures for research in the university are also critiqued. Commenting on the establishment of the Centre for Research on Race in Education at the University of Birmingham, UK, Professor Gillborn wryly notes:

> I do not think it's a coincidence that when we set the race centre up at Birmingham, it was the only University-based centre at an English University looking at racism in education and it's founding Director was a white man. I do not think that's coincidental, it tells you a lot about the Academy. (p. 4)

The role of university affiliation in securing external funding, and university support for certain forms of research, is discussed in the well-publicised and contested case of Noah Carl, a postdoctoral fellow at the University of Cambridge:

> I was one of the people who signed the public letter saying that the Fellowship at Cambridge was a disgrace. I'm also one of the people that Noah Carl in his work kind of identifies as one of the bad guys. So in his paper about so called Stifling Debate about Race and IQ . . . looking for links between race and systematic and/or genetically based differences in ability, they ought to just come clean and say 'well, this is racist research' because that's what it is. (Professor of Education, UK, p. 7)

Transnational funding arrangements between the main campus and its branch campus were commented on by two NYU Professors with experience in the NYU Abu Dhabi branch campus. It was noted that for NYU Abu Dhabi, in particular, the drive for the branch campus is presented as the UAE purchasing soft power:

> So these institutions made these deals with states that were looking to use their soft power and looking to use I guess some of the excess wealth they had in these ways to improve their image, than maybe increase their internal capacity and do something for their people. (Professor, NYU, p. 10)

Funding for NYU Abu Dhabi comes from the UAE, in addition to financial incentives given to NYU, New York: 'So the salaries, so it's not just building the campus for NYU, the salaries are all paid'. (Professor, NYU, p. 13). The transnational flow of money between the NYU branch campus in Abu Dhabi back to NYU New York is further commented on:

> the amount of money that is released from Abu Dhabi funds that flows into the system – the entire operation is bank rolled by Abu Dhabi authorities. That money does not just stay in Abu Dhabi, it comes sloshing over into New York, and it fills the coffers of academic departments here, because if you send faculty to NYU Abu Dhabi, then you are very richly rewarded. You know, the department suddenly has a lot of funds [laughs]. Individuals who go and teach there get very lavishly remunerated. The department also gets rewarded. And so, yes, the department does have Abu Dhabi funds, and it uses them at its discretion. (Professor of Cultural Studies, NYU, p. 5)

4.4.3 Unions

Academic freedom is seen to be protected through the strength of a university's union, referred to by interviewees in the United Kingdom, the United States, and Lebanon:

> Because I am active in my Union and I'm very lucky to be on a Campus that has a Union and a collective bargaining agreement, I feel really strongly that as a tenured Professor it's part of my job to speak out about inequities that I see in the institution, that the junior faculty who do not feel as empowered to speak, it's my job to advocate for them and speak out for them. (Professor of Women's and Gender Studies, US, p. 4)

Another interviewee comments on the important role of the union, in relation not only to the university but to external pressures and restrictions on academic freedom, such as 'Canary Mission', a website established in 2014, documenting cases of pro-Palestinian scholarship in US universities, which is deemed to be 'anti-Semitic':

> I really feel very lucky to be at [] for that reason, we have a very strong union and the union has called me to tell me that they are on top of things and that I should not worry and that they are keeping abreast of this issue. I'm also in a Department where across the entire university the only people who are on these lists are in my Department. (Professor of Anthropology, US)

'Faculty United', a non-profit association serving as the AUB Chapter of the AAUP, operates effectively as a union at AUB. Its mission is outlined as 'to promote substantive faculty participation in AUB's institutional governance, to defend academic freedom, to improve the economic status and terms and conditions of employment of faculty members at the university, and to advance the standards, ideals, and welfare of the academic profession' (AUB Faculty United, 2019). Faculty United developed as a response to unfavourable developments with the Faculty contracts and the impetus to take a collective stand: 'And this is how Faculty United came to be in the first place as a reaction by some Faculty, by a number of small group of Faculty towards administrative decisions that were taking place that were unilateral without consultation with Faculty members and did not engage us' (Professor of Psychology, AUB, Beirut, p. 2).

Professor Jad Chaaban (Economics, AUB, Beirut) describes its development starting with his writing of a secret document in 2011, which was only shared with a few close colleagues. Taking consultation from lawyers:

> We immediately did it as a chapter of the American Association of University Professors, which is the oldest, as you know, association in the US and it organises a lot. And then we just announced it, when it was all done, that now we have an association that is a chapter of the AAUP Association. It was a major surprise here especially for the administration that we could actually pull this off. (Professor Jad Chaaban, AUB, Beirut, p. 5)

Over the following few years, Faculty United developed a strong and sizeable membership and achieved considerable success. However, the change in administration in 2015 has posed challenges to Faculty United:

> Unlike the previous administration, the current administration is very short on dissent and there is unfortunately a culture of fear that has come to the campus that did not exist even at the strongest of opposition times with the previous administration. And that is felt by both Faculty United executives and leadership as well as the Faculty in general. Do you see what I'm trying to say? So the culture of fear, people are afraid to speak up, people are afraid to talk, people are afraid to voice dissent, there are many brown nosers about trying to curry favour and so on and so forth and the others are not feeling comfortable or confident enough to challenge certain decisions that are happening. And that is new. That did not exist before. (Professor, AUB, Beirut, p. 8)

Yet, Faculty United was recognised as having considerable power, which the Founder of Faculty United sees as the guiding rationale for co-opting its senior members into positions of managerial power within the institution: 'He put, so Deans, Associate Deans were appointed from Faculty

United or were invited to run then were selected. And this was from the founding group. So this was the first kind of move to kind of buy the group in or lure them in' (Professor Jad Chaaban, AUB, Beirut, p. 7).

The institution of the university union is also seen to play an important role in relation to raising issues arising from the context of branch campuses. The role operates primarily through interrogating central university management and public discourses within the UK and US contexts, although practically constrained by and in tension with local national law in the UAE context. According to a UCU branch officer, academics have raised a range of concerns pertaining to the operation of UK university branch campuses in the Gulf. Furthermore, the union takes the role of raising the university's legal obligations:

> There's reports from Human Rights Watch that they are part of this ongoing practice of forced labour. So we know it's happening, we know that puts the university in all kinds of trouble in terms of they are, as a charity, they have duties under EU law not to allow forced labour or modern slavery in their supply chain. So we think they are in breach of that. (UCU branch officer, UK, p. 3)

In addition, the UNESCO definition of academic freedom is frequently cited in university statements on academic freedom referring to both the academic's autonomy and freedom from state repression. As such, unions have played a role ensuring academics are aware of their rights with respect to any university requests to contribute to or work at branch campuses.

4.5 EXCEPTIONALISM AND CONTEXT

Historically, the university was conceived as a space separate from its political and social surroundings. This separation was embodied both as a physically separate space, with universities walled off from the city, and as an intellectual space, where the pursuit of knowledge is imagined as transcending the political, social, economic, and legal constraints of society. Critiques of the erosion of the university's exceptional separateness arising from neoliberal imperatives of the market (Giroux, 2002) are, therefore, made on two assumptions: firstly, that the university can, in fact, function as if separate from its context, and secondly, that this separateness is normatively a desirable ideal, framed in terms of discourses of academic freedom.

Arguments that the university should not be conceived of as separate from its surroundings are evidenced in the form of discourses promoting the idea that the rationale of university's mission is to serve the economic and political needs of key 'stakeholders' in society, and also as evidenced in the dominance of discourses, policies, and practices promoting 'impactful' research. This conception is also framed in relation to discourses of the civic university and co-producing communities of knowledge and practice. In the colonial context, the discourse of being embedded within the local community and region is a discourse of authenticity. For example, in 2016, AUB celebrated its 150th anniversary since it was founded, where it has proudly presented itself as 'authentically' embedded in its local communities and the region with a civic mission, a 'liberal' ethos, and a commitment to 'liberal education', whilst also of international significance as a knowledge producer with a wide range of international teaching, research, and business partnerships (Khouri, 2016). The former AUB President described the university: 'AUB is of the region and for the region' (Dorman, 2011), and AUB's 'Neighborhood Initiative', established in 2007, locates 'the histories of AUB and Ras Beirut [as] ... intertwined, shaping each other's identity and place within the city', emphasising its particular geographical location (AUB Neighborhood Initiative, 2015). Its civic mission is explicit in that the rationale of the Initiative which is presented in a discourse of 'giving back to its neighborhood, by mobilising the university's resources for the public good, beginning just outside the campus walls' (Kiwan, 2017b). As such, AUB imagines itself as 'authentic' and embedded in contrast to the branch campus universities in the Gulf.

In contrast, the traditional ivory tower model is proposed as necessary for the pursuit of knowledge unfettered by dynamics of power through political, religious, and economic relationships embedded in society. McGreevy (2018) also argues that non-democratic countries favour such a model of separation to geographically and intellectually limit effects on the surrounding societal context, which may hold different social, political, and religious views.

Yet, McGreevy (2018) argues that universities are in a 'paradoxical' position, as they are simultaneously 'places of closure' and 'places of openness'. The term 'places of closure' refers to the disciplined structure of knowledge, whilst at the same time being open to innovative, critical, and new ways of thinking. He further argues that such 'neo-monasticism' will not preserve and nurture the production of knowledge, but rather the university becomes 'caged and defanged by greater separation' (McGreevy, 2018, p. 6):

> Universities have been conceived up as separate from the world around them. And I think that that is part of their DNA and the way they have always been conceived. But I think that that is problematic. And one of the ways it's problematic is in regards to freedom. Does the university need special freedom? Many people have made this argument that it should be kind of a sanctuary for freedom and for free enquiry and open enquiry. But I sort of feel like this does not work you know. We create these pristine places you know, like Yosemite. We put a fence around them and we say 'Look, we preserved nature'. That's not the problem at all. The problem is living with nature. It seems to me we have a similar problem in universities. You can wall them off and say 'Look we allow these people to have all this freedom and all this, to pursue any topic they want.' (Professor Patrick McGreevy, Former CASAR Director and Dean of Faculty of Arts and Sciences, AUB, Beirut, p. 2)

The question of whether the university or its academics should have special freedoms is raised by the following interviewee:

> about academics is that they exist in a unique positionality where they have access to a much wider range of platforms through which to speak and also a much broader, a much larger audience. And in addition to those two things, a greater degree of authority within the society in which they live. And what that means is that – or this is what I've kind of proposed in my work – is that academics actually pose greater dangers than non-academics who do not have those kind of additional factors relating to their speech, except in the case of course of politicians and celebrities for example. (Lecturer in Philosophy of Science, UK, p. 2)

The concern expressed here is that academics not only have greater public profile and opportunities to reach a larger audience, but they also hold a greater degree of authority that is not necessarily warranted when commented on areas outside their areas of expertise, and this could be conceived as an abuse of power. What is proposed is for constraints on academics in order to protect the public, as well as students.

4.6 CONCLUSION

This chapter has critically examined discourses of the perceived role of the university and how this relates to constructions of knowledge and its implications for pedagogy, research, and academic freedom. Various constructions of the mission of the university, including 'pursuit of truth', 'public good', 'knowledge economy', and 'image of the nation' are interrogated in transnational perspective. Developments of the mission of the university are also examined in the context of the massification and internationalisation of HE globally. Changes in university governance, funding, and pervasiveness of an audit culture are considered in relation to the theory and practice of academic freedom. The following chapter develops this theme through a focus on the 'internal' and 'external' restrictions on the production of knowledge.

5 Challenging Knowledge
Internal and External Restrictions

> So when we defend academic freedom, we defend the complex institutional conditions that make its exercise possible, and we understand those conditions and its exercise as bound up with one another; if the conditions fall away, the exercise becomes impossible.
>
> (Butler, 2015, p. 293)

5.1 INTRODUCTION

The previous chapter critically examined the role of the university in contextualising practices of academic freedom through a consideration of rationales for the mission of the university and in the context of the internationalisation of higher education globally. The interrogation of governance and funding practices illustrates mechanisms that constrain academic freedom, which is further examined in this chapter, in addition to constraints on academic freedom at the level of the university and at the level of the individual. The contextualisation of such constraints is examined through the lens of geographical and sociopolitical positionalities, as well as the positionality of individuals. The constraints of the nature of topics researched, taught, and publicly debated are also examined intersectionally in relation to the situated geo-sociopolitical contexts.

Through an examination of internal and external restrictions (individual, institutional, national, and international) on the production of knowledge, this chapter first explores Butler's (2015) arguments for the conditions for academic freedom, in order to situate various discourses affecting the practice of academic freedom, including 'neoliberalism', 'civility', 'quality', and procedural processes. Second, restrictions imposed by the university are examined, for example, the role of institutional practices, such as the practices of research ethics committees (Hammersley, 2009). The ethical regulation of research in universities globally has increasingly become institutionalised. As such, this regulation gives the university legitimacy in controlling the production of knowledge. The role of students, the university environment with respect to employment security, and diversity are also examined.

Third, the interrelationship between university and state-imposed constraints is critically explored through a focus on the UK Research Excellence Framework (REF) and Impact agenda and the practices of research funding councils for international research with Global North–South partnerships. Examples of critical analysis include examining tensions between contributing to local issues versus gaining international recognition – international collaborations where researchers in the Global South typically contribute data rather than setting the theoretical/research agendas (Connell, 2014) – and blurring of public/private with the establishment of 'offshore' or branch campuses.

This chapter sets the scene for examining what knowledge is considered 'forbidden', the focus of the following chapter, Chapter 6, which will examine restrictions on topics that vary by place, such as Palestine, gender and sexuality, race, government agendas (e.g. anti-extremism initiatives such as the UK Prevent Strategy), and also self-censorship in relation to these topics.

5.2 THE CONDITIONS OF ACADEMIC FREEDOM

Butler (2015, p. 293) argues that academic freedom cannot be separated – logically or in practice – from the 'conditions of its exercise'. This means that any defence of academic freedom is simultaneously a defence of the context that enables its practice. Conversely, if these enabling conditions or context are no longer present, then the practice of academic freedom is no longer possible. Butler (2015) develops this argument using the case of scholars in Palestine working under conditions of underfunding, frequent university closures, checkpoints, and student and faculty detentions arising from their political viewpoints. She argues that these conditions undermine the right to education itself, which is both a precondition and a part of definition of academic freedom. She further argues that the institutional conditions are integral to the definition of academic freedom. The rationale for this argument is not to make a judgement on the legitimacy of the Boycott, Divestment, Sanctions (BDS) movement, but rather to highlight how the aim of the BDS directs attention to 'unacceptable debilitation of the infrastructure of Palestinian universities, inaccessibility by roads controlled by moving and stationary checkpoints, and the regulation of speech that has culminated in the detention and imprisonment of hundreds of students and faculty every year' (p. 296).

This argument highlights that the rights of academic freedom are not abstract rights held only at the level of the individual, but rather must take account of functioning academic institutions, in conditions of safety, mobility, and intellectual exchange: 'We ask how it is that any educational institution can preserve open inquiry under conditions of institutional, legal, and economic constraint' (p. 299).

There is also debate about the hierarchy of rights, with some claiming that academic freedom is not at the top of the hierarchy of public good, but rather that principles of equality and justice may come higher. Commenting on extreme right-wing speakers invited to speak on campuses in the United States, Alex Lubin, Professor of American Studies reflects: 'And so in that regard I think that the academic freedom of the group that brought the speaker is perhaps less important than the basic rights of the students not to be arrested or not to be de-humanised by a sponsored university event' (p. 5).

Lubin also applies a similar logic to the Palestinian context and the rationale for BDS:

> I guess one other example that I think about is in the BDS, my advocacy for the academic boycott, I recognise that the academic boycott, if it were enacted, may abrogate the academic freedom of some Israeli scholars. But I also recognise that Palestinian existence is at stake and the rights of a scholar to do research in a university that might be on illegally occupied land in the West Bank such as scholars at Ariel University, are less important to me. I place those below the rights of Palestinians to their homeland. (Professor of American Studies, USA, p. 6)

Butler (2015) argues that the right to education cannot be separated from the context of academic freedom, and as such the logic of BDS is to effect institutional and structural change in conditions, rather than restrict individual rights. Butler argues that academic freedom is necessarily predicated on and constituted by the necessary conditions to uphold academic freedom; this can also be applied to understanding how hostile university environments constrain the practice of academic freedom. This will be elaborated further in this chapter in the discussion on university restrictions, with reference to institutional racism, sexism, and cases of harassment.

5.3 NEOLIBERALISM AS A FRAMING DISCOURSE

'Neoliberalism' is an increasingly dominant discourse globally that can be understood to correspond to a set of practices, framed in terms of the market, which Ball (2012, p. 18) describes as 'a business dynamic which seeks profit from the buying and selling of education "services"', and where the state ensures the market through deregulation and privatisation (Phipps, 2017). The marketisation of higher education results in competition, where marketing and communication of the university brand take precedence over individual academic autonomy in teaching and research:

> With the marketisation of Higher Education, the corporate interest of the university is much more extensive and so the ways in which you can damage the corporate rep-, or damage the brand, as it's put, have become much more, but I think they were always there and they were always mobilised but now it's much more of a serious issue. (Professor of Sociology, University of Nottingham, UK, p. 8)

A UK professor describes the experience of joining a university department that was closed as a result of the REF, a system for assessing the quality of research in higher education institutions. The rationale for closure is based on a business model for higher education:

> So I went to ... which was a very hierarchical model, it was very clear within a year that there was, you know, that we had something like a £500,000 deficit. I wished to have a plan for dealing with that deficit, that would have been in sort of roundabout 2006, you know, they did not wish to have a ... no they kept saying 'oh there's no need, there's no need' and I thought well it's not right that there's no need to deal with a deficit and of course in a sense they were waiting for the 2008 Research Assessment Exercise. There was no way we were going to do well in that because we'd only been set up in 2005 and so in a way what they were doing was choosing to close the Department after the Research Assessment Exercise, when that was announced. So I experienced that as a completely sort of hierarchical in effect I was offered, well, you know, 'we can make things OK for you so long as you cooperate with the closure of the Department', so that was not something

I was in, so I decided there not to cooperate with the closure of the Department, but it was a difficult and conflictual time. (pp. 3–4)

One UK Sociology Professor commented on how often research foci at the level of the department are determined at a higher institutional level, and as such controlling knowledge production: 'I think most universities are now thoroughly hierarchically managerially organised' (p. 4).

Yet, neoliberalism is also a way of being. According to Ball (2012, p. 18): 'it gets into our minds and souls, into the ways in which we think about what we do, and into our social relations with others. It is about how we relate to our students and our colleagues and our participation in new courses and forms of pedagogy and our "knowledge production"'.

The UK initiative of the Campaign for the Public University was established as a challenge to the dominating neoliberal discourse and practice with its stated aim: 'to defend and promote the idea of the university as a public good. We believe that the public university is essential both for cultivating democratic public life and creating the means for individuals to find fulfilment in creative and intellectual pursuits regardless of whether or not they pursue a degree programme' (Campaign for the Public University, 2019). Similarly, according to a Professor of Sociology, University of Nottingham, United Kingdom: 'the Government was conceptualising Higher Education as a private benefit, either contribution to the economy and economic growth or it was understood as a private investment in human capital. And so that was the focus of the campaign' (p. 10). 'Performativity' becomes the guiding rationale where productivity is the new moral framework for the contemporary academic way of being, illustrated in the pressure to publish, secure grants, and recruit more students, for the benefit of the university's ranking and economic prospects (Ball, 2012).

5.4 UNIVERSITY RESTRICTIONS

5.4.1 Ethics Committees

The history of university ethics committees is embedded in the principles of 'harm' and 'consent' where the researcher undertakes to not *harm* human participants and that participants have *informed consent*:

Well I mean any research that violates ethical codes in terms of how to treat human subjects I think is you know, I mean I think we do now have some kind of guard against that because of codes of ethics. But there's a lot of research historically that I think was deeply disturbing and should not have been conducted. (Professor of Philosophy of Education, UK, p. 6)

Yet, there is ongoing debate in the literature about the role of university ethics committees in relation to knowledge production and academic freedom (e.g. Hammersley, 2009; Holmswood, 2010). Concerns about the role of ethics committees have been voiced particularly from those in the fields of social sciences as an infringement of academic freedom (Hedgecoe, 2016).

This raises the question of legitimacy – on what grounds do university research ethics committees justifiably restrict the freedom of researchers? According to a UK Lecturer in Medical Sociology and Bioethics:

> I do not think it's wrong to go through research ethics committees. Biological research can be physically harmful; social science, I do not know, it's much harder to say. However, the well-known Humphrey's Tea Room Trade study, for example, where he spied on people and went to their homes – there are limits of being 'covert'. I am personally uncomfortable with it – it was an invasion of privacy, and beyond acceptable. But I do not think there are topics that should not be researched.

Humphrey's *Tearoom Trade: Impersonal Sex in Public Places* study was published as a book in 1970 based on his Ph.D. dissertation done at Washington University in the United States on homosexual encounters in public places. The term 'tearoom' refers to public toilets, and the research was conducted in an American city in the mid- to late 1960s. Its findings showed that many of the men lived traditional lives within their communities, with a range of motives and different sexual identities. It entailed Humphrey acting as a 'lookout' in male public toilets whilst men engaged in sex with other men, warning them if anyone was approaching, and they had no knowledge that he was a researcher. In addition, he recorded their license plates and tracked down their home addresses, where he visited them posing as a market researcher, further invading their privacy. It is a well-cited example in the social sciences of controversial research ethics, using deceptive methods and not obtaining consent from the research participants. Yet, some scholars have argued in support of the work, making the case that from the ethical pillars of beneficence and social justice, Humphreys made important positive contributions to the population that he studied, challenging the myth that men engaging in such encounters were deviant or criminal or non-consensual; his work also challenged binary constructions of sexual identity and policies of punitive imprisonment (Lenza, 2004).

The aims of university research ethics committees have been disputed, where it has been argued that the university is primarily concerned with the protection of its brand, rather than the protection of the human participants involved in the research. Through an analysis of university research ethics committees in the United Kingdom and the United States (referred to as the Institutional Review Board – IRB), Hedgecoe (2016) identifies that 'risk' has broadened beyond the remit of risk to human participants to risk to the institution's brand or reputation. Whilst accepting that academic freedom is not absolute, Hedgecoe expresses concern with the rationale and aims of the restriction which he deems as illegitimate.

The dynamics of ethics research committees in evaluating 'risk' in relation to conducting research internationally is highlighted in the following account of a UK-based anthropologist conducting research in Lebanon:

> You can talk about the bureaucracy in the modern university which is not exactly conducive for intellectual freedom. So what I mean by this is as you are probably aware, the kind of hoops you need to jump through to get ethical clearance, you know, if you are doing some research in somewhere like Lebanon which is kind of perfectly, it's not necessarily a more dangerous place than many other places where we have done research, there's sort of an assumption that it's going to be dangerous and should you be going to these places. (p. 2)

Similarly, for a UK Lecturer conducting research in the UAE:

> It was obviously passed through the ethics committee here and I cannot remember actually whether it was considered as being high or low risk. I would imagine high risk, just because of geography and how the UK is in particular very worried about certain parts of the world. But it was somehow made easy because I had an association with a local university in Dubai where I also taught. (p. 2)

The workings of university research ethics committees in Lebanon at the American University of Beirut (AUB) have also grappled with the conceptualisation of 'risk', as well as the scope of what should be evaluated for ethical review. A Professor of Psychology describes the challenges he faced with AUB's IRB (ethics board) with his research on inter-sectarian relations in the Lebanese context:

> My research can be a bit sensitive because it involves inter-sectarian relations, it can involve conflict with vulnerable populations and so on. When I started doing my research, that was like ten to fifteen years ago, the IRB at AUB was quite limited and then eventually it became a full-fledged office that has control over the research programmes that were happening on campus whereby every single

research project had to go through the IRB. I was doing collaborative research with colleagues of mine from New York and we were doing a study on values and we wanted to collect a sample from the Lebanese population and assess specific value profiles within the community. So I sent the project to the IRB and the project had received approval from New York – IRB approval from the university there, and I had contributed to the questionnaire. I sent it to the IRB and the IRB, at that time again was still immature; instead of looking at the well-being of participants and the protection of their rights and so on and so forth, they went into the content of my questionnaire, they were like 'hm, this is a question that you are asking that might be sensitive, what if the data results show that Christians are more x than the Muslims, Sunnis or the Shias or whatever and that can create a problem?' And it continued back and forth and back and forth for literally months on end and then eventually I was summoned for a full IRB defence. So I was summoned to the IRB, the whole IRB was there, like there were twenty people around the table, and for about the entire afternoon I was grilled about the research. And then at the end of the day then it was like 'you know what, you need to remove this and do that' and what about changing this question and what about changing that question and I was like 'you are dealing with content here' and that was it, that was done. They had rejected to give me approval and I had appealed and then appealed and so on and eventually the whole project died. (pp. 3–4)

The IRB's decision illustrates a concern with the political and cultural sensitivity of the topic and the institutional reputation, rather than the ethics of conducting the research itself:

I was telling them 'you are interfering in things that are none of your business' and they were like 'OK, from an IRB point of view, so protection of participants, protection blah blah blah you are not doing any harm, etc., we agree, but now there is another layer that has been created, it's called institution approval which is beyond ethical approval, which is will the institution accept to have its name associated with your research and this requires Provost clearance'. So that was like an extra layer that did not exist before and I was like 'what?!' (pp. 5–6)

5.4.2 The Valorisation of Procedure

In 2015, Steven Salaita was offered a one-year position at AUB in Lebanon as the Edward Said Chair at the Center for American Studies and Research (CASAR), subsequent to the withdrawal of his offer from the University of Illinois, following his tweets that were critical of Israel's bombing of Gaza in

2014. As mentioned in Chapter 3, his subsequent application for a more permanent position as the Director of CASAR was surrounded by controversy. The university-appointed search committee recommended Salaita's appointment; however, the administration blocked the appointment citing 'significant procedural violations'. A student petition in support of Salaita likened AUB's response to that of the University of Illinois, stating concern that the blocking of Salaita's appointment was politically motivated. According to a faculty member at AUB:

> So the Salaita issue, I'm quite aware of what happened there. So I know that there was ... so the administration is citing procedural irregularities ... Ha ha! But we also know that [there were] calls from Senators or US politicians expressing their unhappiness with Salaita being offered a job at AUB because of his assumedly or supposedly anti-Israel tweets. And when we asked about this and we challenged it in the Senate, they said there was an internal audit investigation into the process of the selection. The internal auditor was summoned, we summoned him to the Senate, he gave us a presentation and he highlighted that there were about seventeen or eighteen procedural violations that were around that particular kind of hiring situation, which is not unusual by the way, because if you go into the detail of these violations, you can find a lot of those similar situations across campus. (p. 14)

The current political environment at AUB was contrasted with that of the preceding administration:

> Well, at that time, the Provost and the Dean of the Faculty of Arts and Sciences had a very different understanding of the role of AUB and the role of, you know – I do not know – more leaning to the left, pro-Palestinian attitudes. And they did not care about ... and at that time this was also Obama, right. So I'm not really sure what was happening at the US level and what kind of pressure they might or might not have received from the US side in terms of the decision-making, in terms of hiring or offering Salaita a one-year position, but from a Dean's perspective and Provost perspective, this seemed to be something like they were very comfortable with and that a lot of Faculty members were very happy to see happen. The change happened with the change of administration. The new administration was not one that was favourable to that kind of argument or sentiment or that kind of vision for AUB. For them, this new administration, the way it's dealing with compliance and the way it's reacting to American dictats is not honourable to AUB in general. Now, I do put some exceptions here ... AUB on a couple of occasions made statements that were excellent and unusual, so the

first one was when Trump recognised occupied Jerusalem as the capital of Israel and the President issued a statement rejecting that. (p. 15)

5.4.3 Students

With the marketisation of higher education and the introduction of fees, the construction of the student has changed significantly to a marketised understanding of the student as a 'client' or 'customer', where the 'customer is always right'. The construction of student as 'client/customer', therefore, impacts the academic freedom of the professor/instructor, reflected in students' power to potentially censor and control the curriculum. This experience is reflected in the example of a Senior Lecturer in Education in the United Kingdom, who experienced student confrontation on assigning them an essay to critically reflect on the interrelationship between education and extremism:

> Even now, with the module that I have here, for undergraduates, the essay that the students have to write – and they are not given a choice, it's just one essay question. And when I took the module over, because it's a very interesting topic, it's not something that you necessarily study when you study education studies, it tends to be very kind of race, gender, disability focused. And I thought it's very cutting edge, it's very kind of in the now. It might be interesting to write about the role of education and extremism or counter-extremism policy for example. And I had not quite expected the level of fuss that I would get from some students who felt very strongly that they should not be made to write about this issue – why is it that they have to write about this issue? And my own suspicion is that some of them felt a bit uneasy that they might have to write in a way that could be seen to be defensive actually of Muslim communities, who are being singled out. And I've had quite confrontational, sometimes angry emails from students who have kind of put that point to me. (p. 4)

The ensuing emotional and practical work can lead to self-censorship:

> So it's come to the point now where last year I thought do you know what, is this even worth the headache? I'm just going to change the essay question. I brought this up to the Undergraduate Programmes Director who encouraged me to keep it because he could also see the value and benefit of it as I could. So I sort of revamped it slightly, made it a bit more vague, a bit more broad and ran it again this year. It did run better this year but I've had quite a few issues, in fact one, I had a student just before you in my office in tears because it was related to that assignment, and there was some anger around why do we have to write about this?

This is just not – and it's absolutely shocking to me Dina, completely. It annoys me a lot, yeah. (Senior Lecturer in Education, p. 5)

Similarly, a Professor of Journalism at New York University (NYU) reflects on his experience where some students challenged his reading lists as anti-Israeli. Whilst he had support from colleagues and did not replace his readings:

it just took . . . it did take a little bit of time, it took maybe about half the semester, I mean, there was nothing official, there is no grievance or investigation or anything like that. They were basically conversations within, between myself and the chair and myself and students. (p. 2). He further commented on his sense of vulnerability: 'I think yes at some point, I felt that this could all . . . this could become something bigger' (p. 2).

Procedure or pedagogical protocol is weaponised in some instances to mask attempted censorship:

And there was one issue in particular where one student emailed me with – I mean I will not go into the details but it was a very problematic accusation that effectively, the materials provided did not enable him to answer the essay question. And at that point I got another colleague who was in a position of leadership in that context, I got that person involved and said 'You know what, I think this is . . .' well I did not say it like that but I basically said 'I think this accusation is absolutely ridiculous and' you know 'I'm quite happy for all of it to be reviewed'. And it was just, I mean, it was clear that the whole thing was meant as a way to just agitate and to be difficult, because that accusation that an academic at this university would have designed something to disable the students from answering the question, an easy question, is horrendous. And it's purely because of the topic, I mean I'm absolutely certain of it. (Senior Lecturer in Education, UK)

Concerns relating to curriculum are also evident in branch universities in the UAE, although the restriction primarily operates from the main campus in the Western context. The example of the Australian university, Curtin University, illustrates an approach of avoiding any material perceived to be controversial:

But the course material was basically coming from, you could say the main campus of Curtin here in Perth. Anyway, she basically received a document two weeks before she was supposed to release these materials to be taught in Dubai and it was called Tips for Teaching. And in this document it said that all content, the content needed to be avoided entirely in that course and one of the areas was gender and sexuality, specifically transgender and same-sex relations. She is a queer academic. She was pretty much traumatised by the whole thing because she, it was her first six months here at Curtin University and she was the Unit Coordinator for this thing and she was given the responsibility of making these materials available in Dubai. And the thing was that the whole unit, all the way through – it's a contemporary unit on digital everyday life – the whole thing is full of gender and sexuality issues. (p. 8)

However, the actual practice of teaching in campus university contexts can be contrasted as more fluid, in terms of both curriculum context and pedagogical practice:

So sometimes, I mean they left me quite surprised because things that I was teaching was the sort of foundations of political philosophy, stuff around gender, race, ethnicity, right? So the sort of curriculum is very much Eurocentric because unfortunately there is not organic literature from the Gulf as yet, or as much. But obviously brings a degree of self-censorship because obviously if you are talking about gender, you are not going to talk about the category of third gender and whether that's a useful category and so on and so forth. (Lecturer in Migration Studies, UK and former Lecturer in Dubai, p. 8)

5.4.4 Hostile Environment and Self-Censorship

Bullying and harassment in UK higher education has been shown to be widespread (UCU, 2012). Mirza (2015) reflects that:

In my 30 years in academia, as a student but also as faculty I have witnessed and been subjected to endemic and sustained sexual harassment in higher education. There's not an institution or time when I have not seen it. It oozes out of every lecture hall, lab, classroom, tutorial, eatery and office. It has different forms in different times, but I think the more times change the more they stay the same.

She critically reflects personally on the damaging and misplaced effects of shame, which are internalised and, in effect, nurture a patriarchal regime. Almost predicting the #MeToo movement, Mirza calls for a collective 'sharing' of the shame with institutions, that they feel shame, and victims reclaim their honour.

A Professor of Gender Studies in the United States comments on the problem of sexual assault on US campuses, where the 'honour' or reputation of the neoliberal university and the protection of victims sit in tension:

> I mean it's a sticky problem right because it's true, but here as well the problem is rife. Sexual assault is outrageously prevalent on campuses over here and it's true that frequently students have tried to make this known and it's been covered up. So I understand the feeling that we have to do something. So I guess it returns to the idea of faculty governance and who runs the University, right, these policies were created by Lawyers and University administrators eager to protect the institution and its reputation, not necessarily created by faculty and students who are interested in protecting the lives of survivors. (p. 11)

Phipps' (2015) writing about sexism and violence in the neoliberal university context draws out parallels between 'lad culture' and practices of evaluation in higher educational institutions. Phipps (2015) notes that 'to offend with impunity is a function and exercise of privilege'. That language entails violence is dismissed as 'banter' and as such has been invisible in higher education institutions between staff, staff and students, and between students. Phipps (2015) further argues that such acts can be described as 'strategic misogyny' which functions to 'preserve masculine power and space'.

A UK Professor reflects on her experience as a Ph.D. student and the sexual harassment experienced throughout her Ph.D. supervision:

> He developed a complete obsession with me, a sexual obsession. And so for the whole of my academic career there – it was persistent and consistent over years and years, and I do not know how I survived it but I did. And it was an endemic problem. I can send you the papers I've written on it because you know, young women were fresh meat every term you know. And it was openly done. And he would write all sorts of things on my manuscripts you know. And remember we are typing in these days. He'd write things like 'I'll squeeze your tits if you spell this wrong'. I have dyslexia and my spelling was always bad with a typewriter, there wasn't a spell check. And he would make overt sexual comments. He would put condoms on the table when I would go in the room. I mean it was really difficult. But I had two choices – to leave or to stay. (pp. 2–3)

The hostility of the environment also takes the form of job insecurity, tenure processes, and self-censorship. The following reflections on self-censorship raised the issue of precarity in work from short-term contracts or being an early career academic; as a result of such precarity, self-censorship is a form of self-preservation:

> I have felt it in relation to the things that I say outside of the classroom and I find myself without having planned to be affected by it, I find myself increasingly cautious as, you know, I'm still a very early career academic but, as the years go by,

> I'm finding myself more and more cautious, as I suppose I have more to lose than I did when I was a PhD student or before I was in a job I felt I'd like to keep long term – if that makes sense? (Lecturer in Medical Ethics, UK, p. 4)

The following excerpt makes a direct link between job precarity in the form of short-term contracts and academic freedom in the UK context:

> [The] increasing precarity in academic work which I think also relates to the issues that you are working on which is academic freedom, right? How we navigate or how we define academic freedom is going to be inevitably shaped by the global trend on precarious academic work. So if you do not have anything to eat with, if you do not have any money, you are going to reconsider certain things, how you frame academic freedom or how much you are willing to give away from your academic freedom. And what is happening especially in the UK and to a lesser degree in Europe is shaping what is happening in the Gulf. So I think that's really important to consider. So I mean I work on six months contracts. I do not think anyone should be exposed to working conditions as such. So that is why I think academic freedom relates a lot to what is happening here. (UK Lecturer and former Lecturer, Dubai, p. 9)

Self-censorship is also most evident around topics of controversiality, where academics are aware of the 'red lines' and the potential implications and nature of those implications in different contexts:

> I mean the sort of topics are quite actually critical that we teach there. To be honest, I'd never had the need to censor my class. But there are no goes on such as like the sectarian you know, divide and stuff like that, and gender is also, yeah. And everyone that is working there knows this. I mean it's not written code but everyone who operates in these campuses do know where the boundaries are, or should know. (former Lecturer, Dubai, p. 8)

Reflecting on his academic life in various institutions in the United States and AUB, Lebanon, Professor McGreevy, former Dean of the Faculty of Arts and Sciences at AUB, Lebanon, comments on the subtle, implicit forms of self-censorship that are, for the many academics, common practice:

> In generally I think it has not bothered me. But you never know, because it's sort of a low-level pressure that's on everybody their entire career. And you know how difficult the academic careers are these days. People are often moving and scrambling and trying to keep them together. So even subtle pressures at the edges definitely have an effect on us and might change what we decide to work on, among other things. (p. 3)

In a similar comment on the UK context, the subtle incremental micromessages that lead to self-censure are noted, especially in the almost complete absence of academics' critique of their own institutions:

> It's those sorts of things, the e-mailing, the quiet comments and the conversations as much as anything, they do not give a thought to anything, but make the difference, but create that environment and you only need one person to be criticised and then it becomes more symbolic for what anybody else then ceases to make comments about things. I mean one of the issues that I've raised recently, currently because of HR here is, in the 1997 UNESCO recommendation on higher education teaching has a clause which is very good actually. I know it's only soft law, but it says that academic freedom must apply to give academics the right to criticise their own institution and every HR department and most University managers would see that academic freedom only applies within the classroom. (Dennis Hayes, Professor of Education, University of Derby, UK, p. 8)

This widespread lack of critique of one's own institutions is a function of the neoliberal construct of the university as a corporate employer, in contrast to constructions of the university as a collaborative venture led by its academics, as discussed in Chapter 4. Furthermore, the concern of the unpleasantness of public pressure and the question whether a university is prepared to stand behind 'unwelcomed' knowledge are raised:

> But some people do get tremendous troll on social media and I have actually raised it as an issue at University or 'what's going to happen if somebody starts sending', you get a Twitter storm and they say 'Dina Kiwan should be sacked for researching academic freedom' and if the Vice Chancellor gets 20,000 people saying this, what's going to be the position of the University? They'll cave in, I'm absolutely sure they'll just cave in. But I've not personally had, I sort of keep off Twitter to some extent because life's too short. (Dennis Hayes, Professor of Education, University of Derby, UK, p. 7)

However, these various forms of self-censorship become internalised as a norm, with many commenting that they had to reflect on the extent of their awareness of their self-censorship. This gradual fixity of boundaries is summed up by the comment: 'You bend and you bend and you bend and then it becomes your natural posture!' (former Professor, AUB, Lebanon, p. 10)

I propose that the hostility of the higher education environment is an infringement on academic freedom as, to draw on Butler's (2015) argument, an environment free of hostility, harassment, and violence is a precondition of and a necessary constituent of academic freedom. The production of knowledge is necessarily restricted in racist and sexist contexts and contexts of other forms of exclusion and violence.

5.4.5 Scholars' 'Responsibility'

It has been argued that, in contrast to 'freedom', there should be self-imposed limits on academics' freedom, in particular in relation to extramural speech. But rather than constructing this as self-censorship, this should be understood in terms of academic responsibility and speaking within one's own area of expertise. Shahvisi (2018) extends this argument proposing that academics in fact have a 'responsibility', given their respected position in society, to not abuse this position by publicly commenting outside their areas of expertise. Given that academics are privileged in potentially being able to access a wider audience and having (perceived) authority, this carries greater risks.

5.5 NATIONAL AND INTERNATIONAL RESTRICTIONS

As stated in the introduction of the chapter, constraints on academic freedom are a nexus of state and international policies and practices, university processes, and those at the level of the individual. A UK study conducted in 2017 examined both the *de jure* protection, via examination of legal instruments, and the *de factor* protection, by means of a survey which was completed by +2,500 University and College Union members (Karran and Mallinson, 2017). Regarding de jure protection, the United Kingdom does not have a constitutional protection for the freedom of speech nor elements of academic freedom. With regard to national legislation, the freedom to speech and research is protected. With regard to UK's relationship with UNESCO's, 1997 statement on academic freedom, the United Kingdom is not compliant in terms of academic freedom being protected in law nor in terms of academic staff electing the majority of representatives to decision-making bodies. Karran and Mallinson (2017) produced a 'scorecard' for countries in Europe for academic freedom constituting protection in the following areas: freedom to teach and research, institutional autonomy, university governance, institutional governance, and international agreements, where the United Kingdom was ranked twenty-eighth out of twenty-nine countries. In addition, at the individual academic level, the level of knowledge regarding academic freedom was significantly lower than their European counterparts, when comparing survey data collected by the European Union. Respondents also perceived a decline in their individual academic freedom and the autonomy of their institutions (Karran and Mallinson, 2017).

In this section, a series of cases are drawn upon to explore the nature of national and international constraints and lack of protections, including the UK REF, the requirement for US Compliance at AUB, Lebanon, and mobility restrictions into the United States and the UAE.

5.5.1 UK REF and Impact Agenda

The 'Impact' agenda and concerns relating to the UK REF provide an illustration of the state's marketisation of higher education, where knowledge equates to capital, and individual academics are conceptualised as 'units of resources' (Ball, 2012) as 'cogs in a machine of mass production' (Stanonis, 2016, p. 133). Measures of performativity and productivity are the means enabling such evaluation. The four higher education funding bodies, namely Research England, the Scottish Funding Council, the Higher Education Funding Council for Wales, and the Department for the Economy, Northern Ireland, carry out this evaluation, with the stated aims emphasising accountability for public investment in research and an appropriate allocation of resources. As a consequence, universities are ranked for their 'research power' (Stanonis, 2016).

As a consequence, this agenda determines what research is considered important and has the temporal bias towards measurable short-term impact. It also encourages a faster rate of publication, and it has been argued that the system results in mediocre research. Another effect has been to affect the nature of disciplines, themselves. For example, commenting on the shifts in emphasis within the discipline of Sociology:

> When I argued that people were quite sceptical but Les Back who's at Goldsmiths and, you know, I'd had an exchange with him and he did a study of the impact cases for the last REF in sociology and said not one impact case study in sociology addressed what conventional sociologists would regard as a critical or social justice topic. So I think students will move towards behavioural disciplines rather than critical social science disciplines so, in that sense, sociology will be affected.
> (Professor of Sociology, University of Nottingham, UK, p. 5)

Debates pertaining to REF also relate to what constitutes 'excellence' and 'world leading', with critics noting that relatively few panel members evaluating research are from outside the United Kingdom (Stanonis, 2016).

In addition, higher-ranking faculty members tend to dominate submissions, which Stanonis (2016) argues constrains academic freedom by reinforcing disciplines and suppressing intellectuals' creativity and openness to new ideas, citing Kuhn (1970, p. 152): 'particularly the older and more experienced ones may resist indefinitely' the work of younger scholars. In a similar vein, Sayer (2014) argues that 'REF panels give extraordinary gatekeeping power to a disproportionately older, male, white – and overwhelmingly Russell Group and former 1994 Group – academic elite'.

There is a tension between certain forms of perceived 'lower' status locally embedded work and 'higher' status international collaboration. Beyond the context of the UK REF, this tension can be illustrated, for example, where universities contributing to the local community are also simultaneously concerned to accrue status for international relevance. This tension can be particularly acute in the Global South, where pressures to publish 'internationally relevant' as opposed to 'locally relevant' work result in what Hanafi (2011, p. 291) refers to as 'Publish globally and perish locally vs. publish locally and perish globally'. Typically, contemporary universities take the model where the three mission areas of teaching, research, and civic engagement are separate, and, subsequently, civic engagement becomes sidelined in a competitive system, where rankings focus predominantly on research and global networking. This separation into the three streams results in a fragmentation of work illustrated, where some academics writing for non-academic audiences are requested to add a disclaimer that their work does not represent the institution and sometimes academics find themselves separating their public and professional identities for professional reasons (Hanafi, 2011).

5.5.2 Compliance with US Regulations

The role of the United States is significant for academic freedom at AUB in Lebanon:

> I do not think there is any threat to academic freedom at AUB as large and as looming and as threatening as the issue of compliance with US regulations. But in this situation, we have an institutional ban on research topics, research interactions, talks and academic freedom that infringes upon freedom, rights, basic rights. (Professor of Psychology, AUB, Lebanon, p. 19)

Whilst in law, the local law takes precedent, there is an international political dimension:

> I know that the university and the administration and the board of trustees have enough power and clout to resist infringement from the state onto the campus, we are really an island in that regard, although the current administration is trying to reach out with sectarian kind of undertones at least. But to get back to the original question of academic freedom – and this is the issue that I want to be the centre of our conversation. And this is the issue of compliance. (p. 11)

Compliance affects who the university can engage with and what populations academic researchers can research. A Professor of Psychology at AUB, Lebanon, describes the case of the university hosting a United States Agency for International Development–funded event as background 'engaging in work that involved members of Hezbollah' and being sued because Hezbollah was on a US sanctions list. This is based on funder clauses that work cannot be undertaken by organisations perceived to be terrorist by the US administration.

He goes on to describe how the issue of compliance has expanded from conditions of funding to all forms of interaction, as it is being interpreted and applied by the university administration:

> So Trump decides that Iran is a terrorist state and that means that anyone dealing with Iran is . . . we cannot do that. The same applies, they have Syria as a regime, so if you are working with anyone who happens to be a Government employee, like for example if you are at the University of Aleppo or you are at the University of Damascus, these universities are public government funded and then that means that you are dealing with the Government and that's a problem, you cannot pay them money. And now, they are asking Faculty members on campus that anyone who's coming to AUB, so originally the assumption was AUB cannot pay or give expertise to groups that are perceived, that are on the terrorist list, so we cannot go and say to Hezbollah, 'here is some money, come to our university', or 'hey, Iran University professors, come to AUB, we are flying you over, you cannot do that. So originally it was really very much the money transactions and so on and so forth, but the last one, the last interpretation of compliance by the censor, or whatever you want to call him, is that anyone coming into AUB to give a talk, right, so I'm inviting somebody, I know a colleague of mine is coming, he happens to be dropping . . . you are coming to AUB from the UK, you are happening to visit your family and I tell you 'hey, why do not you drop by into my lecture and give me a small talk about what you are doing' or whatever. This has to be vetted. (pp. 11–12)

He elaborates on the increasing extent of transnational infringement on his academic freedom, showing how this severely undermines the ability to conduct research in his field and context:

> For me, it's something that is outrageous. It's a violation of my mission. But many people, they are like 'well, you know, because of the US's situation, we need to follow US law' and I'm like 'no, if the law is unfair, it should not be followed', I mean, it's one of our roles, one of our functions is to challenge unjust rules and bigotry that is out there. But even if we are not talking about this, even if you are talking about research, so let us say I'm doing research that involves Syrian refugees or I want to go and do research in Syria, I cannot do it anymore as an AUB Faculty. And the number of organisations that are put on the terrorist list by the US who happen to be in our region is tremendous – they have Palestinian organisations on the terrorist list, they have Syria's government on the terrorist list, they have Iran, they have Hezbollah and half the Lebanese population – what am I supposed to do, stop doing research? (p. 13)

5.5.3 Mobility Restrictions

A Professor from NYU and visiting Professor at NYU Abu Dhabi comments on the issue of accessibility of movement in comparative perspective, noting that denial into the United States for some scholars is understood differently than the denial of entry into the UAE, for example:

> Is it accessibility of movement of people across borders and academic freedom ... or is it academic freedom when someone does not get into one of the countries in the global network or is it a question of the sovereign independence of the country in question, which controls its borders? So we speak to people here when there's an outcry about someone not getting into say the Emirates, then people here will really say 'well', they like to remind people that people do not get into the United States quite often, for example [X] was recently barred from entering to the United States and so, you know, there's equivalent, there is a kind of equivalent about the border question, it's never satisfying, it does not make people happy about the fact that a colleague can be denied entry to this or that branch campus but did not we remember that access to the United States can be equally problematic especially in these times. (p. 2)

5.6 CONCLUSION

This chapter has examined a range internal and external restrictions on academic freedom and the production of knowledge, across and between the four contexts of Lebanon, the UAE, the United Kingdom, and the United States. Consideration of the conditions of academic freedom provides a challenge to decontextualised constructs of academic freedom, whereby the case is made that certain conditions are a prerequisite for and also a constituent part of academic freedom (Butler, 2015). Discourses of neoliberalism frame the examination of institutional, national, and international, as well as individual-level restrictions. Forms of restrictions relating to topics such as Palestine/Israel, gender and sexuality, race, security, and extremism will be examined in the following chapter examining the idea of 'forbidden knowledge'.

6 'Forbidden' Knowledge

> Forbidden knowledge cannot refer to any particular body of knowledge, but is a dynamic category, the contents of which shift depending on culture, political climate, and the interests of researchers.
>
> (Kempner et al. (2011, p. 479)

6.1 INTRODUCTION

Developing Chapter 4's focus on the role of the university in producing knowledge and Chapter 5's focus on internal and external restrictions, this chapter interrogates the concept of 'forbidden' knowledge (Kempner et al., 2011). Kempner et al. (2011, p. 476) recognise that the 'knowable unknown' is fluid and expansive, but they use the sub-category of 'forbidden knowledge' in their work, constructed in terms of being 'too sensitive, dangerous or taboo to produce'. The related construct of 'negative' knowledge has also been used to designate knowing what knowledge not to produce (Cetina, 1999), as it can threaten powerful interests mediated through institutions and sociopolitical and religious cultures. The operationalisation of these non-knowledges can entail both formal and informal processes including self-censorship, internal university restrictions, and external sociopolitical restrictions as discussed in Chapter 5, as well as Chapter 4's contextualisation of the production of knowledge within the institutional framework of the university, its mission, public funding, and its national and international contexts. Kempner et al. (2011, p. 475) identify the phenomenon of 'the production of nonknowledge' as a neglected area of research, in contrast to sociologists, philosophers, and historians of science focusing on the production on knowledge and the 'structures and processes that impede that knowledge'.

This chapter turns its attention to the question of forbidden knowledge deemed too dangerous or 'taboo' to produce, approached in relation to the structural and sociopolitical processes, rather than in terms of gaps in knowledge. As such, agency must be accounted for in such absences of knowledge. For example, the terms 'undone science' (Hess, 2007) and 'agnotology' (Procter, 1995) have been coined in this emerging field to gesture towards agency (Kempner et al., 2011). There is a relative lack of interrogation of how discourses and sociopolitical and historical contexts shape the absence of certain knowledges. Given my transnational approach to the study of the production of knowledge, including 'forbidden' knowledge, my empirical data provides accounts of daily lived experiences of academics operating in and against this terrain. Kempner et al. (2011) highlight how the existing literature on forbidden knowledge takes a universalist approach towards the content of forbidden knowledge, and so this approach focusing on the nature of power, agency, socio-politics and history in relation to forbidden knowledge is both theoretically and empirically novel.

In the first section of this chapter, I conceptualise dominant discourses of forbidden knowledge with respect to three framing rationales arising from the empirical data. These include concerns arising from the applied use of knowledge, discovering 'uncomfortable truths' and 'taboo' topics. Based on the empirical data, the next section of the chapter focuses on four areas of 'forbidden' knowledge: 'bioethics, psychology, and genetics'; 'Palestine'; 'gender and sexuality'; and 'race, religion, security, and extremism'. This is then followed by an examination of academics' experiences of difficulties in publishing and disseminating their research – what has been called 'boundary work' (Kempner et al., 2011).

6.1.1 Conceptualising Rationales of Forbidden Knowledge

6.1.1.1 Fear of the Misapplication of Research Findings

On asking interviewees whether they believe there is some research that should not be conducted, the majority of interviewees had a permissive approach to academic freedom, often only highlighting a concern relating to the application or, indeed, misapplication of research findings, particularly in relation to science. For example, Professor Peter Singer, Professor of Bioethics at Princeton University, is well known as one of the intellectual founders of the animal liberation movement and for his work on global poverty. However, some of his philosophical positions on euthanasia and disability have raised significant public controversy. As such, his own research operates within and against the terrain of 'forbidden' knowledge. Singer answered this question in terms of what ought not to be published, constructed in terms of weighing dangers and benefits – the language of ethics:

> Some research that should not be conducted ... I guess there might be some things that ought not to be published, you know, an example of this would be, say, I did once object to a ... there was a magazine called *The Progressive* that published an article called 'The H-Bomb Secret', in which it described how to make a hydrogen bomb. I thought that should not have been published but that's rather different from saying that I thought the research on which it was based should not have been done. I do not think there's, I'm generally in favour of finding out the truth ... as I say, sometimes it might be – I suppose you could say 'well, if you do this research someone will find out about it and it could be extremely dangerous', like enabling people to build terrible weapons or maybe a more realistic example now is to bio-engineer a virus that creates a pandemic. So there could be cases of that sort where the dangers clearly outweigh the benefits, then I think it might be better not to do it. But they'd be pretty rare cases I think. (Peter Singer, Professor of Bioethics, Princeton University, US, p. 3)

This kind of argument is also reflected in other public discourses typically concerned with the misapplication of technology. This is evident, for example, in the history of assisted reproductive technologies, leading to ethical debates on applications leading to single parenting, same-sex parenthood, increased multiple births, sex selection, and the usual prohibitive costs, creating a classed marketplace. There have also been anti-racist, gendered, classed, and ableist critiques of eugenics – not only of historical 'positive' eugenics practices but also of contemporary 'negative' eugenics practices such as prenatal screening, and as mentioned, Singer's positions on euthanasia and disability.

In the United States, the heightened sociopolitical and religious contexts around abortion debates have also affected assisted reproduction technologies. The case of assisted reproductive technologies illustrates that what is perceived as 'dangerous' is not fixed, but has changed over time, and varies according to geopolitical, cultural, and religious contexts. The determination of what becomes dangerous and then forbidden can be seen through state law-making, as evident in cloning and nuclear weapons. Singer distinguishes further in proposing boundaries around publication as opposed to the research itself, which Klein (2021) refers to as boundary work that occurs during the peer review process, where knowledge becomes forbidden for normative reasons, examined later in the chapter. Public and disciplinary discourses also become internalised by researchers themselves, as elucidated in the previous chapter.

6.1.1.2 Fear of Alternative Positions: Discovering 'Uncomfortable Truths'

Another set of concerns raised by interviewees relates to the notion of uncovering 'uncomfortable truths'. In the two accounts below – one academic working on the conflict in Northern Ireland and the other academic working on sectarian differences in Lebanon – self-restraint and institutional mechanisms such as the institutional review board (IRB) or ethics committee act to harness the perceived potential dangers of the findings:

> I'm not sure whether it's academic but more sort of intellectual freedom – openness about pursuing ideas and feeling a sense of confidence that there's not going to be any boundaries or kind of borders in doing it. I mean occasionally in doing research in conflict and peace building you find out very uncomfortable truths, you know, whether it's in Northern Ireland, whether it's the State and its counter-insurgency processes or whatever. You know, that's kind of a slightly different issue because that makes you think about, you know, how your research can potentially be used or how can we deploy it in different ways which may not have necessarily the intention which you originally hoped. (Professor of Sociology, Queen's University Belfast, UK, p. 2)

The conception of the strategic use of not knowing (Gross and McGoey, 2015) is an emerging concept in the interdisciplinary emerging field of 'ignorance studies'. In relation to policymaking, strategic not knowing is not addressed by collecting evidence, but is rather a 'constitutive feature of policymaking than an external disturbance' (Paul and Haddad, 2023). Paul and Haddad (2023) argue that ignorance can be conceived of as a material good which can be weaponised in policy disputes, which they illustrate in their examination of the COVID-19 pandemic, which they coin as 'institutionalised ignorance' (p. 224). The above example with respect to Northern Ireland politics and sensitivities about making visible 'uncomfortable truths' in research illustrates a policy collusion through self-censorship. The following case, in contrast, shows the institutional boundaries imposed based on a rationale of ethical concerns:

> IRB, instead of looking at the wellbeing of participants and the protection of their rights and so on and so forth, went into the content of my questionnaire, they were like 'hm, this is a question that you are asking that might be sensitive, what if

the data results show that Christians are more 'x' than the Muslims, Sunnis or the Shias or whatever and that can create a problem. We were similarly frustrated over a period of years after that, the first years when the IRB was operated where every single research that was proposing that involved intergroup relations or intergroup contact or whatever was scrutinised beyond the issue of wellbeing of the researcher and/or the participants. (Professor of Psychology, AUB, Lebanon, p. 4)

The potential of dangerous statistics, despite policy knowledge typically favouring quantifiable empirical data, is not deemed strategic in this instance. In conflict or post-conflict contexts, the policy logic is one that is strategically forward-looking, and therefore, inconvenient statistics do not fit such policy aims. In a similar vein, Paul and Haddad (2023) show how statistical data in the context of COVID-19 was, in fact, deleted in Brazil; in several countries, varying decisions were made on the extent to which data on numbers of infections or death rates were collected and published; inconsistent data has also been collected on vaccinations and disaggregation of statistics by various ethnic and religious groups, those with disabilities, gender, etc. They argue that this non-knowledge enables a 'high degree of uncertainty' which is not accidental but, in fact, strategic.

6.1.1.3 Taboo Topics

At a fundamental level, interviewees talked of research that either they or others perceive as 'taboo'. One UK Senior Lecturer proposes a hierarchy of 'controversial' topics in the UK context:

> So the topics, just to be completely explicit, the topics that I'm talking about, probably three things primarily – one is Israel, the other is masculinity and men more generally and the other is Whiteness as an institution. I think Israel is more controversial than the other two. And I feel those are three things which I feel personally very, very critical of. They're three things that worry me greatly. And I do not hold back from criticising them, I do criticise them, but I am cautious when I do in a way that I'm generally not cautious about other things. (p. 5)

The intellectual history of research on race and cognitive difference, characterised as 'pseudoscience', was also raised by a number of interviewees: 'Well, I mean I suppose we are getting into the whole thing about supposed links between race and intelligence' (Professor of Education, University of Birmingham, UK, p. 7). One of the most significant works in this field by Herrnstein and Murray is their book, *The Bell Curve*, arguably underpinned by a eugenics logic both methodologically and in terms of its policy applications, where they argued that race and intelligence are correlated with Black Americans being the lowest performers on IQ tests (Kiwan, 2022). Contemporary academic efforts to decolonise knowledge are predicated in modern theories of race that are situated in the history of European justifications for colonisation in the eighteenth and nineteenth centuries based on notions of differential intellect. The rise of eugenics in this context provided a pseudo-scientific rationale for creating not only raced but also classed and disabled 'others'. The intersection between race, class, and disability has also played an important role in US immigration discourses and policies (Kiwan, 2022).

Research philosophically exploring arguments about the comparative fluidity of constructs of gender and race was also mentioned:

> The case of ... the woman who wrote the article was raising questions about why if it was OK to change your gender, to identify as a gender that was not your biological sex, wasn't it OK to identify as a member of a race that wasn't your biological heritage, if we don't think of race as a biological concept? So she got a lot of flak for that. So that's one example and I was in touch with her and she was certainly somewhat intimidated by what happened. (Peter Singer, Professor of Bioethics, Princeton University, US, p. 4)

This case refers to Professor Rachel Tuvel, who wrote an article entitled 'In Defense of Transracialism' in 2017, published in the feminist philosophical peer-refereed journal, *Hypatia*. In the article, she considers whether one can select one's race, as is accepted for gender. This article provoked strong criticism, accusing Tuvel of transphobia and racism and engaging in 'epistemic violence', with an open letter calling for its retraction and members of the journal's editorial board apologising for its publication and the editor resigning.

In addition, a number of interviewees talked of the ethics of conducting certain topics of research, often in certain scientific fields:

> I think that when we have restrictions in the United States on some research involving subjects, and particularly children, or preborn, you know, foetuses and the like, I do think that's an issue. And obviously the question of surrogacy comes up and the use of biology, of testing to try to create three parent children and try to get around biological norms in the United States. Those are all issues that are a concern. So yeah I do think there are some that should not be conducted. (Emeritus Professor, Law, US, p. 8)

In the following section of this chapter, four key areas of 'forbidden knowledge' are examined arising from interviewees' own experiences of working on topics considered controversial and the challenges they have faced in producing this 'forbidden knowledge'.

6.1.2 Areas of Forbidden Knowledge

6.1.2.1 Bioethics, Psychology, and 'Controversial' Science

As highlighted in the section above on areas interviewees consider research should not be conducted, interviewees working in the areas of bioethics, psychology, and genetics provide personal accounts of their first-hand experiences. For example, Peter Singer, Professor of Bioethics at Princeton University in the United States, has worked on the issues of abortion, euthanasia, and infanticide with positions considered to be controversial. He has argued that the right to life is linked to the ability to hold preferences and a capacity to feel pain. Based on these assumptions, he has argued that foetuses and newborns do not have the characteristics of personhood (Singer, 1993). His work has been criticised from religious perspectives and also those working in the field of disability rights. In his interview, Singer traces the development of his research interests:

> That was partly as a result of the birth of the first in-vitro fertilisation baby back in 1978 and the fact that the first one who was born in Britain was rapidly followed by the second one who was born – no, the third one I think actually – was born in Australia. So it became a big issue in Australia and that's why I got involved in bio-ethics and that led me to some controversial topics, to some extent including in-vitro fertilisation although what I have to say on that topic is no longer controversial. But issues about euthanasia and especially about euthanasia for severely disabled newborns which clearly were, and still are, controversial and those are questions which simply arose from the fact that I was working in bio-ethics so I'd founded Australia's first university-based bio-ethics centre. (Peter Singer, Professor of Bioethics, Princeton University, US, p. 1)

Similarly, Robert Plomin, Professor of Behavioural Genetics at King's College, London, locates the intellectual development of his research interests in historical perspective and in relation to the norms of the discipline which have changed over time:

> This was in the early 70s – and back then in psychology in America at least, probably in the rest of the world too, psychology just did not consider the possibility of biological genetic influences. Psychology was dominated by

environmentalism. The view that you are what you learn. And so it was kind of dangerous professionally, and sometimes even personally, to even talk about genetic influence. And the psychology textbooks did not say anything about genetics. There's been a mountain of data from different sources: twin adoption studies, and now DNA, that often verge on the conclusion that genetics is important. So I think there is increasing acceptance of it. But when my book came out in October of last year, I was still quite worried about what the reaction would be. Some friends of mine, academic friends, thought it was like a suicide note in a way, in that I could become a pariah, because for the first time I did not pull any punches on it. You know, I just said as the title suggests, that DNA is the major systematic influence making us who we are. You know, the environment's important, but it does not work in that systematic way we always thought it worked when we used the word nurture. I was asked to write this book 30 years ago, and I did not want to do it then because I thought we needed more evidence, more research. But really, as I say in the book, the main reason was cowardice. I knew at that time that it was still politically incorrect in psychology – and maybe the behavioural sciences at large – to talk about genetic influence. (Robert Plomin, King's College, London, UK; formerly Penn State, and University of Colorado, US, p. 2)

He discusses the reception of his work and the unwelcome knowledge that 'genetics could affect behaviour' and that 'parents do not have as much control as they think'. In addition, he perceives the hostility in the reception of his work, in part arising from a lack of understanding in how to interpret the findings, stating:

> I was just amazed to find that inherited DNA differences account for so much of psychological traits, when it had been ignored for a century. So I found that very exciting and it led to lots of new ways of thinking about individual differences in psychology. It does not lead to a determinism, which is what some people worry about. (p. 9)

Noting that whilst the environment is important, Plomin explains that it does not work in a systematic way, but rather in terms of chance events. In addition, he clarifies that the findings of genetic influence are descriptive rather than making a normative claim that:

> no necessary policy implications [arise] from that – you can have a right-wing view or a left-wing view. The left-wing view is like the Finnish model where you say OK kids differ genetically, but what we are gonna do is put all the resources into that lower end to make sure that no kids are left behind, in terms of literacy

and numeracy. And a right-wing position could be oh well, just educate the best, forget the rest, which does not seem very wise because it's the intellectual capital of the society that's important. (p. 6)

He notes how this is also reflected in the priority of some funders, commenting on the ESRC: 'I think there's still quite a bit of resistance there to genetics' (p. 7).

6.1.2.2 Palestine

A number of academics interviewed commented on the challenges of conducting research on Palestine, both in the US and UK contexts. These observations were made by both academics who themselves work or have worked in the field, as well as those outside the field. Matthew Abraham, Professor of English, University of Arizona, USA, and author of *Out of Bounds: Academic Freedom and the Question of Palestine*, reflects on his career journey through academia:

> So my dissertation focused on ... issues around critical speech on the Israel-Palestine conflict asking if within the American Academy there's even academic freedom when it comes to Israel-Palestine, and my resounding answer is no, there is not really academic freedom when it comes to this issue. And really everything I've said in the last fifteen years has proven that to be true. I have faced obstacles in various points in my career, as a graduate student, as an assistant professor, where I was given subtle warnings, even veiled threats to stop writing on these issues and that I would not get a job or would be denied tenure, or would not be able to get key grants to support my research. I've lost grants before, after they were guaranteed to me in writing under the cover of bureaucratic error. At DePaul I went through various type of exclusions because of my support of Finkelstein and because of this focus on Israel-Palestine. I never was able to become Chair of my department even though I tried several times and people would say 'Oh he's too much of a lightning rod' and 'He's too political' and 'His criticism of Israel is not something we can tolerate.' (p. 2)

For some scholars, the precarity of doing this work is too great:

> I think if you are on tenure for example, it can be very hazardous to engage in certain types of research, particularly about, you know, Israel-Palestine's conflict if you are being critical of Zionism, if you are being critical of the Zionist lobby, if you are looking at the conditions of the public sphere that are constraining debate about Palestine. Sure, if you are visible enough, you are probably going to get on somebody's radar and you are going to be attacked and you could very well face

calls for your firing or being denied tenure. And within the university there are all kinds of people monitoring scholarship on Israel-Palestine ... I've really drifted away from doing this work in the last five, six years, just because it's just too much, you know, it takes emotionally and just from the standpoint of energy, it's just too draining and it just, it makes far more sense from the standpoint of one's energy and mental health to just stick to more conventional things. (Matthew Abraham, Professor of English, University of Arizona, US, p. 4)

The constraints of working in the field are illustrated in similar accounts:

I led a field school into the West Bank of Palestine – it was the Israel-Palestine Field School, that I co-taught with an anthropologist here. And when people found out that we were leading this class, there were hysterical emails about how we were anti-Semitic and the university should not support this kind of work. And then lastly I would say that when we host pro-Palestinian or Palestinian speakers on campus, we get criticism from Jewish organisations in our state saying that the speaker should not be supported by the university, that university funds should not be used and on and on. (Alex Lubin, Professor of African American Studies, Penn State, US, p. 3)

The case of Professor Miller, sociologist at the University of Bristol in the United Kingdom, acts as a 'cautionary tale' (Kempner et al., 2011) in the field with his sacking in 2021 following a formal investigation of a complaint of anti-Semitism made in 2018, which was unsuccessful. It was reopened for an appeal in 2020. In an interview after being fired, Miller says that there was a reactivation of the complaint under new rules introduced in 2019 based on the International Holocaust Remembrance Association's definition of anti-Semitism (Politics Today, 2021). Although his speech was ruled lawful, it was concluded that he 'did not meet the standards of behaviour we expect from our staff' (The Guardian, 2021). At the same time, a university statement said that it regards the 'principle of academic freedom as fundamental' and would like to 'reiterate that we take any risk to stifle that freedom seriously' (BBC, 2021).

6.1.2.3 Gender and Sexuality

Research on increasing youth identification with transgender identities has been a controversial domain. In 2018, Professor Lisa Littman at Brown University in Rhode Island, United States, coined the term 'rapid-onset gender dysphoria' to describe the increased incidence of gender dysphoria in young people (Littman, 2018). Littman proposed that this phenomenon could be explained by peer influence and that identifying as transgender is a social coping mechanism. On publishing her paper, Littman faced a number of criticisms on the methodology and conclusions from academics as well as transgender activists, and it was also critiqued by sociologists as a moral panic. The publication agreed to a post-publication review, and it was subsequently framed more clearly as a study of targeted parents' views predominantly from anti-transgender websites. It was also made clear that the medicalised term coined by Littman did not have diagnostic standing. The case also attracted a lot of controversy in the mainstream media. In a subsequent response from Littman in 2022, she addressed assumptions behind her motivations for the study stating her research had been a 'very good-faith attempt' to 'find out what's going on' and that 'As a person I am liberal; I'm pro-LGBT. I saw a phenomenon with my own eyes and I investigated, found that it was different than what was in the scientific literature' (Kessien, 2022). Commenting on this case, a UK Professor expresses concern in such research being 'shut down':

> There's been a massive increase in the number of, particularly girls, presenting with various forms of gender dysphoria, a huge increase, like a kind of five hundred-fold increase. And it seems to me that any good social scientist or anyone concerned with ensuring that children you know, vulnerable children or children presenting with whatever kind of problem get the most appropriate therapeutic or medical interventions, that you need to understand what the underlying cause is for what's being presented. But anyone trying to do research that suggests that there might be a broader cultural or social reason for these phenomena is blocked from doing so. And that's just, you know we know that. And this seems to me deeply worrying. So there's a famous example that you are probably aware of, of Lisa Lippman at Brown University in the States who's developed the idea that based on quite a lot of qualitative data that there is an element of social contagion amongst girls presenting for gender reassignment. And this is seen as hugely problematic by the trans activist community, [who] have tried to get the research shut down, tried to discredit it. And I think well you know, maybe they are right, maybe the research is flawed, but this is such a new area and this is such an important area to get right. I mean we are dealing with children's development, we are dealing with people making potentially irreversible decisions to undergo medical transition and take puberty blockers and all sorts of things. We need to make sure we are getting it right. And I just think in a climate like that, the more research you have the better, you know provided the research itself is not doing anything unethical and if it turns out that that hypothesis is not borne out by the

research then do more research and show it. But I just do not think we should be shutting down research into particular attempts to, in a particular attempt to understand what's going on in a case like this. So I do think there's some worrying things going on at the moment. And this seems to be an area that a lot of people just will not get involved in. (pp. 7–8)

Subsequent large-scale research analysing data from 2017 to 2019 in the United States has not replicated Littman's claim that there is a trend of increase in transgender identification (Turban et al., 2022). Kempner (2017) proposes that such controversial cases of 'horror stories of academic persecution' act as 'cautionary tales' to make public and share the boundaries of forbidden knowledge – often cited well-known cases such as Milgram's (1974) obedience to authority studies, Humphrey's tearoom trade study, and Herrnstein and Murray's *The Bell Curve* (1996). Kempner also found that academics self-censored on the basis of disciplinary norms.

The experience of infringement of academic freedom as a result of an ensuing bullying environment and the ensuing culture of self-censorship is also highlighted as a means of securing the boundaries of forbidden knowledge:

In the last year, when I started to speak out about the current debates around transgender rights and feminist issues ... that's when I really came up against what in my mind is a very, very worrying culture of actually a lot of sort of self-censorship of people who are scared to speak up on things that are seen as controversial, because of the amount of harassment and bullying that's taken place really about people speaking up on this. So it's really in the last year that this has become an issue for me. It's never been an issue before ... People speaking at those events have been bullied, physically bullied, targeted with threats. Meetings have been shut down. I mean any meeting that I've attempted to go to has had last minute venue changes because of bomb threats to the venue. Quite aggressive people demonstrating outside and shouting targeted abuse and harassment at people. I personally know people who have had death and rape threats on social media, from activists who are aware of the stance they are taking ... I have had student activists tweeting about me on their accounts, warning students to stay away from my classes because I'm apparently a dangerous transphobe so my classes are not safe spaces for trans students which is very upsetting to me as a lecturer, as someone who's worked really hard to make my classes as inclusive as possible, and would never you know, say anything that I thought would offend or make students uncomfortable. (UK Professor, UK, pp. 3–4)

The importance of the complexity of power dynamics within transgender pressure groups, calling for attention to the intersectionality of class, sex, and gender/sexuality identity, is raised to nuance the understanding in situating certain forms of research as taboo and threatening to transgender identities:

> Because historically male body persons – and I include in that group trans women and gay men and bisexual men – have always had power. That's historically true. Particularly white upper-class persons in those groups. Unlike women and unlike racial minorities, LGBT people have always had a segment – and I want to stress, a segment of people within them, who have always had significant power. And they have oppressed not just other groups but they have oppressed, not just other vulnerable minorities but they have oppressed other LGBT people. And so it should not shock anybody that they have corporate ties, they have university ties. I do not think the behaviour of those groups is the majority but they have the power to shut down other groups. And I think it ties right into our discussion of academic freedom. They have the economic power to shut down other groups. So that's what's been happening. (Emeritus Professor of Law, US, p. 6)

Forbidden knowledge is also evident – not only in terms of research but also in terms of what is 'forbidden' knowledge in the curriculum. The perception of topics from the main university campus that may be considered to be controversial on branch campuses tends to result in a cautious approach from senior management with regard to what is taught in the curriculum. In the case of Curtin University, Australia, and its branch campus in Dubai, the perception of topics from the main university campus that may be considered to be controversial on branch campuses, tending to result in a cautious approach from senior management with regard to what is taught in the curriculum, is detailed in the previous chapter.

A concern was expressed that staff may publicise dissatisfaction around any perceived restrictions on their academic freedoms, especially in the humanities and social sciences:

> So I think part of the reason of them focusing them kind of more technical and vocational subjections is because they probably know it's not very viable to take certain things to Dubai, because the staff will not do it, you'd have to change the syllabus so much, and that creates controversy in and of itself. And then people can go public with that and leak things as well which they really do not like. So I think that definitely must have been part of the logic I presume ... The university have a process where they review anything that's going to go to Dubai. So they are appointing people working with Directors of Education and then

down within the schools to review and check that they are compliant with Dubai's laws. (UCU Branch officer, UK, p. 5)

The concern to control curriculum on branch campuses from the main campus in perceived controversial topic areas differs from the situated experiences of lecturers teaching on branch campuses. Accounts from lecturers express their perceived sense of relative freedom to teach in this field, although being aware of 'boundaries': 'It wasn't as if you could not deal with some of those issues about gender inequality or whatever, you know, it was just a question of framing more than anything else' (former Lecturer, UAE, p. 7). UAE lecturers report relative autonomy in developing their courses, whilst also taking personal responsibility for content:

> Well I mean to be honest no, everything was left to me in terms of, you know, delivering and teaching the courses, but you are kind of expected just to use basic textbooks and teach from that, you know what I mean? So I did not really kind of stray too far on this. I mean one of my colleagues who was teaching a course on like – it was Clinical Sociology. I would have like a debate each week and one of them was a debate about gender equality and like a bunch of the women students were really into it and arguing for gender equality. Another bunch of students just walked out. So you know, I found the boundaries out – I did not get into trouble or anything like that but I think in terms of self-censorship, you know, obviously Judith Butler and LGBTQ stuff, you know. I mean I do not think the students would have been angry or anything like that; they would have just kind of sat there thinking 'why are we being told this?' (p. 7)

Academic freedom and the production of knowledge relating to gender and sexuality at the American University of Beirut (AUB) in Lebanon has been perceived to be increasingly restricted within a certain construction of gender studies. Commenting on the Gender Studies faculty search at AUB in 2015, a US professor commented on the dominance of a more conservative conception of gender studies, excluding possibilities of knowledge production in alternative framings of gender that intersectionally incorporated sexuality.

6.1.2.4 Race, Religion, Security, and Extremism

Previous chapters have highlighted that whilst 'race' work goes on in UK universities, this takes the form of institutional objectives on equality and diversity, such as the Race Equality Charter. Academics working in the field do not perceive their research and teaching to be directly constrained but cite lack of funding as the most significant indirect form of restricting the production of knowledge:

> So I've never felt that a University or the requirements of the role stop me from speaking out directly. I'm never told 'you cannot say that'. But funding is probably the most powerful, single mechanism that restricts critical anti-racist research because you simply cannot raise lots of money to do research looking at how white supremacy saturates the economy, the education system and society at large. (Professor of Education, UK, pp. 6–7)

On being asked if there is some research that should not be conducted, a number of academics commented on 'racist pseudo-scientific' research in particular, where there was institutional support and external funding for this research. There were mixed views on whether such research should be done, ranging from arguments that such work is not responsible research to arguments that academics have the freedom to choose their research. As mentioned in the previous chapters, views were expressed on the case of Noah Carl, who was awarded a Fellowship at the University of Cambridge but was then dismissed after over 500 academics signed a public letter calling the research racist pseudoscience being legitimated through the University of Cambridge. It is argued that hosting such research at elite universities accords it with credibility and legitimacy, that such research should not be conducted and is a misuse of academic freedom: 'There is no legitimate science around the argument race and intelligence are genetically linked, because race is a social construction, it varies from one time to another and from one society to another ... I think it's a hangover from the scientific racism of the 19th Century' (Professor of Education, University of Birmingham, UK, p. 7).

In contrast, a UK sociologist expressed the view that racist research will continue and would not take the position that such research should be 'forbidden':

> I cannot just simply say that they should not do their research. They're going to do their research whether I like it or not. So I'm not empowered in this debate. They will get huge funding and they will continue. The racist pseudoscience has been for millennia, you know, it's been the foundation of the Empire, it's been, it's used to explain everything from gun crime in the inner cities to single mothers. It's a whole gamut of race science that's been there and yeah, there might, you know the highbrow research centres doing it but there's also a lot of low brow everyday racism of that ilk of pseudoscience ... As far as I'm concerned it gives me meat to my grist. I can argue against it. I can do my alternative thinking and my alternative ideological stances and I guess you know, I would not have written the work

Introduction

I've written and influenced the students that I have and produced the body of work that I have been privileged enough to do, if I wasn't counteracting these bastards, if I wasn't saying you know, Charles Murray is pseudoscience – I mean that was my inaugural lecture, you know, looking at The Bell Curve and looking at how it pervades everyday common sense thinking about races being fundamentally different and the right of some people to dominate others. (Professor Emeritus, Sociology, UK, p. 6)

The different institutional contexts within the United Kingdom are also perceived to have differential restrictions on the production of knowledge, as reflected on by another academic researching on education and extremism, comparing the experience at the School of Oriental and African Studies with other universities:

In fact I became quite naïve because I was under the impression that I could say and do whatever I wanted and it was only when I started taking my research outside of the university, whether it was quote, unquote in the community, or it was in some other universities. And the kind of questions, the sort of questions that I got, that I started realising well maybe some of what I'm saying is not going down so well with people. Maybe I have to be careful how I present my ideas. So at SOAS I did not have an issue. (UK Senior Lecturer, p. 2)

The constraints on researching security, in particular, in relation to the Middle East take the form of perceived limited funding opportunities:

I think that certainly with the ESRC in the past, although I have not done it for a while, but in the past when I've put in applications – and I think they have been strong applications ... for example there's a project that I wanted to look at regarding peace narratives between Israeli and Palestinian youth, and we did not get funding for that. And actually, I thought it was a very, very strong bid. A couple of years later I put another bid in, a similar kind of thing, from the ESRC. We did not get that again. And looking at the feedback that we were getting, it seemed to me that the ESRC – and again I have no, and I'm saying this in a very subjective sense, so make of that what you will – but it seemed to me that the ESRC does not seem to want to fund projects that relate to Israel. (Professor of Regional Security, UK, p. 9)

In addition, it is noted how funding calls present certain framings of security, thus indirectly shaping the development of disciplines and fields of study:

If you look at it purely in hard security terms, the honest answer's probably no. I think if you are looking at security in terms of soft security, so that could include things like environmental security, human security, societal security, I think there's more of a sympathy towards those constructs of security. And by the way, that's not a bad thing. I think these projects, if they are good enough, should be funded. (Professor of Regional Security, UK, p. 9)

Research on religion in contemporary everyday life is highlighted as 'forbidden' knowledge from a range of different disciplinary perspectives and contexts. For example, critically examining religious claims-making in politics is seen as a neglected and taboo area of knowledge:

> If you think about for example the deployment of religion and religious claims that are made in religion and politics and so on, so forth, these are areas that should be researched and there should be serious soul searching and thoughtful reflection on these areas, because they are affecting everything, they are affecting the present and the future. (former Professor, AUB, Lebanon, p. 12)

The reception of historical research on the Muslim Brotherhood in Egypt is an example of the misconstrued politicisation of Professor Baron's work:

> There were reviews that interpreted my book as I supported the Muslim Brotherhood. I mean I was writing about the, the founding of the Muslim Brotherhood in the early nineteen thirties, so I'm not talking about the Muslim Brotherhood in Egypt or anywhere else today. The book takes, argues that the Brotherhood arose in response to, in part, in response to, and in the image of the missionaries, that it learnt from missionaries certain tactics about forming certain kinds of institutions. So for example if the missionaries had educational institutions, the early Muslim Brotherhood, some of the first things they did was start schools, to draw kids out of missionary institutions. So the argument was really built on things that were going on on the ground in certain small towns and cities throughout the delta region and canal zone of Egypt. But in this kind of superficial reading there was this sort of sense that if you are researching the Brotherhood you are obviously of a certain position. (Beth Baron, Professor of Middle East History, US, p. 8)

Research considered taboo in the UAE made reference to research on the politics of ethnicity and national identity:

> No, they [interviewees] were just saying that 'By the way, we were never asked these questions because as you know these are taboo here, treated as taboo' and you know if you think about the questions that I was asking, it was just whether their ethnic or tribal background sort of had any impact on the way they experienced their national identity on an everyday basis. So there's a total concealment

of diversity within the ... national narrative [which] is on homogeneity and being Arab and being tribal. (UK Lecturer, and former Lecturer, UAE, p. 5)

In the final section, I examine what I refer to as 'agentic boundary work', where academics talked of their personal experiences of publishing and disseminating 'forbidden' knowledge.

6.1.3 Agentic Boundary Work: Publishing and Disseminating 'Forbidden' Knowledge

Academics spoke of their varied experiences and repercussions of publishing or disseminating forbidden knowledge. One initiative is the *Journal of Controversial Ideas*, cofounded and edited by Peter Singer, Francesca Minerva, and Jeff McMahan, a multi-disciplinary peer-refereed journal, where academics can publish under pseudonyms, with the first issue published in 2021. It describes itself as 'the first open access, peer-reviewed, interdisciplinary journal specifically created to promote free inquiry on controversial topics', where controversial is understood in terms of 'certain views about them might be regarded by many people as morally, socially, or ideologically objectionable or offensive' (Journal of Controversial Ideas website, 2022). Singer explained the role of a hostile context in the development of the idea:

> The original idea of it is not mine, it's Francesca Minerva's idea, my co-editor and probably you should talk to her about it if you are interested in that. But she's somebody who did publish an article defending infanticide and she and her husband actually co-authored it. They got death threats that frightened them and a lot of hate mail as well and I think she also feels that it has actually made it more difficult for her to get a tenured position, or a tenured track position. So she approached me and Jeff McMahan as well with the idea of providing a venue whereby people could publish anonymously or under a pseudonym, but still be subject to the usual academic scrutiny and then they could, if they wished under specific circumstances, the Journal could tell, let us say, a selection committee that they were going before that they were the author of this article if they wanted it to be known that they were. (Peter Singer, Professor of Bioethics, Princeton University, US, p. 4)

The journal's first two issues have covered topics including transgender, race, freedom of speech, queer theory, paedophilia, Nazi education, and 'wokeness', with four out of fourteen articles using pseudonyms. All articles are from the Global North, except for one substantively different article by authors in Saudi Arabia on Saudi Arabian universities' rapid rise up the academic rankings, not evidently 'controversial'. The journal states that its remit includes considering articles 'that discuss issues or policies in non-Western cultures that may not be controversial in the West but are sufficiently controversial elsewhere that critically discussing them could endanger authors (Journal of Controversial Ideas, 2022). The Eurocentric/Global North bias is reflected not only in the knowledge production of the journal's contents but also in the language and framing used, where all knowledge from outside the Global North is designated as 'other' in the use of the term, '*non*-Western'. The journal is also presented as a 'safe haven' for knowledge production assumed to be curtailed by those countries curtailing academic freedom; the remit does not include, for example, ideas from the Global South that are controversial in the West.

In contrast, in Lebanon, the peer-refereed journal, *Kohl*, publishes academic and practitioner perspectives on gender and sexuality throughout the Global South, located as an independent initiative operating outside the more conservative constraints of academic institutions in the region. It describes itself as a progressive feminist journal on gender and sexuality in the Middle East, South West Asia, and North Africa regions and is a multilingual publication. It locates its mission of producing knowledge transnationally and as a corrective to orientalism and the exclusion of the region in the production of knowledge about itself: 'This journal hopes to trouble the hegemony of knowledge production and ensure that our regions and communities play a central role in redefining their own intersections and challenges when it comes to feminist and sexuality research' (https://kohljournal.press/about). Given the relative conservatism of gender studies within university contexts, *Kohl* is not embedded within any such university or institutional framework. According to one of the editors, a former academic at AUB, Lebanon, and currently a UK-based Lecturer: 'I mean, definitely there was no real positive appetite to be involved with any university. There would not have been a very clear home for it. Some of the stuff on sexuality in particular and sex within the journal has been I think beyond what either university would have been happy for us to be publishing under their name.' (p. 14)

Academics in the United States talked of subtle censures in the form of difficulties in publishing:

> I have had experiences as I've said you know, but they have not come from my university, they come from outside the university. They've come from the people

who control speech. I have a book – I did not mention this to you but I'm writing a series of books on LGBT people who are outed in newspapers going back to the seventeen hundreds. And there's a lot of information out there. And I have been writing it for some time. And finally now I have the time to try to finish it. But I sent out a couple of proposals of subsets of that work and I did not get any bites from publishers. And I was told by a friend of mine that they do not want to publish that because they think it will affect the litigation that is going on in the country. So I sent it out to academic publishers. Now this wasn't my institution that was blocking and it wasn't, you know these publishing companies are associated with institutions but they aren't actually directly run by them. But it's that kind of thing you know, the ability to have a platform infrastructure which I always stress is the key issue. (Professor Emeritus in Law, George Washington University, US, p. 14)

Preserving the intellectual history of lesbian, gay, bisexual, and transgender (LGBT) in the United States, where such knowledge was historically controversial, is detailed in the account of a US Professor:

Lesbian Herstory. It's a US thing, right. So it was started in 1974 as part of the gay liberation movement and an intentional effort to respond to the fact that research on gay and lesbian lives is not supported by regular libraries and out of the suspicion that no regular research library would ever house these materials in such a way that they were accessible to the whole of people who might call themselves lesbians, right, this is warnings from 1974 so warning sounds a little dated but the goal was to make these materials available to the whole of the lesbian community and therefore they should not be housed in an institution where you had to have credentials to get in, right. So it started in somebody's kitchen in 1974 and it has grown and is the largest collection in the entire world and they do have regular international contributors (p. 12)

Experiences of difficulties of publication and dissemination are evident across the different country contexts from Lebanon, the UAE, the United Kingdom, and the United States. Andrew Ross from NYU comments on the lack of visibility of research on labour conditions in the Gulf and the potential consequences of trying to conduct such work:

We published a report of our field trips with the Gulf Labour Coalition. Subsequent to that, I have not really seen any field research of that kind published, and maybe it's undertaken, but it has not certainly been reported or published. I think, you know, people have either been scared off, or organisations with the resources like Human Rights Watch, are barred from entering. And my colleagues at NYU Abu Dhabi, who are in a position to conduct research – as far as I know, they do not do it. (Andrew Ross, Professor of Social and Cultural Analysis, NYU, US, p. 7)

In the UK context, production of knowledge with alternative narratives is seemingly blocked both from public domains and in academic fora. A UK Professor of Sociology describes his difficulties in publishing on the highly publicised case of 2019 protests in Birmingham against the inclusion of LGBT (No Outsiders) in primary education curricula:

> But I think that's where I would see the big free speech issue, the position of Muslims on campus. I mean, I cannot get anything, I mean, do you know of the No Outsiders issue in Birmingham schools at the moment at Parkfield Primary School? So I've not been able to get anything published around the No Outsiders. Within newspapers, no letters to a newspaper, no offer to write something for a paper, article for *The Conversation*, which is like the house newspaper of universities, they were not interested in having anything on No Outsiders ... They do not wish to publish on this topic with a view that is other than the mainstream view of a deficit in the attitudes of Muslim parents. (Professor of Sociology, UK, pp. 6–7)

Other academics gave accounts of difficulties in either having invitations for visiting lectures on their work or even being banned. One US Professor researching on the Gulf recounts offering to give lectures at universities in the region and receiving no response:

> I reached out to all of my networks of colleagues that are in the Gulf, they all know the book is out, telling them that I'm already going to be in the region, invite me for a talk, you know? And, ... people know who I am, you know, because there's not a lot of [disciplinary scholars] that work on the Gulf, so ... it caught my attention that nobody answered me, you know! (p. 7)

Peter Singer, Professor of Bioethics at Princeton University, details his experiences on being banned to give lectures in parts of Europe. The sociopolitical and historical contexts of the reception of his work are also evident in the protests being in certain European contexts:

> No, those protests have been exclusively in Western countries. Yeah, as I said they started off in Germany and I think they had something to do with Germany's past and with the Nazi so-called Euthanasia Programme for disabled people which was not really a euthanasia programme at all of course. But then it spread to Austria and the German speaking part of Switzerland and there have been some

protests – well, one of the universities that refused to allow me to speak on campus was actually in Warsaw and also there was a protest – I wasn't even there – but at the Victoria University in British Colombia. (p. 6–7)

This is contrasted with the reception in other parts of the world and the widespread translation of Singer's work:

Certainly my books have been translated into probably something like thirty languages at the moment and in terms of what you were talking about, developing countries, I've just recently signed a contract for Animal Liberation to be translated into Swahili. So that would be my first book in Swahili or I think in any African language, unless you count Arabic I guess working in North Africa. But anyway, any sub-Saharan language. But my books have certainly been translated quite a lot into Asian languages, particularly in Korea I have maybe eight or nine of my books have been translated into Korean. I get regularly, they are taught in Korean universities and high schools as well so I regularly get emails from Korean students asking me to basically answer their exam question for them. And some of my books are now in China and they have been for many years in Japan. So yes, certainly in Asian languages as well ... Yeah, I do not think that that kind of disability rights movement exists in Japan or China or Korea for example, as far as I'm aware. (pp. 6–7)

6.2 CONCLUSION

This chapter has identified four domains of 'forbidden' knowledge drawing on academics' accounts across all four contexts of Lebanon, the UAE, the United Kingdom, and the United States. What emerges is that the nature and content of forbidden knowledge is fluid over time – as illustrated, for example, by the *Lesbian Herstory* account of LGBT history and its archiving in the US context. It's fluidity is also geopolitically situated, with the accounts illustrating the differences in how forbidden knowledge is constructed and negotiated in both teaching and research in the domain of gender and sexuality in Lebanon, the UAE, United Kingdom, and the United States. Pedagogical approaches to mediating this forbidden knowledge in the classroom emphasise a direct engagement with the ideas in an open context:

Academic freedom, you know, freedom of enquiry, freedom to make mistakes, freedom of trying to articulate ideas, freedom to get it wrong in the classroom is something that I support every day in my teaching, well a couple of days a week anyway, in my teaching. And I'm pretty good at allowing unpopular ideas to be expressed, not hate speech, I have not had people say really hateful things in class but I do encourage people who make mistakes who get it wrong to try again and I tell them in advance at the beginning of the semester, look if something comes up that's provoking we are going to slow down and stop, and I might ask you to slow down, reiterate, ask where that idea comes from, what received wisdom are you repeating, what's the history of it, how do we want to dig into it in order to understand its effects, right. So I do that whole thing at the beginning and I've been wholly in support of people trying out ideas, even if they have racist impacts and effects or homophobic impacts and effects in a class where they are actually trying to engage with the ideas and we can handle that. (Professor of English and Women's Studies, US)

The empirical data collected in transnational perspective illustrates that rationales underpinning forbidden knowledge are socially constructed in several ways, including framing as 'taboo', concerns relating to perceived and actual applications, and the discovery of 'uncomfortable truths'. Forbidden knowledge is a *strategic* construction, shaped geographically, politically, and socially, in contrast to being gaps in knowledge or data that have not been collected. This reinforces understandings of knowledge and non-knowledge as constructed within an interpretivist lens, as opposed to constructions of knowledge as uncovering 'truth', as described in Chapter 4. For those working on controversial topics, the agentic boundary work that these academics engage in producing this forbidden knowledge is labour that takes its toll – emotionally, economically, and physically – through hostile environments, challenges to publishing, travel bans, and imprisonment.

7 'Legitimate' Knowledge

Methodological Debates and the Political Sociology of Knowledge Production

> Sociologists seem to have forgotten, to paraphrase Raymond Williams, that education is not a product like cars and bread, but a selection and organisation from the available knowledge at a particular time which involves conscious or unconscious choices.
>
> (Young, 1971, p. 18)

7.1 INTRODUCTION

The previous chapter examined the notion of 'forbidden' knowledge conceptualised in terms of knowledge that is considered 'taboo' or dangerous to produce. The content of this knowledge as well as the processes and lived experiences of academics' accounts took a transnational approach in situating such forbidden knowledge in relation to sociopolitical, historical, and geopolitical contexts. In this chapter, I turn to the conception of 'legitimate' knowledge. I examine the construction of 'legitimacy' drawing on political, sociological, and philosophical conceptions and interrogate what constitutes legitimate knowledge. Foucault's work has enabled the recognition of the influence of the relationships of power on constructing fields of knowledge (Foucault, 1969; 1975; 1976), and Bourdieu, using the concept of 'capital', has argued that knowledge must be accepted as important within a given field of power and its relationship to other fields of power (Bourdieu, 1986).

Examining examples of various systems of legitimation, for example, disciplinary methodology, university world rankings, impact, employability, and publications, I propose that 'legitimate' knowledge not only is the opposite of forbidden knowledge but also relates to the dynamics and relationships of power in what knowledge is deemed acceptable and validated.

7.2 CONSTRUCTIONS OF 'LEGITIMACY' AND 'KNOWLEDGE'

In the political science literature, the notion of 'authority' is central to understanding legitimacy. This entails both the perceived 'right' of the authority and its 'acceptance'. In philosophical terms, the notion of 'legitimacy' has a normative status, with implied validation – implicit or explicit. In examining individuals' beliefs in societal context, Weber (1978) argued that there is a tendency to conformity in line with cultural beliefs, as the perception of support for this social order seems valid, and this is therefore taken as a 'norm'. As such, 'legitimacy' in sociological terms can be understood as a collectively formulated process resulting in 'the taken-for-granted support of an aspect of social life (e.g. an action, a procedure, an individual, a position, or a structure of positions) by a real or an implied audience' (Johnson and Watson, 2015, p. 823). Thus, it entails social, cognitive, and normative dimensions.

The sociological theorisation of 'legitimacy' entails a complex and dynamic interrelationship of the conceptions of belief, truth, and justification. Goldman (2002), drawing on the literature of social epistemology, distinguishes between four constructs of the term 'knowledge': (i) knowledge as equated with belief; (ii) knowledge as institutionalised belief; (iii) knowledge as true belief, and (iv) knowledge as justified true belief. Goldman places the first two constructions of knowledge as typically used by sociologists, whereas the latter two constructions tend to be represented in philosophical theories of knowledge.

The notions of truth and justified truth in relation to knowledge are illustrated in the account below, where truth is socially understood in the context of an audience and where the justification arises from an agreement of what is true:

> And I think the only way you get to truth, or at least an agreement as to what we should decide is true, is by having different perspectives and people from different perspectives providing input into the process as well as into the final result. Without that I really do not think we can arrive at either an assessment of what is true, but also an assessment of what we would all agree upon is fair and decent. So for me academic freedom is the pursuit of that end result that we call can at least be comfortable with as opposed to just one side winning because one side has all of the power. (Professor Emeritus of Law, George Washington University, US, p. 2)

It could be argued, however, that the notion of agreeing on what is true differs from Goldman's (2002) notion of 'justified' true belief. Justification in the given account is not constructed in terms of a logical process or on the basis of perceived irrefutable empirical evidence. Rather, it comes closer to Goldman's (2002) notion of institutionalised belief, arrived at through a process that is perceived to have legitimacy through inclusivity. What is clear in this account is the central place of process that is deemed to be 'fair' in arriving at a conception of truth that is justified, and therefore legitimated.

The notion of justice or a sense of the 'right' is raised in the following two examples given of research entailing 'epistemic violence', and as such deemed to lack legitimacy:

> Is the research in itself, does it have epistemic violence or ontological violence within it? And not just about the human but also about nonhuman, if I can extend it into that. These are really deep questions. And I think it's that whole thing about resurgence of eugenic research which is really what that empire and stuff, you know the pushback now at the moment. I think there's subtle eugenics coming back into research and legitimated as such. (Professor of Cultural Studies, Curtin University, Australia, p. 11)

> I mean for me, there is no legitimate science around the argument race and intelligence are genetically linked, because race is a social construction, it varies from one time to another and from one society to another. So for me the argument ... would be the same argument as somebody saying we should not stifle debate about the possible dangers posed by women who could be witches. I mean there is no legitimate debate about whether a proportion of women are witches and I do not think there's any legitimate debate about whether there's a genetic link between social race and fixed levels of ability. I think it's a hangover from the scientific racism of the 19th Century and it just continually every 10 or 20 years puts on new clothes, wraps itself in the latest scientific kind of language and pretends to be different to the previous versions. (Professor of Education, University of Birmingham UK, pp. 7–8)

In the second excerpt, the analogy with research on women as witches is based on a contemporary social agreement of the preposterousness of any such belief as truth. The logic of the account is that any such claim lacks justified scientific or empirical basis and, therefore, lacks 'truth'. Drawing on this logic, the science of race and intelligence is delegitimated as an outdated racist science of the nineteenth century, based on unjustified and false belief. Goldman (2002) argues that knowledge necessarily entails belief, and so understanding how we reach knowledge requires a consideration of the routes to belief, which are largely social.

7.3 WHAT CONSTITUTES LEGITIMATE KNOWLEDGE

That truth is a social institution was illustrated in the preceding account equating research on women as witches with research on race and intelligence. Shapin (1994) highlights that a claim 'is never determined by the individual making the claim' but rather can be understood in terms of a collective judgement, which is then used as a standard in the future by which this 'truth' becomes 'stabilised'.

The literature on the sociology of knowledge has highlighted various types of factors complicit in the formulation of knowledge, including class, political interests, gender, and so on. Science was considered to be beyond such influence by early sociologists of knowledge (Mannheim, 1936; Merton, 1973), although later sociologists of science from the Edinburgh School did not consider science to be outside the influence of society (Goldman, 2002). Longino (1993, p. 260) has gone further arguing that not only is there the social context within which science takes place, but also this context is 'an integral part of the epistemic nature of science'. Similarly, Kitcher (1993) locates social within the epistemic, pointing to how science is organised through practices of consensus, which is necessarily social and associated with a scientific community. The use of statistical evidence in the field of race equality in education is an example of how 'quantitative approaches often encode particular assumptions about the nature of social processes ... that reflect a generally superficial understanding of racism', yet, such knowledge of 'race inequality' is legitimated (Gillborn, 2010, p. 253).

The issue of what knowledge is taught in schools and higher education institutions is operationalised on the basis of a belief that 'some areas of knowledge are more worthwhile than others' (Young, 1971, p. 34), and so 'worthwhile' knowledge reflects sociopolitical dynamics of power in society. Social consensus of belief stabilises into truth.

This section examines a range of factors and processes implicated in the legitimation or delegitimation of knowledge including positionality; university diversity initiatives; discourses of civility; disciplinary constructs of methodology, 'quality', and the 'Canon'; skills, employment, and research assessment; funding and international partnerships; and university world rankings and publications.

7.3.1 Positionality

Legitimate knowledge is framed in relation to *positionality* – in terms of both *who* is the knowledge producer and *where* the knowledge is being produced.

The positionality component of legitimate knowledge relates to the perceived 'right' of the authority. The second component of legitimate knowledge entails the processes by which it is recognised as legitimate. This component relates to the 'acceptance' of the authority.

As a White UK researcher on race in education, David Gillborn reflects on his positionality in conducting research in schools: 'As a White researcher I would be able to hear things from staff that I would not hear if necessarily I was a minoritised researcher' (p. 4). In addition, his positionality as a White male researching racism gives a greater legitimacy to the knowledge produced: 'Members of the oppressor class are taken more seriously as witnesses to oppression' (p. 4). In addition, career progression and positionality raise ethical issues: 'White researchers come along, do their research, go off and build a career and nothing changes for the Black folk experiencing the inequalities' (p. 3). Gillborn formerly directed the Centre for Research on Race in Education at the University of Birmingham, the only university-based centre at an English university focused on racism in education. He comments wryly that: 'I do not think that's coincidental, it tells you a lot about the Academy' (p. 4), aware of the politics of his positionality as a White male in the production on knowledge and its legitimation in the field.

Gillborn reflects on the reception of his work by Black academics, professionals, and communities, noting that positionality is definitely present in the room, but that he believes his work is well received. However, the status of the knowledge is always filtered by perceived positionality by the audience:

> So after a talk once about institutional racism a White, young woman asked me she said 'can I ask you a personal question?' and I said 'yes' and she said 'are you White?' and I said 'well, yeah all my family have always identified as White' and she kind of looked thoughtful for a second and then said 'oh OK' and then walked off. And I could not go after her to say 'hang on let us talk about what do you mean?' because there were lots of people around who wanted to talk to me and I've always thought that was interesting because whatever my answer, if she wanted to disregard what I said she could do it. So if she says 'are you White' and I say 'no, I'm mixed race' she could say 'ah well that explains it then, you would say that wouldn't you, it was the special pleading'. But if I say 'no, I'm White' she can go 'oh, so you admit you do not know what you are talking about'. So either way I think racism always has the stronger hand. (David Gillborn, Professor of Education, University of Birmingham, UK, p. 5)

Positionality is invoked in the following excerpt with a reflection on *who* can legitimately do what research:

> There are certain projects that I'm just not the right person to do. I might be someone who could be brought into the team, as a member of the team or as a part of an advisory group. But very clearly there's work, for example, around, I do not know, Black families' parental support. I mean there's some brilliant, radical work in those areas, but I'm just not the right person to do it. That's not self-censorship in a kind of 'oh I must not talk on these issues' it's just simply I would not be able to do that as a White-identified researcher. I do not have the knowledge, I do not have the tools, culturally or sociologically to do the best piece of work. So that's work not for me to do. (David Gillborn, Professor of Education, University of Birmingham, UK, p. 9)

Conversely, for ethnic minority academics, positionality can play an invisible role in self-censoring, where in the following account, the Lecturer is aware that her perceived positionality by students may be weaponised to delegitimise her intellectual contributions, invoking Fricker's (2009) concept of testimonial injustice:

> And we were just like talking about Edward Said and how that applies to these Hollywood productions or depictions of the Middle East. And one student, in an ... angry voice said 'Well I think some people in the Middle East are so emotional about things. So what if they are portrayed as terrorists? I mean as English people we are portrayed as scone eaters and tea drinkers, so we do not get offended with that' you know. So that sort of thing. Then I do not push that further, even though when I tell this to my English colleagues, they say, 'I would not be able to hold myself back'. And I was like no, I do not want to do that because of my positionality or how my positionality is perceived by the predominantly English classroom. (UK Lecturer and former Lecturer UAE, p. 10)

Epistemic injustice (Fricker, 2009) is also evident with the institutionalised racialisation of legitimate knowledge as illustrated in the account below discussing decisions made by funders about 'expertise':

> There was a scandal in geography, not amongst the White geographers but everyone else: so there was a grant that was issued on migration and all the grants of the people who were actually the experts – Black and Asian geographers, they did not get picked but the White geographers, they did get picked. And because people did not have the expertise they tried to then hire the Black and Asian geographers. (Lecturer in Geography, University of Leicester, UK, p. 6)

Debates about the democratisation of knowledge and contestation over notions of 'expertise' raise the issue of who holds the 'authority' to produce legitimate knowledge. Inherent in the concept of democracy is the notion of the critical citizen, challenging established norms, which is evident in de Tocqueville's (1990; orig. 1835) theorisations of American democracy. Expertise can be conceptualised in terms of acquired skills and knowledge through education and experience. In addition, the willingness to accept assessment and evaluation by others from a community of experts is conceived to be a part of a dynamic notion of expertise (Nichols, 2017). Nichols (2017) laments the 'death of expertise' and derides the elevation of opinion over research-informed knowledge, where there is an elision between belief and knowledge. He argues that whilst there is an intellectual history of the relationship of expertise to authority, both the hostility to 'knowledge' and the belief that all opinions are valid are new. The question of presumed 'authority' is challenged regarding the practice of academics publicly commenting on issues outside their areas of expertise:

> So you'll get academics speaking out on all manner of things which they are not qualified, so Jordan Peterson speaking about gender for example – Jordan Peterson does not study gender, is not an expert on gender – but many people's opinions on gender are formed through hearing or reading Jordan Peterson talking about gender. So I think there's this danger, you know, of academics getting a kind of general authority granted to them by the world at large. (Senior Lecturer in Ethics, University of Sussex, p. 3)

Jordan Peterson, Professor of Psychology at the University of Toronto, has raised controversy for his views on race, gender, and Islam. In March 2019, the University of Cambridge rescinded his visiting Fellowship offer. Responding to concerns expressed by both students and faculty, a university spokesperson was quoted as stating: '[Cambridge] is an inclusive environment and we expect all our staff and visitors to uphold our principles. There is no place here for anyone who cannot' (The Guardian, 2019). Rather than this being an infringement of academic freedom, the reference to the University of Cambridge 'principles' invokes Chemerinsky and Gillman's (2017) distinction of professional standards in the academic community from broader speech rights extending beyond into the community and Baer's (2019) arguments for such principles being equivalent to rules and standards within the workplace.

Similarly, responsibility is invoked as a necessary basis for authority in the following account on the discipline of History:

> We clearly are in a classic crisis of kind of hegemony that the old verities that drove and represented Britain and British history for centuries have broken down

in the last thirty or forty years, for reasons which are in a way obvious. And that has given rise to a crisis of authority and of legitimacy in academia. I think that academic freedom to me means, in summary, the right and the responsibility to undertake evidence-based research. It's obviously omitted from the statement from Academics for Academic Freedom, just passed over completely, that notion of responsibility. It's not a privilege but a responsibility. So that would be the first thing. And the second is that statement from Academics for Academic Freedom refers to opinions as explicitly that is what is being defended. I can see absolutely no justification for treating the opinions of academics as being in some way more or less sacrosanct than anybody else's opinions, but that's not what, I think, academic work should be about, and that's why I stressed the evidence-based. (Professor of History, UK, pp. 1–2)

There is a literature on the notion of lay expertise, which has developed in particular in the field of health and personal experiences of illness (Calnan and Williams, 1992; Prior, 2002). Such experiential knowledge has increasingly been recognised as having legitimacy, with funding often requiring the participation of the public in research (Harris et al., 2015). Yet, it is argued that such lay 'expertise' is wholly experiential, and as such, the use of 'expertise' in conjunction with 'lay' has been seen as an oxymoron (Prior, 2002). This leads us back to Goldman's distinctions of the contested different conceptions of knowledge and notions of 'truth'.

Contestations over legitimising different kinds of knowledge are also evident in debates surrounding indigenous knowledge. Indigenous knowledge has been conceptualised as a 'lived world, a form of reason that informs and sustains people ... a bridge between human beings and their environments' (Akena, 2015). The production of knowledge has also been studied in the field of social movements, including the affective production of knowledge (Kiwan, 2017a). Here, such knowledge entails emancipation, is emotive, and is inter-subjective. Western knowledge is taken as 'legitimate' rational and objective knowledge, and in its colonial interactions, this knowledge has been universalised as legitimate over other forms of indigenous knowledge. The fluidity and dynamic nature of knowledge production necessarily entail its contextualisation. Akena (2012, p. 600), in examining the marginalisation of indigenous knowledge, argues that the social, economic, and political contextualisation of the knowledge producers within these colonial contexts elucidates the 'domination and subjugation of indigenous knowledge'.

Working in the field of Native American Literature, a US Professor in Women's Studies recounts her growing awareness of her positionality as a non-native scholar in the field whilst doing her PhD:

> And it was my first time, you know not talking to indigenous people but talking to indigenous people with PhDs who asked me point blank 'what's in your research for us?' and I'm embarrassed to say that at the tender age of 29 I had never really thought about that ... I found that they had really amazing abilities and institutions set up for archiving and taking care of and remembering their own literary histories in ways that non-Native institutions did not. Rather than being in need of what is referred to in the field as 'recovery work' – the discovery of forgotten literature, I found when I started talking to Native people that they did not need me to recover their stuff, they did not need non-Native scholars digging through archives to find their stuff, they already had it. So I had 12 tribal editors who each chose literature from their Tribal Nation and chose how to present it and really all I did was frame it (p. 1-2).

The issue of audience for this knowledge has implications for understanding academic freedom. Whilst noting that initially the assumption was that the primary audience would be her students, it unfolded that the anthology had a significant audience within Tribal communities, and in some instances, it was not deemed appropriate that some knowledge be shared outside the community:

> So it has wound up having an audience among Tribal communities and Tribal communities have done their own sort of readings and gatherings, using the book and it's grown into a website with an evolving digital magazine. And then it also shows up in places like historical societies and museums, places that have interests in indigenous history. But along the lines of academic freedom one thing that comes up with indigenous history is that scholars tend to think that academic freedom is the freedom to publish whatever we want and whatever interests us and of course indigenous people were telling me that that's not necessarily so. There may be stories that are sacred, that are not supposed to be shared outside the community. So academic freedom in that sense became more of a conversation with Native people and a desire to be guided by them in what was appropriate for distribution and not all scholars agree with this. Some scholars think that that's the ultimate infringement on our academic freedom if I allow a Tribal Elder to tell me not to publish something, that's an infringement on my academic freedom. I respectfully disagree, I do not think freedom means very much if we are trampling on the wishes and desires of other people, especially marginalised people. (p. 2)

7.3.2 University Diversity Initiatives

Diversity initiatives in UK and US contexts are a common feature in universities. In the United Kingdom, Athena SWAN was established in 2007 and is managed by the Equality Challenge Unit, with the stated purpose being to bring about structural and cultural change in higher education for women in the sciences, technology, engineering, maths, and medicine (STEMM). The scope of subjects expanded in 2015 to include arts and humanities, social sciences, and business and law; the geographical reach includes Ireland and a pilot in Australia (Tzanakou and Pearce, 2019). Institutions can apply for recognition at three levels of award, namely bronze, silver, or gold. A version of this scheme was piloted in the United States, called SEA Change for STEM subjects, hosted with a non-governmental organisation, the American Association for the Advancement of Science (AAAS, 2022). In a similar vein, the UK (England, Scotland, and Wales) Race Equality Charter introduced in 2014 focuses on race equality, particularly in terms of representation of staff and students in higher education institutions, with thirty-one institutions involved in the trial. In 2022, universities expressed disapproval of government pressure to 'reconsider membership of the race equality scheme', in what has been characterised as culture wars, with the Minister of Education at that time describing the scheme as in tension with university duties to uphold free speech (The Guardian, 2022b). Less prominent, there is also a scheme relating to disability equality in the United Kingdom – '2 ticks' – positive about disability symbol which is awarded to employers who have 'made commitments to employ, keep and develop the abilities of disabled staff' (UCU, 2016); there is also the UK Stonewall Diversity Champions, which is a programme for employers on sexual orientation including trans.

It has been argued that the UK Athena SWAN (Scientific Women's Academic Network) is 'a product of neoliberalisation with the UK's academic environments, reflecting the tendency towards accountability, metric, and the performative "doing" of equality work' (Tzanakou and Pearce, 2019, p. 1191). Given the market logic, such initiatives typically prioritise outcomes that take the form of extra support, rather than addressing systemic institutional barriers. Tzankou and Pearce (2019) use the construct of 'moderate feminism' to refer to an approach of 'reasonableness'. This reasonableness invokes the dichotomy of rationality and emotion, where any affective response must be neutralised or contained as inappropriate. As such, this discourse does not recognise that emotion is actually a sociopolitical practice, rather an individual-level feeling (Ahmed, 2014). In addition, this discourse is embedded in a marketised construction of individual competitiveness as opposed to social solidarity (Peck et al., 2009). Furthermore, it is often those who are marginalised (typically women and ethnic minorities) who are tasked with the burden of this work (ibid., 2009). Below, a senior ethnic minority academic in the United Kingdom whose work focuses on race and who has also held 'race equality' roles elucidates the paradox of these initiatives:

> I have been asked to champion race equality ... So I'm allowed to spout off whatever I like. And they do not come, they never come to my sessions but they are happy I'm doing them. Happy 'Oh [she's] doing that. We've ticked that box, it's fine'. It allows the status quo to just be you know. (Emeritus Professor of Sociology, UK, p. 4)

Whilst 'being allowed to spout off', there is a concomitant undermining of legitimacy in that the dissemination of such knowledge is contained within sessions that 'they never come to'. Furthermore, whilst such initiatives are supported, there is a lack of support in terms of funding, and hence the challenge in producing 'strong research' as opposed to being based on 'our experiences in higher education':

> So going back to the whole thing of academic freedom, you can spout off as much as you like, we are allowed that, but we cannot get the goodies and we cannot necessarily get that kind of very strong research. So I find that a lot of the work we do around race and gender and intersectionality, and our experiences in higher education are just based on our experiences, and not on hardcore big research grants you know. And I've noticed this across the board. And a lot of young people, young scholars are doing their own research without any funding at all. (p. 7)

The construct of 'strong research' as opposed to experiential research further delegitimises those whose research is already marginalised. Disciplinary and methodological constructions of 'quality' consolidate this process of delegitimisation, discussed in the following section.

7.3.3 Disciplinary Quality, Methodology, and the 'Canon'

Whilst semantically the understanding of 'discipline' as a noun describes content, it is pertinent to note that its origin stems from the verb form 'to discipline', corresponding to training in the methods associated with the content (Williams, 2016). Scott (2019) comments on the role of disciplines as performing a protective function, yet concomitantly recognising that disciplinary structures are hierarchical and can act as a 'regulatory tool' (p. 49). Therefore, discipline denotes a 'practice', which can be inclined to 'policing and punishment of non-conformist thought and action' (Hudson, 2016, p. 34). Conversely, interdisciplinarity transgresses disciplinary boundaries and has been linked to thinking 'outside the box' – 'the activity of thinking – and its correlatives of teaching and research – exists precisely when one goes beyond the disciplinary' (Docherty, 2016, pp. 102–103).

The concept of a self-regulating disciplinary community based on expertise arose in practice, emerging from this conceptual framework. Although the content and practices of a discipline are not static, they entail a recognition of the legitimacy of the shared norms of the discipline. If the disciplinary norms are transgressed, there is the threat of exclusion from the disciplinary community. Debates on the role of the disciplines in knowledge production, therefore, entail the issue of quality and methodological rigour and are used in discourses legitimising or delegitimising research.

The well-publicised case of Lisa Littman, Assistant Professor at Brown University in Rhode Island, United States, is revisited. Her work on 'rapid onset gender dysphoria' came under attack from academic colleagues framed in terms of concern about the research design and data collection, where she was required to make post-publication amendments. The university posted a statement saying explicitly that the case was not about academic freedom, not because the research was deemed controversial, but rather because it was about 'academic standards' (Brown University, 2019). However, the context surrounding the case is highlighted in the following account, where scepticism over the discourse of 'quality' is evident:

> I think what Brown did was despicable. I mean I think it was not defensible because first of all, they were under pressure from groups to not even print the article and so they had the article on the website and then they withdrew it. Here is a person who is not tenured, who is going to be coming up for consideration, and now apparently the article's been reviewed again, it's been re-posted, there have been a few changes made but she still got to produce a scholarship. But they were successful in having the article taken down. And the reason I say that it's despicable is because other people's scholarship does not get the same review. Let us review everybody's scholarship the same way you know. If we are going to do that, let us do it to everybody. And the end result was that she had to make some adjustments in the article but I think the core of the article stands. But there was a chilling effect on other people doing that kind of research I think. (Professor Emeritus, Law, US, pp. 4–5)

Robert Plomin, Professor of Behavioural Genetics at King's College, London, and author of *Blue Print: How DNA Makes Us Who We Are* (2018), recounts that one of his greatest concerns in publishing his work was the reaction from academic colleagues, and that this has been the main reason for publishing his book at a much later stage in his career. He reflects on the challenges in publishing his work throughout his career. This was especially the case during the earlier career stages, and at a time when behavioural genetics in the discipline of Psychology was unpopular: 'The extra hurdles you had to go through if you were studying something controversial. So, and also for publication, the research had to be a lot better to get it published, because people needed to be convinced – if you publish something saying the environment's important, you know, no problem – everybody accepts that' (p. 3).

Conversely, 'quality' is inferred from 'legitimate' evidence used to validate argument, as evident in the following account on legitimate historical evidence:

> So we have faced pressure from corporations whose work or whose histories we have identified ... 'Are you sure? Show us the evidence. Are you clear that what you are saying is supported and is the way that you are saying it consistent with the evidence?' And that is in the end an easy conversation because we have done the work, we know where the documents are and we can demonstrate that what we are asserting is true, historically true, in relation to particular companies and concerns. But business corporations have been the most active in if you like, seeking to correct us. (Professor of History, UK, p. 3)

Similarly, quantitative research is associated with objectivity, neutrality, evidence, and truth and contrasted with qualitative research as political, subjective, partisan, and relative. As highlighted by Gillborn (2010, p. 272), statistics are 'generally equated with scientific rigour and objectivity'. As discussed earlier in the chapter, quantitative research evidence is not excluded from the influence of assumptions and context. Gillborn (2010) warns of the dangers and responsibility of researchers in recognising the power of numbers and their influence on policy and practice.

Debates on disciplinary quality are also central to discourses on the 'Canon'. The Canon is assumed to be a universal recognition of works of quality, based on 'objectively' agreed standards. Tracing the intellectual history of the disciplines, Williams (2016) notes that before the twentieth century, 'liberal education' consisted of humanities-related disciplines, based on the rationale and assumption that this approach best prepared men for elite leadership of the Empire. The legitimacy of religious foundations of knowledge was increasingly challenged through the Enlightenment with a shift towards secular knowledge.

The 'Canon' has been challenged by post-colonial, critical, and feminist theorists, with growing recognition of the sociopolitical and historical construction and positionality of knowledge and its embedded values (Arday and Mirza, 2018; Banks, 1993; Giroux, 1983; Habermas, 1971). The recognition of the positionality and particularity of the 'Canon' is evidenced in various university initiatives on decolonising the curriculum. That the decolonisation of the curriculum entails a process of legitimating alternative ways of knowing, feeling, and thinking to address the epistemic violence of the Canon is recounted below:

> We all had to learn the British Canon. We learnt British history, we learnt British literature, we had to read Shakespeare, we had to do you know, we learnt the canon of the master. But we were able to use that, the tropes and the literary expressions and all of that, we were able to use that to write our post-colonial stories you know. (Emeritus Professor of Sociology, UK, pp. 11–12)

7.3.4 Discourses of Civility

As discussed in the previous chapters, the concept of 'civility' has been used to discredit critique by focusing on *how* this critique is delivered. The critique of a large-scale externally funded UK-based project entitled 'Ethics and Empire' led by Nigel Biggar, Professor of Theology, University of Oxford, resulted in a heated expression of concern and frustration at the perceived controversial premise and aims of the project, its funding, and University of Oxford's support, and hence legitimation for this work. The interdisciplinary project aims to develop a 'Christian ethics of empire'. On asking Professor Biggar if he felt that his academic freedom had been infringed, he focused on the ways in which the critique had been delivered and its lack of civility:

> but the ***manner*** in which various groups of people decided to register their objections, the manner really does not invite discussion, in other words so I'm not averse to take what I've written or said and say 'you said this, I disagree, here are the reasons', when we have a kind of rational responsible conversation and we give and take reasons. But when you have got 60 Oxford colleagues denouncing a project or 170 worldwide denouncing a project, it's not designed to dialogue at all, so that was one of my objections. That was not even addressed to me, it was

addressed to my university ... so that certainly was not designed to start a conversation with me about anything, it was designed to put pressure on my university to reconsider its support for the project, in other words, it was designed I think quite explicitly to make the project, 'Ethics and Empire' unviable. (Nigel Biggar, Professor of Theology, University of Oxford, UK, p. 5)

The high-profile case of Stephen Salaita has led to debate regarding 'civility' and its relationship to academic freedom. As mentioned previously, Stephen Salaita had been offered an academic position of employment at the University of Illinois as a Professor of Native American Studies which was subsequently withdrawn, as a result of university donor objections to Salaita's tweets criticising Israel and Zionism in the context of a fifty-one-day Israeli military assault of Gaza. His offer was rescinded by the chancellor in August 2014 presented in terms of civility: 'What we cannot and will not tolerate at the University of Illinois are personal and disrespectful words or actions that demean and abuse either viewpoints themselves or those who express them' (Moshman and Edler, 2015). The statement notes that in the US context, 'uncivil' speech is protected in law by the First Amendment, although not in educational contexts. Whilst there is no legal requirement for civility, nor sanctions against it, it was argued that civility creates a supportive respectful learning environment ideally modelled by academic faculty.

Yet, Salaita (2015a) defends the use of incivility, claiming incivility is the only civilised response to barbarity. Arguing for the importance of contextualising the positionality of the incivility, Salaita elaborates: 'My tweets might appear uncivil, but such a judgment cannot be made in an ideological or rhetorical vacuum. Insofar as "civil" is profoundly racialised and has a long history of demanding conformity, I frequently choose incivility as a form of communication. This choice is both moral and rhetorical.' Puar (2015, pp. 64–65) argues that certain bodies are deemed disposed to incivility, and as such, it is not just an issue of the incivility of linguistic expression, but rather that the 'ideological evaluation of speech is used to reinforce the production of certain bodies as threatening, dangerous, and uncivil'. Puar highlights the contrasting language used in the Charlie Hebdo case, where rather than a discourse of the 'incivility' of Islamophobic cartoons, it is referred to as 'political satire'.

It is argued that the history of the discourse of incivility has operated as a form of 'racial and class denouncement' in US and European contexts since the nineteenth century (Massad, 2014). The binary of civility/incivility can be seen as a more politically correct yet masked reformulation of the cultured/uncultured binary which is 'openly colonial'; it is relevant to note that 'civil' derives from civilization, with its settler-colonial and imperial legacies (Salaita, 2015a). Tracing the use of discourses of incivility used against Eastern European Jews' perceived lack of assimilation in the United States, Massad (2014) draws a parallel with the case of Steven Salaita and, indeed, the challenges he himself has faced whilst at Columbia University, with concerns – expressed also by Arab-American colleagues pertaining to his 'vulgar Arab incivility' and 'immoderation'. He contrasts this reaction with the support from his 'liberal Jewish colleagues who gave [him] their unequivocal support and showed no discernible concern about the question of "civility"'(Massad, 2014). This positionality not only is a historical position but also continues into the contemporary lived context of various forms of discrimination, as Salaita tweeted on 21 June 2019: 'Because "civility" compels people to work with racial segregationists, corporate hacks, colonial settlers, sexual predators, and war criminals, I'll go ahead and proudly remain uncivil' (@stevesalaita, 2019). The discourse of civility also reflects assumptions of the rationality and objectivity of knowledge, as opposed to experiential, subjective, or affective constructions of knowledge. As such, the use of the term 'civility' excludes and delegitimates such knowledge.

Related to discourses of civility, the terms 'snowflakes' and 'wokeness' are used to delegitimate any critiques of dominant forms of knowledge production. It is commonly argued that the political left wing is limiting academic freedom, with its concerns relating to 'controversial' speakers or research projects or unnecessarily protecting 'oversensitive' students. Furedi (2017) refers to the 'therapeutic' construction of education and society and the infantilisation of young adult students; he critiques 'trigger warnings', concerns of protecting minorities from hate speech and calls to decolonise the curriculum and the established centuries-old canon, as illegitimate attacks on academic freedom. This discourse is predicated on the abstraction of knowledge from the existing power relations between groups and its sociopolitical context, and instead assuming the neutrality and equality of different knowledges, as if on a 'level playing field'. In contrast, the importance of historicising power relations is elucidated in the account below:

> the cost . . . is disproportionately borne by people who are already the targets and already disadvantaged by White supremacy, by male supremacy, heteropatriarchy and no society should tolerate, no community, academic community should tolerate people who are already precarious, bearing the brunt, carrying the burden of the principle of free speech. (Professor of English and Women's Studies, US, p. 8)

7.3.5 Skills, Employment, and Research Assessment

As discussed in the previous chapters, neoliberal and market pressures on higher education are evident in the dominant functionalist interrelated discourses of skills, education for employment, and research *impact*. That this is a widespread globalised discourse is commented on:

> There is a big debate now about the value of education ... is it worth the investment and so on. And ... they think of employability and, you know, what is the expectation, you know, how are you expected to make money on graduation and so on. And I think, as a result of that, there is an attempt to come up with metrics and these metrics are connected to employability and to define certain areas where it's OK to provide the funding. (former Professor, AUB, Lebanon, pp. 1–2)

The internationalisation and privatisation of higher education globally drive a logic of the monetary worth of qualifications and the operationalisation of a qualification into employment and earning power. This impacts the perceived legitimacy of those humanities and social sciences disciplines compared to professional degrees. Whilst the discourse of skills and employment is a global one, in the Arab world it is particularly dominant given that most universities do not have a liberal arts–based requirement. In contrast, in the US context, typically professional degrees at high-status institutions have liberal arts requirements, thus providing a form of legitimation for such knowledge.

The governance of research in the Arab world is typically centrally organised through government ministries of education, although in Lebanon, which is a highly decentralised system, this governance is managed by an independent council; this is also the case for the UAE, although its governance is described as 'trade-oriented' (Hanafi and Arvanitis, 2015). The UAE scores the highest for innovation in the region, with Lebanon scoring significantly lower (ibid., 2015), measured using a World Bank Global Innovation Index. The World Bank has also devised a Knowledge Economy Index which ranks the highest in the UAE, championing the UAE as a model for the future based on the liberalisation of the economy, privatisation, entrepreneurship, innovation, and less state control (Hanafi and Arvanitis, 2015). Of note is that Lebanon, with a more established research tradition, does not perform well on the Knowledge Economy Index. Hanafi and Arvanitis (2015) question the 'objectivity' of the index and advocate a more diversified model.

This emphasis on skills for employment is also reflected in terms of funding of teaching programmes and research. This is evident in the example of the UK Research Evaluation Framework (REF) as noted in Chapter 5. The REF is a national assessment exercise of research 'quality' upon which funding of universities is decided, the concept of 'impact' is prioritized, and research meeting these criteria is legitimated. The REF has been critiqued as a manifestation of the 'neoliberal audit culture that infests universities' and a form of governance to ensure 'appropriate returns' on public investment (MacDonald, 2017, p. 706). It has also been critiqued that it curtails creativity through constraining research to produce narrow outcomes (Watermeyer, 2016). The REF illustrates both the commodification and the regulation of universities (Burawoy, 2011). The REF and the impact agenda act as a legitimising or delegitimising mechanism shaping what research is conducted. The rise of systematic research reviews supporting evidence-informed policymaking in education illustrates this logic, where knowledge is produced to meet the aims determined by policymakers. In this framework, knowledge is 'beholden to the strategic and technocratic frameworks' of the research councils and government (Watermeyer, 2016). A UK Professor of Sociology comments on how the discipline of Sociology has been shaped and delegitimated by the REF and impact agenda:

> You see that in the declining number of submissions to the sociology REF panel, so if you look at most sociologists in Britain I think are now submitted to the social policy REF panel, but the social policy REF panel is putting less emphasis upon sociology as one of its background disciplines. So it's increasingly reaching out towards psychology and towards economics as part of the interdisciplinary foundation of social policy and that's following this sort of behavioural shift. And what you notice is most places that are, you know, most degrees in social policy have collapsed undergraduate degrees. So we have social policy REF submission supported by sociology undergraduate degrees. So sociology I think is being shaped in that direction and, at the same time, the nature of the work in that area becomes less sociological, so people start describing themselves as working on a particular applied topic 'oh my interest is in health', not as 'I'm a sociologist working on health'. (Professor of Sociology, University of Nottingham, UK, p. 1)

This account illustrates the shift to legitimating more applied constructions of the discipline that are topic based and related to policy, such as health and influence by more behavioural disciplines.

7.3.6 Funding and International Partnerships

International networks and 'North–South' partnerships have gained prominence in social science funding over the last two decades. This rationale supports the participation of relatively marginalised partners in co-constructing research agendas and building research capacity in the Global South. Yet, it has been argued that there is still the 'fundamental problem' that the Global South provides the data but does not usually set the theoretical or research agendas, which is central in the larger social process of knowledge production (Connell, 2014). A number of interviewees commented on the political use of transnational partnerships to legitimise knowledge, through institutionalised research council grant requirements: 'There are research agendas and when you are collaborating with the UK or the US, by the fashion you are collaborating with, I mean, with people who have many more resources, you know, larger institutions, a larger number of researchers and so on and quite often what they are looking for is a token local partner' (former AUB Professor, Lebanon, p. 8).

In the field of migration research, international networks and North–South partnerships are requirements for funding. The objectives for such funding schemes entail the inclusive production of knowledge and building regional research capacity in the Global South. Whilst laudable objectives, the structural constraints and historical power relations expose the inequalities between North and South and inadvertently may be reified (Landau, 2012). In addition, the agenda of impact and addressing global challenges direct the nature of research towards policy-driven research, and so research councils retain the authority over funding and the legitimation of research (Landau, 2012). The 'business of refugees' is used to describe the legitimated policy-driven research on refugees: 'The business of refugees, you know, it became a business and there are literally hundreds of NGOs and so on and there is a card that goes to the locals and, you know, quite a bit of the money, the funds go to international NGOs and so on. So it becomes a business' (former AUB Professor, Lebanon, p. 9).

Indeed, Hanafi (2010) has illustrated how international sources of research funding in the region have channelled social science research away from higher education institutions and towards policy-oriented consultancies. Yet, he notes that European Union (EU) funding schemes in the region have been a relative success with 300 million euros spent on research in the region between 2007 and 2013 (Hanafi and Arvanitis, 2015). In Lebanon, in particular, international research collaborations have increased particularly with

European partners, with co-publications increasing from 22 percent in 1987 to 55 percent in 2006 (ibid., 2015). In examining research collaboration across the region, looking at the Qatar National Research Fund, less than 15 percent are with collaborators in the Arab world, and there is also little within-country collaboration (ibid., 2015).

Whilst there have been efforts to respond to critiques of unequal partnerships, the focus has been relatively more on the implementation and dissemination of research, rather than interrogating processes of agenda setting and research governance (Fransman and Newman, 2019). As such, the practice of partnerships is the focus, rather than examining epistemological conceptions and the political economy of knowledge. There have been calls for partnerships between the Global North and Global South to be understood as ethical concerns. Walsh et al. (2016) note that typically broader power relations are not treated as an ethics concern in the field of health research, and they propose a Bourdieusian lens to understand North–South inequalities in research collaborations. They use Bourdieu's notion of habitus to explore the legacy of colonialism in North–South partnerships and the maintenance and legitimacy of the status quo; considering economic, symbolic, and scientific capital, they also critically examine funding arrangements.

These structural and economic inequalities between North and South impede competing on a level playing for large-scale EU and US grants, which can be understood in terms of discrepancies in 'capital' and 'habitus':

> There were certain funds which were non-competitive which were reserved for partnerships with less competitive institutions because, you know, you have to compete, it's almost impossible, you really cannot compete. The European funding, they have opened it up so you will be competing, it's by and large competitive. They will not reserve anything for let us say this other part of the Mediterranean which they used to do, but they are now opening globally so you are competing with US scientists and with Japanese scientists and of course with German scientists and so on and it's impossible to compete, but they continue to reserve a little bit of funding for ... they encourage collaborative funding and collaborative projects but, at the same time, it's next to impossible to compete for these collaborative projects. (former Professor, AUB, Lebanon, p. 7)

The politics of research that does not even get funding is raised in the account below, referred to as 'neglected diseases'. This term in itself illustrates that it is recognised that research is not being conducted on these diseases despite sizeable populations suffering:

> They [diseases] are neglected in relation to their disease burden, so they are often the diseases which are causing the most suffering and affecting the greatest numbers of people but are just, you know, getting a disproportionately small amount of research funding and attention compared with diseases which primarily affect Global North populations and also diseases which pose threats to Global North populations, so ones which are easily transmissible, things like HIV for example, which does get a fair amount of funding, and tuberculosis and also malaria. But beyond that, there are all these other ones called neglected tropical diseases and they do not get funding. And the reason for that is because even if we were to develop effective treatments there would be nobody to pay for those treatments to get them out to the populations who need them. So it's sort of a dead end in a way by virtue of the way the global economy works and the marketisation of health. (Lecturer in Ethics, UK, p. 11)

This illustrates the politicisation of global funding, where funding is available for those diseases affecting populations in the Global North as opposed to those in the Global South, where there is not deemed to be a market for the development of treatments arising from such research. As a result, the marketisation of the application of such research delegitimises the perceived need to undertake this research.

7.3.7 Global Legitimating Systems

Global university rankings play an important role in higher education, in spite of having been critiqued as part of the neoliberal and audit culture (Ball and Olmedo, 2013) and of succumbing to the rise of metrics and data (Lim, 2018). In examining the practices of various ranking systems, Lim (2018) argues that the processes of legitimation entail using 'hard' data such as bibliometrics and also input from a range of stakeholders including students. The interactions with stakeholders are the means by which audience 'trust' is built for the ranking system – in effect, the legitimation of their knowledge. Contestation over university rankings entails, firstly, a methodological debate about the reliability of such rankings. It has been argued that objective ranking systems cannot exist as they necessarily entail 'adding up a converted value by means of an a priori (e.g. subjectively) assumed system of weighting' (Rocki, 2005, p. 179). As such, the legitimacy of rankings is questioned. In addition, it is important to contextualise the increased use of university rankings in relation to the globalisation and massification of higher education and the marketised logic of the student as 'customer'. There is also contestation over what constitutes a 'good' university.

Turner (2008) analysed various university ranking systems and identified that many UK higher education institutions, which did not appear in the top 200 global ranking, performed better than Oxford and Cambridge on national rankings. He gives the example of the University of Lancaster and University of York, which were very effective at converting input into research outputs – in effect, a type of 'value-added' score. However, many universities in Europe and the Asian Pacific have adjusted their strategic objectives to meet the criteria of 'world-class' universities as defined by the global rankings methodology. This heightened legitimacy does not take into account the significant inequalities in resources between universities in the Global North and Global South. Jons and Hoyler (2013) illustrate that the global circulation of knowledge aligns with Anglo-American publication cultures and publishing in the English language. However, they identify the emergence of new 'knowledge' hubs' which increasingly may have significant transnational influence in the production of knowledge. They argue that the partiality of such global ranking systems undermines their authority and legitimacy, and that 'other measures and subject-specific perspectives would produce very different geographies' (Jons and Hoyler, 2013, p. 57).

There is a significant literature on the international division of knowledge labour between the Global North and the Global South, whereby Northern scholars in North–South collaborations have outcomes of publishable knowledge, whilst Southern scholars play more of a role of 'sub-contractors' (Kreimer and Zabala, 2008). Collyer (2018, p. 57) reminds us that 'knowledge is not just a product of individual knowledge-makers', but rather it entails 'systematic boundaries and mechanisms of exclusion across and between countries and regions of the world'. Furthermore, whilst scholarship in the Global North tends to claim universality, scholarship in the Global South typically locates the research in context (Baber, 2003). Citation practices also diverge, with the Global North showing patterns of self-citation, with rare citation of Southern scholars by Northern scholars (Collyer, 2018). In contrast, Southern scholars are outward looking in their citation practices. Such differences in publication and citation practices reify and consolidate the inequalities in transnational knowledge production. This politics of citation has been critiqued by critical feminist and anti-racists scholars in the Global North, who argue that current practices of citation consolidate 'the continued hegemony of white heteromasculine knowledge production' and the marginalisation and delegitimation of 'subaltern and otherwise othered populations' (Mott and Cockayne, 2017, pp. 956–958).

An example of this can be seen in the study of who were the dominant knowledge producers on knowledge of the 'Arab Spring' (AlMaghlouth et al., 2015). In a network analysis, it was found that the majority of published articles on the topic (75 percent) were from outside the Arab region, with 30 percent accounted for by US authors. Furthermore, of those articles published within the region, there was a slight majority published in Arabic, thus constraining it to a more domestic audience. Furthermore, the majority of publications are located with the disciplines of political science/international relations, with only 14 percent being based on field research. AlMaghlouth et al. (2015) conclude that there is a hierarchy of three levels of knowledge production; first, authors with the greatest 'legitimacy' are from the US Ivy league universities considered to be 'experts' given their theoretical expertise; second, there are less-cited scholars in spite of their scholarly expertise – often local scholars or French-speaking scholars; and third, there are those scholars writing in Arabic from the region. Whilst the third level in the hierarchy cites the authors in the first level of the hierarchy, those authors from outside the region rarely cite the local experts, thus delegitimising their knowledge on the global stage.

However, examining the distribution of academic knowledge production, there has been a shift towards a 'non-English speaking periphery' in Brazil, South Korea, Taiwan, and China; as such, this reflects a shift from a centre-periphery model to a more multi-polar model of knowledge production (Hanafi and Arvanitis, 2015, p. 88), challenging this epistemic injustice (Fricker, 2009). Yet, the publication output of the Arab world remains low: 'Now in terms of the production of knowledge, there is a lack of accurate figures. So there is less investment, there is less production, I mean, we could look at number of dissertations produced, whenever there are records, you know, for some of the largest universities, I mean, we are not even talking here about quality. It's quite dismal' (former Professor, AUB, Lebanon, pp. 2–3).

However, Hanafi and Arvanitis (2015) have shown that the rate of growth over the last two decades are above world averages and comparable to the emerging powers of Chile, South Africa, and Thailand. They make the case for the region being an emerging knowledge producer, with Morocco, Tunisia, Lebanon, and Jordan contributing to this, as well as huge growth in the UAE and Saudi Arabia.

Yet, citations of publications in the region are low, excluding the role of a language effect. Whilst impact cannot be inferred from citation, influence, recognition, and status within the academic community are invoked by such measures. As such, citation confers legitimacy. Composite H-index calculations by country are low for the region; however, Lebanon and the UAE score fourth and fifth in the region, respectively (109 and 100, respectively), compared to 943 and 1,518 for the United States and United Kingdom, respectively, for the period 1996–2013 (Hanafi and Arvanitis, 2015). Legitimacy also comes from publishing in internationally recognised journals, rather than local journals, and can at least account in part for relatively few academic books published in Arabic geared towards a local audience (Hanafi, 2010). Hanafi and Arvanitis (2015) analysed publication databases for publications produced at the American University of Beirut, and they illustrated that 68 percent of knowledge is invisible to international audiences. This also impacts the world rankings of universities, as this knowledge is invisible.

7.4 CONCLUSION

This chapter has critically examined the concept of legitimate knowledge, in terms of how it is both constructed and operationalised. Examining the concepts of 'legitimacy' and related concepts of 'authority', 'right', and 'acceptance' in political science literatures, I juxtapose this with different constructs of knowledge and how this relates to 'belief', 'justification', and 'truth'. I examine a range of factors and systems that shape how knowledge is legitimated transnationally, including positionality, university diversity initiatives, disciplinary debates and the 'Canon', modes of communication, national systems of research assessment, funding and international partnerships and global systems of university ranking, publication systems, and citation. I illustrate how these systems of standardisation located with globalised discourses of internationalisation are predisposed to favouring the status quo. However, multi-polar nodes of knowledge production are increasingly challenging this hegemony and universalising constructs of legitimacy inherent in national and global systems of knowledge production.

8   Conclusion

A Transnational Theory of Academic Freedom and the Production of Inclusive Knowledge

This book has sought to build the case for a transnational theoretical framework for the understanding of academic freedom and the production of knowledge drawing on original empirical data from Lebanon, the UAE, the United Kingdom, and the United States, in order to take into account the complexities of globalisation and the geographical and historical interconnectivities. Through a critical examination of the various contested constructions of academic freedom and knowledge at different sites in different contexts beyond the dominant Global North frame, the case is argued for academic freedom premised on inclusivity, and in turn inclusive knowledge premised on an inclusive conception of academic freedom. Examining the structures and processes within higher education and society more widely illustrates the challenging dynamics in the production of knowledge and the methodological implications for the very structure, content, and form of learning and knowledge itself.

8.1 SHIFTING CONCEPTIONS OF ACADEMIC FREEDOM

In Chapter 2, constructions of academic freedom were critically interrogated across the different national contexts of Lebanon, the UAE, the United Kingdom, and the United States. Yet, the transnational reality of the production of knowledge challenges the dominant methodologically nationalist framings of constructions of academic freedom. On examining key legal and policy statements at the international level, there is no explicit protection for academic freedom in the two United Nations Human Rights Covenants. The 1997 United Nations Educational, Scientific and Cultural Organization (UNESCO) statement focuses on the status of higher education teaching personnel explicitly noting the importance of academic freedom as a prerequisite that affirms the right to education, teaching, and research and 'provides the strongest guarantee of the accuracy and objectivity of scholarship and research'.

The American conception of academic freedom is codified in the American Association of University Professors (AAUP) 1915 Statement of Principles of Academic Freedom and Tenure. This contrasts with the UK context where at the elite universities of Oxford and Cambridge, academic freedom could be attributed to a de facto rather de jure construct of academic freedom based on historical privilege. Of note, the United Kingdom does not have a written constitution with a form of protection for freedom of speech. A statement of the University and College Union in 2009 invokes the 1988 Education Reform Act as having established the legal rights and protections of UK academics to 'test received wisdom and put forward new ideas and controversial or unpopular opinions', also making reference to the 1997 UNESCO statement. In the Middle East post-colonial context, 'imported internationalisation' is evident in initiatives such as Dubai's Knowledge Park, where there has been an expansion of branch universities partnered with US and UK universities. In Lebanon, the American University of Beirut (AUB), established by foreign missionaries in 1866, based on a US liberal arts model of education, has a US charter and is bound by the AAUP Principles of academic freedom; all these different contextual examples raise the relevance and importance of contextualising academic freedom in transnational perspective.

There are ongoing polemical debates that principles of academic freedom sit in tension with principles of diversity of inclusion. Philosophers of education Callan (2016) and Ben-Porath (2016, 2017) have proposed that inclusivity is a threshold condition for academic freedom or, in effect, a 'precondition' for academic freedom. Using the concept of 'dignity safety', Callan (2016) argues that this is a necessary precondition for the inclusive practice of academic freedom. Without the condition of dignity safety, academic freedom is not upheld. Without such an inclusive context, research cannot be conducted with academic freedom, which in turn undermines the inclusive production of knowledge. The notion of a hierarchy of rights is also invoked where academic freedom is contextualised in relation to other rights necessary for the inclusive production of knowledge. For example, the nationalistic lens can also obscure how academic freedom is undermined for those in legal precarity, such as refugee scholars or academics working under occupation. Dominant constructions of academic freedom implicitly require legal citizenship as a prerequisite to practice academic freedom. Butler argues for a broader notion of academic freedom, where freedom from violence, freedom from hunger, and freedom of movement both internally and across borders are recognised as an integral precondition for academic freedom, clearly invoking a transnational frame. She argues that academic freedom cannot be separated – logically or in practice – from the 'conditions of its exercise' (Butler, 2015, p. 293). As such, the defence of academic freedom necessitates a defence of the conditions that enable its practice. Conversely, if these conditions are not met, the practice of academic freedom is not possible. The preconditions for academic freedom that include the right to free movement illustrate the necessary transnational nature of academic freedom.

Five thematic discourses relating to academic freedom are identified, the first relating to *'free speech, responsibility, and expertise'*. Responsibility is conceived in various ways by interviewees, including notions of 'expertise' and 'evidence-based' research, as well as invoking 'legitimate' disciplinary methods. Responsibility is also contrasted with traditional notions of privilege and also linked to the conception of the university as a privileged space. Therefore, it has been argued that there should be an emphasis on responsibility that comes with their status in society, in the context of academic freedom. This is especially the case with extramural speech and the issue of academics not speaking outside their spheres of expertise, which, it is argued would be an abuse of their position (Shahvisi, 2018). Hence, we see the notion of privilege as a geopolitical project in such understandings of academic freedom. The elasticity of the conception of responsibility also entails notions of its performance as 'civilised', 'reasonable', and 'rational' in its delivery.

The interrelationship between constructions of academic freedom and knowledge emerges in discussions of the notions of 'truth' and 'public good'. These ideas underpin a second discourse of academic freedom in terms of **power, knowledge, and morality**. The positionality of the academic within society and in relation to their research is highlighted as significant, both in terms of the construction of knowledge and in terms of the academic freedom accorded to the individual; this positionality affects the perceived 'truth' and 'legitimacy' of the knowledge as well as the freedom to seek such knowledge. Despite the hegemony of knowledge from the Global North, examples of reconstructions of fields of knowledge, for instance, the case of American

Studies at AUB, Lebanon, illustrates the transnational turn in various fields and disciplines. Rather than these knowledges being anchored as 'local' subjective knowledge, the transnational turn has illustrated how disciplines 'at the centre' have been affected. The position of Palestine in American Studies is no longer an 'absent present' in American Studies (Lubin, 2016).

The relationship between seniority, or job security, and academic freedom illustrates the relevance of positionality in understanding the relativity of academic freedom in practice. This issue is particularly emphasised in the US context. In addition, the coupling of moral responsibility with seniority is normatively held up as an ideal particularly in the US and UK contexts. This takes the form of supporting and advocating for those academic colleagues in more vulnerable positions with respect to job security – those who are 'untenured' in the US context or on temporary contracts. However, it is often minoritised senior academics with respect to gender and race who take on this supporting role. In the UAE context, vulnerability also comes in the form of legal status, where academics enter into both a legal and a 'psychological' contract, invoking personal responsibility with regard to academic freedom as an 'expat'.

A third discourse relates to the **context of the university** as the space within which academics practice their academic freedom, which varies across the different national contexts depending on different constructions of the mission of the university. With the discourse of the 'civic university', the development of the critical citizen is based on the construction of the university as a public space where controversial ideas can be explored and authority can be challenged (Giroux, 2002). It is argued that this model is increasingly undermined by the neoliberal logic and the marketisation of higher education. In the Arab world, few universities constitute such a critical public space, with the exception of AUB in Lebanon, which has a long history of academics engaging with the public on social and political issues of the day (Hanafi, 2011; Kiwan, 2017b).

A fourth discourse relates to **individualisation and psychologisation,** where it is argued that the 'infantilisation' of society and, in particular, students can be located within a therapeutic turn in the UK and US contexts (Furedi, 2017). This therapeutic turn is evident in the protection of legal and market-oriented interests of higher education institutions. However, rejecting the measures of inclusion required to meet the needs of a wide range of students invoked in such discourses dismisses calls for dignity safety as prerequisite conditions for academic freedom as argued by Callan (2016) and Ben-Porath (2017).

The fifth discourse relates to the ways of delivering knowledge. Discourses of *civility* are linked to notions of literally being 'uncivilised', being 'over-emotional'/'too sensitive', and, therefore, lacking rationality. Moral virtue is also invoked from the manner of expression which is critiqued; however, moral virtue of those acting in the name of social justice and inclusion is also highlighted as problematic in that 'truth' is fixed through belief, and either legitimised or delegitimised, as was critically examined in Chapter 7.

8.2 THE RELATIONSHIP BETWEEN CONCEPTIONS OF ACADEMIC FREEDOM AND CONCEPTIONS OF KNOWLEDGE

Chapter 3 examined a range of contested constructions of knowledge with regard to the implications for academic freedom. Two contrasting constructions of knowledge are considered: first, where knowledge is conceived as separate from its producer, which describes reality, and the second, where knowledge is conceived as constructed, negotiated, and embedded in geographical and historical contexts and in relationships of power. Contemporary Western constructions of knowledge have been significantly influenced by the Humboldtian nineteenth-century tradition of teaching as embedded in research, where knowledge is co-constructed by students and teachers. This model conceives of knowledge as subjective and fluid, in contrast to traditional models of knowledge as reflecting entry into a disciplinary field through the mastery of a body of knowledge and methods.

Different conceptions of knowledge underpin different expectations of who the knowledge is for and its purposes. The global neoliberal marketisation of higher education and its implications in constructing the purposes of knowledge is evident across the different national contexts of Lebanon, the UAE, the United Kingdom, and the United States. This is reflected in the language of 'capital', 'value', 'entrepreneurship', 'marketability', 'skills', 'impact', and 'employment' used by academic interviewees across all four contexts. This constellation of concepts illustrates a conception of external knowledge to be discovered, with research positioned in the service of policy and practice. As a result, the funding of research prioritises research questions deemed to be policy relevant and, as a consequence, favours certain methodologies. As such, the scope of knowledge is curtailed, and academic freedom is limited by certain constructions of knowledge. The humanities and social sciences, as reflected in their funding, have been particularly affected, with their status being particularly low in the Arab world. This, in turn, affects curriculum and programmes offered, as well as research.

Examining constructions of knowledge in a transnational frame raises the question of whether the political economy of knowledge has been sufficiently recognised. Positionality with respect to the production of knowledge is increasingly being recognised as relevant, in contrast to the assumed objectivity of 'scientific' evidence-based knowledge. Not only has this challenged the assumed elevated status of the Canon, but this has also challenged the 'epistemic injustices' (Fricker, 2009) evident in Enlightenment theories of natural rights that denied women and colonial subjects rights and a voice on the premise of their lacking rationality.

The temporal and spatial situatedness of knowledge is brought into view by calls for the decolonisation of knowledge. It challenges both the content of knowledge and its methods and ways of thinking. Yet, the recognition of the relationality of power is important to consider in understanding the colonisation and decolonisation of knowledge. Whilst some more radical theories of 'colonising the mind' (Dascal, 2007) construct power as directly hierarchical, Foucauldian understandings of power as relational open up possibilities to understand the complexities of knowledge production and its legitimisation beyond polemical binaries of colonial or decolonial knowledges. Indeed, Connell (2014, p. 527) notes that in the field of gender, some of the most creative work in the Global South arises from the 'critical appropriation of Northern ideas, in combination with ideas that come from radically different experiences'. However, there is, nevertheless, a tension between agentically resisting hegemony and concomitantly experiencing powerlessness in interviewees' accounts.

That temporal and geographical positionality of knowledge as a necessary contextualisation is increasingly recognised in scholarship on knowledge production. There have also been calls to recognise diachronic models in place of a synchronic model of knowledge to replace the premise of European coloniser where colonial is seen as a pedagogic mission towards the same destination but at a slower pace (Nandy and Darby, 2018). The geographical positionality of academic freedom can be clearly witnessed in the accounts, where the production of certain areas of knowledge has differential political and ethical values ascribed to them. For example, the production of knowledge on Palestine in the US and UK contexts attests to experiences of a hostile working environment and constraints on academic freedom in several interviewee accounts. Some researchers with experience of conducting research at institutions in both the United Kingdom/the United States and

Lebanon recount very contrasting environments for conducting their research on Palestine. Producing knowledge on Whiteness/race and gender/masculinity is also commented on in the UK and US contexts, in particular. For those conducting research in the UAE, the internalised 'red lines' are frequently referred to in relation to producing 'sensitive' knowledge relating to gender and sexuality, security, and sectarian politics. The transnational politics of knowledge is also evident in restrictions on the production of knowledge at AUB, Lebanon, as a result of US compliance regulations, where research on certain groups designated as 'terrorist' is banned.

The production of academic knowledge has traditionally been organised through the disciplines. Disciplines denote both a practice and a policing of non-conformity. The rise of interdisciplinarity speaks to the contestations around disciplinarity, arising from contestations around different conceptions of knowledge. It has been argued that disciplines risk the reification and legitimation of unchallenged knowledge. A number of interviewee accounts raise this issue, challenging the acceptance of an objective canon. Yet, interdisciplinarity is also contested, with different forms of interdisciplinarity conceived in relation to different conceptions of knowledge and the aims of such knowledge production. Whilst a form of 'market' interdisciplinarity is promoted through funding for large-scale international impact-oriented research, this contrasts with the guiding logic of an 'intellectual' interdisciplinarity which works across disciplines to critically reconstruct them, illustrated by examples of feminism and decolonising research movements. The promotion of interdisciplinarity by funding councils has been accused of a 'banal' instrumentalisation, which is conservative and takes the approach of bringing together disciplines to deal with a complex multifaceted problem.

Drawing together Chapters 2 and 3, which examined conceptions of academic freedom and conceptions of knowledge, what emerges is that there are different implications for academic freedom arising from different conceptions of knowledge. In the United Kingdom and the United States, challenges to the canon and disciplinarity have shaken conceptions of how knowledge is understood, as well as related conceptions of 'truth' and 'evidence'. This debate has become politicised between right-wing conservative and liberal left-wing positions. Right-wing conservative responses to challenges to the Canon lament the 'death of knowledge' (Williams, 2016), whilst left-wing responses perceive such arguments as disingenuous attempts to weaponise academic freedom against inclusive knowledge. The recognition of the positionality of the knowledge producer located in geographical, historical, and sociopolitical context challenges the view of knowledge as external, to be discovered, and value-free. Rather, it calls for the recognition of the knowledge as relational, contextualised, and positioned within the politics of power relations, beyond national boundaries. Rather than being perceived as a posteriori infringements of academic freedom, Butler and others propose that there are preconditions for the practice of academic freedom entailing an a priori commitment to inclusion and social justice.

8.3 THE ROLE OF THE UNIVERSITY

The role of the university in producing knowledge is discussed in Chapter 4. The literature on the role of the university in producing critical citizens informs the intellectual history of academic freedom and its contemporary and contested constructions. Yet, it is important to recognise this theoretical framing assumes a democratic and national context. The emerging field of critical university studies locates the university as an institution with historically embedded structures of inequality, exploitation, and marginalisation. The case is made for interrogating the role of the university transnationally, examining the post-colonial legacies and nation-building projects of the higher education institutions of Beirut and Dubai. The transnational positioning of the university will necessarily have implications for academic freedom and the production of knowledge. Three key themes are examined in the chapter, which include contestation over the ***mission of the university***, the ***internationalisation of higher education***, and the role of ***governance and funding***.

The mission of the university continues to be a contested one, ranging from the idea that universities are producers of 'true' knowledge to the idea that universities exist to serve the economic growth of the nation, to the idea that the university is an agent of change in a globalised world (Bogelund, 2015). These different missions are underpinned by different constructions of knowledge. The construction of the university as a producer of 'pure knowledge' conceives of knowledge production and knowledge as truth as central to this mission, whilst the application of knowledge for social and economic purposes underpins university missions centred around creating economic growth. The third model of the university as a change agent is informed by an emphasis on social and political contextualisation of knowledge. A traditional US liberal arts education is seen as supporting a mission of promoting democracy through the production of critically informed citizens. This model is also evident at AUB, Lebanon, as well as at the US branch campuses in the

UAE. As an American model, it is accorded status. Yet, this liberal education approach is not a widespread model in the Arab world, where there is a focus on professional education, premised on a mission of educating students to meet the needs of the market. This can be understood, given the region has the highest levels of youth unemployment in the world, coupled with political instability (Campante and Chor, 2013). However, the humanities and social sciences are also seen to be potentially controversial, where issues of academic freedom are most tested. The university is also conceived of as the protector of knowledge and its production, particularly in the case of humanities and social sciences, which are perceived to be more vulnerable to infringement (Scott, 2019).

The mission of the university has also been linked to discourses of a nation's imagined futures. As noted in the US context, the mission of the university has been linked to a discourse of upholding democracy. In the Arab world, colonial rule used education policy as a means of 'soft' power, and post-independence, education has played an important role in nation building, where the national university is seen as a symbol of national identity. The massification of higher education in the last few decades has witnessed an exponential increase in the number of universities in the region, where this massification is also linked to privatisation and internationalisation. These nationalising projects, however, were preceded by a long history of knowledge production in the region.

The nationalising projects in the Arab region have been superseded by the internationalisation of higher education globally. Global enrolment rates continue to rise, with rates in the Arab world having more than doubled since 2000 (UNESCO, 2018). This is coupled with the rapid expansion of private higher education, where education is constructed instrumentally as a means to enable access to the global economy. Lebanon's higher education system is largely decentralised with most of the sector being private, as is the case with AUB. In the UAE, the concept of establishing a 'knowledge economy' drives the 'imported internationalisation' of branch universities in concentrated 'cities' or 'parks' such as Dubai's Knowledge Park. There have been a range of critiques of these branch universities, with some characterising such ventures as 'imperialist'. However, such characterisations do not take account of the agency of the host countries of these branch universities. For example, in the UAE, there has been a strong local drive to establish a knowledge economy, with the initiative for branch campuses instigated from within. In addition, imperialist narratives fail to recognise the relational transnational power dynamics reflected in the UAE being recognised as one of the leading transnational education hubs in the world, with very high rates of outward bound and inward bound student mobility leading to a highly diverse student body (World Education News and Reviews, 2018).

There have also been concerns that the branch campus lacks a coherence in mission with the home institution. As such, this nation-bound conception of higher education institutions is being challenged by a shift in conception of not only the mobilities of people and policies but also the mobility of academic institutions and the development of transnational education and the transnational production of knowledge through teaching and research. As illustrated in Chapter 3's consideration of the geographical positionality of knowledge production, knowledge is constructed differently based on the geopolitics of the context. This is illustrated in the transnational framing of the field of American Studies in Lebanon's AUB, which has challenged and influenced the field within the United States.

The role of the university is also exercised through its governance and funding. Its link to academic freedom can be traced historically in the US context to addressing the conflict arising between power and knowledge (Scott, 2019). We also witness the growth in managerial and accountability discourses, as evident through research assessment evaluations, such as the Research Excellence Framework in the United Kingdom. This shift has been described as the 'hollowed out' university where governance is top-down hierarchical, rather than the self-government of an academic community (Cribb and Gewirtz, 2013). Such managerial shifts have implications for academic freedom, in part arising from the neoliberal framing of the student as customer and also in governing what research is legitimated. These dynamics are increasingly transnational, as evidenced through both funding arrangements of branch universities and funding of international research collaborations. The institution of the university union plays an important role across all four contexts, in terms of both the practice of academic freedom within the local bounds of the university and also transnationally raising issues arising in the context of branch campuses in the UAE, and in relation to issues of legal compliance in the case of AUB in Lebanon.

The governance of legitimate research is mediated through systems of tenure in the US context and the issue of job security in part-time contracts in both US and UK contexts. Furthermore, these forms of vulnerabilities are gendered and racialised, where statistically more women and ethnic minorities work under more precarious work conditions. In addition, funding of certain areas of knowledge, for example, research on race and gender, is not prioritised by research councils.

As can been seen, the university has a multivalent spatial positionality – at the same time, both embedded in its local and national contexts and positioned within transnational dynamics. As such, the argument that the university is a separate decontextualised space, an 'ivory tower' to produce objective knowledge unfettered by the dynamics of political, economic, and religious relationships in society, is undermined. McGreevy (2018) describes this as the paradox of universities being both a 'place of closure' and a 'place of openness'.

Examining the role of the university in contextualising practices of academic freedom illustrates how university governance and funding practices are mechanisms that constrain academic freedom. Chapter 5 further examines such constraints, extending this to an interrogation of both 'internal' and 'external' restrictions. The transnational positionality of academic freedom and knowledge production is further elucidated by the contextualisation of such constraints through the lens of the geographical and sociopolitical contexts, as well as individual positionality.

8.4 INTERNAL AND EXTERNAL RESTRICTIONS

Neoliberalism is a framing discourse globally within which we can understand internal and external restrictions on academic freedom. The marketisation of higher education results in competition, where marketing and communication of the university brand take precedence over individual academic autonomy. Ball (2012) also refers to neoliberalism as a way of being, affecting even the ways in which academics think and relate to others. This framing discourse of neoliberalism is the context of various university-level restrictions, including ethics committees, university procedures, students, and pedagogical dynamics and self-censorship. The role of **ethics committees** in acting as gatekeeper for the production of knowledge has been critiqued by some as an infringement on academic freedom (Hammersley, 2009; Hedgecoe, 2016; Holmswood, 2010), as well raising the issue of legitimacy with respect to curtailing the academic freedom of university academics. The basis for determining legitimacy can be contested in terms of, for example, whether the aims for such restrictions are deemed legitimate. This issue has been contested where it has been argued that the university is primarily concerned with the protection of its 'brand', rather than the protection of the human participants involved in the research. The evaluation of 'risk' is also contested in research conducted internationally, in particular in the Global South, which can unfold to unmask inequalities in power between collaborating partnerships between institutions in the Global North and Global South.

Procedural regulations were also discussed by interviewees as a means by which universities maintain control, with the example of Steven Salaita's reappointment process at AUB, Lebanon. His application for a more permanent position following his one-year visiting position was blocked citing 'significant procedural violations'. Another area of university restrictions is raised in relation to the marketised construction of the *student as client/ customer* and their role as potential censor and gatekeeper of the curriculum. As a result of this power dynamic, academics report that the ensuing emotional and practical work can lead to *self-censorship*. Concerns relating to curriculum are also evident in branch universities in the UAE, although the restriction primarily operates from the main campus in the Western context. Self-censorship and personal responsibilisation in branch campus contexts operate in tandem with the main campus curriculum constraints.

Self-censorship is a feature that emerged as an issue across all four contexts – Lebanon, the UAE, the United Kingdom, and the United States. Commenting on the UK and US contexts, the issues of bullying and harassment in higher education were raised. Following from the premise that there are necessary preconditions for the practice of academic freedom, academic freedom is undermined in such contexts where there is a hostile or non-inclusive environment for minorities by gender, ethnicity, religion, race, class, and disability. A hostile environment may also take the form of job insecurity, short-term contracts, and the tenure system. Such vulnerability leads to self-imposed censorship as a preservation mechanism and, thus, undermines academic freedom. This is especially evident around topics deemed to be controversial, heightened by incremental micro-messages from within the university environment including colleagues and managers.

Restraints on academic freedom also operate at *state and international* levels, and there is an intersectionality of the different levels of restrictions. In addition to variations in national and legal protections of international freedom, there are also a range of national mechanisms, as evidenced by such examples as the UK Research Evaluation Framework (REF), the Requirement for US Compliance at American universities in the Middle East, and mobility restrictions into the United Kingdom, the United States, and the UAE. With the example of the UK REF, its market logic framed in terms of impact determines what research is legitimated and affects the nature of disciplines themselves, as was illustrated examining the trends over time within the discipline of Sociology. It has also been argued that the REF, through reinforcing disciplines, can suppress risk-taking and creativity (Stanonis, 2016). At AUB, Lebanon, the role of US compliance has a significant effect on academic freedom, where operating through university governance structures such as the Board of Trustees and senior management, research is restricted based on political ideology, with the banning of research on those organisations listed as terrorist by the US administration. Initially operationalised in relation to US-funded projects, this has been expanded to all forms of interaction. Mobility restrictions have been high profile in the media, in particular relating to the cases of US-based New York University (NYU) professors visiting the UAE and NYU Abu Dhabi, whilst mobility restrictions into the United States do not gain the same level of coverage, with a significant number of cases being of academics travelling from the Middle East.

8.5 FORBIDDEN KNOWLEDGE

Internal and external restrictions on academic freedom in part act as gatekeeper mechanisms in the production of knowledge deemed permissible. Chapter 6, in its focus on 'forbidden' knowledge, examines this construct, elucidating different facets to this 'knowable unknown', as knowledge that is deemed to be 'too sensitive, dangerous or taboo to produce' (Kempner et al., 2011, p. 476) and knowing what knowledge not to produce (Cetina, 1999). As such, forbidden knowledge entails not only content but also the structural and sociopolitical processes that operate in policing this sensitive/taboo knowledge. I propose three dominant discourses of forbidden knowledge, which include, first, concerns relating to the misapplication of research findings, second, 'uncomfortable truths', and third, taboo topics. Furthermore, four areas of forbidden knowledge were highlighted by interviewees.

The first area relates to *'bioethics', psychology, and 'controversial' science.* In particular, in UK and US contexts, research on abortion, euthanasia, infanticide, and behavioural genetics were highlighted and also positioned in relation to religious and political perspectives. The temporal and spatial fluidity of the construct 'controversiality' is illustrated by how its associated content is not fixed but rather shows change over time and by geographical location. Disciplinary norms change over time, as do sociopolitical priorities and sensitivities, also reflected in state funding priorities.

A second controversial area relates to conducting research on Palestine and Israel, particularly in the UK and US contexts. A range of societal and institutional restrictions, pressures, and exclusions make doing such work precarious, with some researchers leaving the field to work on less controversial topics. Some scholars' concerns about job security, in particular those without tenure in the US system, perceived there to be significant risk in pursuing such research. This sense of vulnerability can be compounded by being blocked from leadership positions within the university, difficulties in getting funding, and being listed on such websites as Canary Mission and Campus Watch. The positionality of the scholar mediates the extent and nature of the exclusion with those of Palestinian, Muslim, or Arab heritage experiencing the highest levels of exclusion. The geopolitical positionality also mediates the experience and nature of restrictions, as illustrated in the case of the study of Palestine through American Studies at the Centre for American Studies and Research at AUB, Lebanon.

Gender and sexuality is another area deemed to be controversial across the four examined contexts, although nuanced with respect to context. The United Kingdom and the United States have seen controversy relating to research on sexuality and transgender, with restrictions often coming from fellow colleagues presented in terms of a critique of the 'quality' of the research. Ensuing bullying and self-censorship is reported to make this knowledge non-knowable. There is also considerable controversy surrounding gender and sexuality knowledge in the curriculum, evident, in particular, in the UAE context. In some instances, the main campus takes pre-emptive measures to avoid any controversy, resulting in gaps in curriculum on this topic. This stands in contrast to reports from UAE lecturers of the perceived relative freedom to teach on this topic, although the issue of self-regulated censorship and knowing what is contextually appropriate is commented on. In the Lebanese context, whilst there is research on gender, the field is typically constructed relatively conservatively, where sexuality is not part of the construct of the field. More innovative approaches within the field do exist, but sit outside higher education institutions, and are funded by international funders, as in the case of *Kohl*, the journal for Body and Gender Research.

The fourth area of controversial research highlighted relates to 'race, religion, security, and extremism'. Again, this area is seen across the four contexts, as well as constructed transnationally. Academics working in the field of 'race' and 'gender' in the United Kingdom comment on the institutional mechanisms and initiatives that can potentially undermine or neutralise their work by occupying the space and defining the terms of 'diversity' work. Funding priorities can also redirect critical work on race and gender into more 'acceptable' forms. Constraints relating to work on extremism in the UK context face similar pressures and can sit uncomfortably in relation to government initiatives such as Prevent – whose aim is to tackle extremism – and the co-opting of higher education institutions into this policy work. The difficulties in conducting research on security in the Middle East were seen with the case of a UK Ph.D. Student, Matthew Hedges, in Dubai in 2018. Funding priorities also present certain constructs of security, directing research within these constructs.

The processes of forbidding knowledge also act through the transnational processes of publishing and dissemination. This occurs at the level of the individual researcher trying to publish their work and/or being blocked from giving guest lectures and is also evidenced by initiatives such as the establishment of the anonymous peer-refereed *Journal of Controversial Ideas*. The rationale is that such a forum enables both the publication and the dissemination of unpopular or controversial ideas, as well as providing a level of protection to individuals who feel vulnerable, having suffered hostility to their work in the past.

In contrast to forbidden knowledge, Chapter 7 examined the conception of 'legitimate' knowledge, where legitimacy is constructed in terms of the 'right to authority' and its public acceptance. Legitimate knowledge is not merely the opposite of forbidden knowledge, rather, it has a wider remit. Delegitimation not only may be a process used to block forbidden knowledge, but it may also be used to drown out alternative sources of knowledge, for example, of formerly marginalised groups with less relational power, nationally or transnationally. Legitimation entails social, cognitive, and normative dimensions and has a complex and dynamic interrelationship with the related concepts of belief, truth, and justification (Goldman, 2002). The literature on the sociology of knowledge has highlighted various types of factors complicit in the formulation of knowledge, including class, political interests, gender, and so on. It has been argued further that it is not only the social context within which the research takes place, but also that this context is embedded in the epistemic nature of the research. Kitcher (1993), for example, highlights how research is organised through practices of consensus, a social practice.

Highlighting the notion of the 'right' to 'authority' and the public acceptance of this authority, I interrogated a number of factors and processes implicated in the legitimation (or delegitimation) of knowledge. These include, for example, positionality; university diversity initiatives; discourses of civility; disciplinary constructs of methodology, 'quality', and the 'Canon'; skills, employment, and research assessment; funding and international partnerships; and university world rankings and publications.

Legitimate knowledge depends on the positionality of the knowledge producer and where that knowledge is being produced. Positionality is also invoked with respect to perceptions of who can legitimately do what research, as given in examples of race research in the United Kingdom. In addition, positionality affects self-censorship, due to hyper-consciousness of positionality, which is often the case for ethnic minority academics. This stands in stark contrast to the assumed universality of knowledge produced by White researchers. Notions of expertise are also important in relation to the production of legitimate knowledge, as previously mentioned. The notion of expertise invokes a particular construct of 'knowable' externalised knowledge, standing in opposition to subjective or experiential forms of knowledge, critiqued as the elision between belief and knowledge. Contestations over legitimate knowledge arise in debates relating to indigenous knowledge. Global North knowledge is associated with legitimacy, objectivity, and rationality, in contrast to Global South knowledge and marginalised indigenous knowledge associated with affect and subjectivity.

Diversity initiatives have become a common feature in universities, especially in the UK and US contexts. In the United Kingdom, Athena SWAN is one example where it has the stated purpose to effect structural and cultural changes in higher education for women. Similarly, the UK Race Equality Charter focuses on race equality and, in particular, representation of students and staff in higher education institutions. However, these initiatives, whilst lauded for raising these issues and having some success, have been critiqued for the marketised construction of individual competitiveness, as well as the burden of this work typically falling on those marginalised groups. It is also argued that these 'reasonable' initiatives neutralise a more radical and emotive bottom-up advocacy.

The construct of quality is used to delegitimise different forms of knowledge production, which operates through disciplinary and methodological constructions of quality, as raised in Chapter 3. Returning to the construct of legitimacy as 'right' to authority, and its public acceptance, we see that the concept of a self-regulating disciplinary community based on recognised expertise enacts this legitimacy of the shared norms of the discipline. If these norms are transgressed, there is the risk of exclusion from the disciplinary community. Academics whose work challenge disciplinary norms typically recount the reaction of academic colleagues as one of the greatest concerns, exacerbated by career stage, where the threat of exclusion is a greater risk for those at earlier career stages. Contestation relating to methodological quality also features strongly in relation to legitimisation of research findings evident in debates relating to quantitative and qualitative research, and in particular, the power of statistics (Gillborn, 2010). These debates of disciplinary quality are also central to discourses on the 'Canon', assumed to be a universal, objective recognition of works of quality. Again, we see the invocation of legitimacy through the notions of right to authority and its public acceptance. With the rise of feminist, critical, and post-colonial theory, the legitimacy of the Canon has been challenged, with calls to recognise its sociopolitical and historical positionality and the political nature of knowledge (Arday and Mirza, 2018; Banks, 1993; Giroux, 1983; Habermas, 1971).

The effect of neoliberal discourses of skills, impact, and employment has been examined through the book, in relation to the production of knowledge, the role of the university, and as a form of restriction of academic freedom. This restriction is operationalised through the legitimisation of knowledge within the neoliberal discourses of skills and impact. Research that is deemed outside this frame is delegitimised. This is not only a discourse in the United Kingdom and the United States but is also evidenced in the UAE and Lebanon and indeed is a global discourse with the internationalisation and massification of higher education. This discourse, in turn, affects the status, in particular, of the humanities and social sciences and its funding by legitimating or delegitimating what research is conducted. There has been a shift to legitimating more applied constructions of disciplines, often related to policy. This effect is particularly exacerbated in the UAE and Lebanon, where many universities do not have liberal arts–based requirements, and professional degree programmes dominate.

Impact agendas also dominate in the funding for large-scale international partnerships, where often North–South partnerships are a requirement of funding. These initiatives have raised the issue of the nature of such partnerships, with calls for more inclusive and equitable partnerships. Yet, there is a legacy of the Global South producing the data, rather than setting the theoretical or research agendas, central to the larger social processes of knowledge production (Connell, 2014). There is a significant challenge in overcoming structural constraints and historical power relations, inadvertently reifying the inequalities between the Global North and the Global South (Landau, 2012). Whilst there have been efforts to respond to critiques of unequal partnerships, the focus has been relatively more on the implementation and dissemination of research, rather than interrogating processes of agenda setting and research governance and epistemological conceptions and the political economy of knowledge (Fransman and Newman, 2019).

For example, the political economy of knowledge production operates in the delegitimising of research on 'neglected diseases' – defined as neglected in terms of the relative disease burden. The lack of funding illustrates the delegitimisation of this knowledge, which can be understood in terms of the political economy of knowledge production. Funding decisions relating to research to develop effective treatments of certain diseases in the Global South are made on the basis that these disadvantaged populations would not be able to afford the treatments. As a result, this marketisation of the application of such research delegitimises the perceived need to undertake this research.

Delegitimation of knowledge also operates through critiques of the 'way' in which information is delivered. The discourse of civility illustrates how critique of the content of knowledge production is deflected by a focus on the nature of the manner of critique. It has been argued that the history of the discourse of incivility has operated as a form of 'racial and class denouncement' in the United States and Europe (Massad, 2014) and is a reformulation of an 'openly colonial' cultured/uncultured binary (Salaita, 2015). A premise underlying such discourses contrasts 'legitimate' knowledge constructed in terms of rationality and objectivity in contrast to non-legitimate subjective and affective knowledge. There is a disingenuous abstraction of knowledge from the existing power relations between groups and the sociopolitical and historical contexts.

Global systems such as university rankings, publications, and citations all play an important role in the legitimation of knowledge. Yet, there has been contestation over the methodology of university rankings and its implications for shaping what constitutes a 'good university'. In addition, there is contestation surrounding the use of such rankings, with concerns pertaining to the reification of the marketised logic of the student as customer. Furthermore, the rankings do not take account of the significant inequalities in resources between universities in the Global North and the Global South. This is also illustrated in global publication practices where publication in the English language dominates. In addition, international division of knowledge labour between the Global North and the Global South often results in Northern scholars in North–South collaborations having outcomes of publishable knowledge, whilst Southern scholars play more of a role of 'sub-contractors' (Kreimer and Zabala, 2008). Citation practices also diverge, with the Global North showing patterns of self-citation, with rare citation of Southern scholars by Northern scholars (Collyer, 2018). In contrast, Southern scholars are outward looking in their citation practices. Such differences in publication and citation practices reify and consolidate the inequalities in transnational knowledge production. However, new knowledge hubs are emerging, for example, in Brazil, South Korea, Taiwan, and China, challenging the hegemony and legitimacy of dominant global systems, with a shift towards a multi-polar model of knowledge production (Hanafi and Arvanitis, 2015).

8.6 FINAL THOUGHTS

Understandings of academic freedom have been defined predominantly through the methodological nationalism of the field. Much of the literature has situated the study of academic freedom in the Global North, in particular, in US and UK contexts. In contrast, this book has made the case for a transnational theoretical framework for academic freedom in recognition of the transnational production of knowledge and the internationalisation and massification of higher education globally. In addition, this book interrogates the interrelationship of academic freedom and the production of knowledge in transnational perspective across and between the four national contexts of Lebanon, the UAE, the United Kingdom, and the United States. The relationship between academic freedom and production of knowledge has been relatively under-researched, and so this book has aimed to theorise their inter-connectivity, drawing on original empirical data from interviews with academics in the four national contexts, whose own positioning in relation to their research interests is often transnational. Interrogating the conceptions of knowledge and the mission of the university, I have illustrated how different conceptions of knowledge have differing implications for academic freedom.

Arguing for a contextualised approach to understanding academic freedom, I also call for consideration of a broader concept of academic freedom – one that entails its preconditions, as outlined by Butler and others. I argue that a construct of academic freedom that also necessarily entails the 'conditions of its exercise' (Butler, 2015, p. 293) concomitantly enables an accommodation between the principles of academic freedom and the principles of inclusion – often portrayed to be in tension with one another. As such, there need be no theoretical dissonance between freedom and diversity/inclusion. Future work may focus on the practical dichotomy between these polarised positions, with further empirical data, especially from the Global South and its emerging knowledge hubs.

Finally, the book also considers the issue of the hegemony of knowledge, its forms of legitimation, and the politics of forbidden knowledge, situated within a transnational framework, illustrating, on the one hand, qualitative similarities between the different national contexts with respect to the operationalisation of legitimacy through internal and external restrictions; on the other hand, however, the transnational framework highlights the political economy of knowledge in the legitimation of knowledge, often consolidating the hegemony of the Global North. Future work on emerging knowledge hubs in the Global South will enable our understanding of how to address these historic and ongoing epistemic injustices (Fricker, 2009), thereby shifting knowledge production to a multi-polar model with its ensuing implications for academic freedom.

REFERENCES

American Association of University Professors (AAUP) (1915). General Report of the Committee on Academic Freedom and Academic Tenure, *Bulletin of the MUP1*, no. 1.

AAUP (1940). *1940 Statement of Principles on Academic Freedom and Tenure*. Accessed 22 April 2019 at: www.aaup.org/file/1940%20Statement.pdf.

Abi-Mershed, O. (ed.). (2010). *Trajectories of Education in the Arab World: Legacies and Challenges*. London: Routledge, published in association with Contemporary Arab Studies, Georgetown University.

Abu-Orabi, S. T. (2013). Scientific Research and Higher Education in the Arab World. Presentation to 5th IAU General Conference Higher Education: A Catalyst for Innovative and Sustainable Societies, 13–16 November 2016. Accessed 21 July 2023 at: http://knowledge4all.com/admin/Temp/Files/678a4cd0-3671-460f-9edd-1ad8b6471638.pdf.

Ahmed, S. (2014). *The Cultural Politics of Emotion*. Edinburgh: Edinburgh University Press.

Akena, F. A. (2012). Critical Analysis of the Production of Western Knowledge and Its Implications for Indigenous Knowledge and Decolonization, *Journal of Black Studies*, 43(6), 599–619.

Al Fanar Media (2017a). In Egypt, Harsh Measures against Academic Freedom Persist. Accessed 22 April 2019 at: www.al-fanarmedia.org/2017/05/egypt-harsh-measures-academic-freedom-persist/.

Al Fanar Media (2017b). UAE Jails Economist: The Silence Is Deafening. Accessed 22 April 2019 at: www.al-fanarmedia.org/2017/04/uae-jails-economist-the-silence-is-deafening/.

AlMaghlouth, N., Arvanitis, R., Cointet, J. P., and Hanafi, S. (2015). Who Frames the Debate on the Arab Uprisings? Analysis of Arabic, English, and French Academic Scholarship, *International Sociology*, 30(4), 418–441.

Altbach, P. G., Riesley, L., and Rumbley, L. E. (2009). *Trends in Global Higher Education: Tracking an Academic Revolution: A Report Prepared for the UNESCO 2009 World Conference on Higher Education*. Paris: UNESCO.

American Association for Advancement of Science (AAAS) (2022). SEA Change. Accessed 7 October 2022 at: https://seachange.aaas.org/.

Amin, T. (2020). Prospects of Knowledge Economies in the Gulf. Accessed 15 July 2022 at: www.orfonline.org/expert-speak/prospects-of-knowledge-economies-in-the-gulf-59881/.

Anderson, B. (2011). *The American University of Beirut: Arab Nationalism and Liberal Education*. Austin: University of Texas Press.

Andrews, K. (2018). The Challenge for Black Studies in the Neoliberal University (pp. 129–144). In G. K. Bhambra, D. Gebrial, and K. Nisancioglu (eds.), *De-colonising the University*. London, UK: Pluto Press.

Aperio Bella, F. (2021). The COVID-19 Pandemic as a Challenge for Academia and Academic Freedom: An Italian Perspective. In M. Seckelmann, L. Violini, C. Fraenkel-Haeberle, and G. Ragone (eds.), *Academic Freedom under Pressure?* Cham: Springer. https://doi.org/10.1007/978-3-030-77524-7_7.

Arday, J., and Mirza, H. S. (eds.). (2018). *Dismantling Race in Higher Education: Racism, Whiteness, and Decolonising the Academy*. Basingstoke and New York: Palgrave Macmillan.

Athanasiou, A., Hantzaroula, P., and Yannakopoulos, K. (2008). Towards a New Epistemology: The 'Affective Turn', *Historein*, 8, 5–16.

AUB (1979). *The Liberal Arts and the Future of Higher Education in the Middle East*. Beirut: American University of Beirut Press.

AUB Centennial Lectures (1967). *The University and the Man of Tomorrow*. Beirut: American University of Beirut Press.

AUB Faculty United (2017). About. Accessed 22 February 2017. https://aubaaup.wordpress.com.

AUB Neighborhood Initiative (2015). The Neighborhood Initiative. Accessed 27 October 2015 at: www.aub.edu.lb/neighborhood/Pages/home.aspx.

Baber, Z. (2003). Provincial Universalism: The Landscape of Knowledge Production in an Era of Globalisation, *Current Sociology*, 51(6), 615–623.

Bacevic, J. (2022). Academic Freedom Is Not Freedom of Speech', *Critical Legal Thinking*, 21 April 2022. Accessed 15 October 2022 at: https://criticallegalthinking.com/2022/04/21/academic-freedom-is-not-freedom-of-speech/.

Baer, U. (2019). *What Snowflakes Gets Right: Free Speech, Truth and Equality on Campus*. Oxford and New York: Oxford University Press.

Ball, S. J. (2012). Performativity, Commodification and Commitment: An I-Spy Guide to the Neoliberal University, *British Journal of Educational Studies*, 60(1), 17–28.

Ball, S. J., and Olmedo, A. (2013). Care of the Self, Resistance and Subjectivity under Neoliberal Governmentalities, *Critical Studies in Education*, 54(1), 85–96.

Banks, J. (1993). The Canon Debate, Knowledge Construction, and Multicultural Education, *Educational Researcher*, 22(5), 4–14.

BBC (2021). Bristol University: Professor David Miller Sacked over Israel Comments. 1 October 2021. Accessed at 21 July 2023 at: www.bbc.co.uk/news/uk-england-bristol-58765052.

Ben-Porath, S. (2016). Safety, Dignity and the Quest for a Democratic Campus Culture, *Philosophical Inquiry in Education*, 24(1), 79–85.

Ben-Porath, S. (2017). *Free Speech on Campus*. Philadelphia: University of Pennsylvania Press.

Bhabha, H. K. (1994). *The Location of Culture*. London and New York: Routledge and Kegan Paul.

References

Bhambra, G. K., Gebrial, D., and Nisancioglu, K. (2018). Introduction. In G. K. Bhambra, D. Gebrial, and K. Nisancioglu (eds.), *Decolonising the University*. London: Pluto Press.

Biesta, G. (2007). Towards the Knowledge Democracy? Knowledge Production and the Civic Role of the University, *Studies in Philosophy and Education* 26(5), 467–479.

Biggar, N. (2019). Cambridge and the Exclusion of Jordan Peterson. Accessed 18 April 2019 at: www.thearticle.com/cambridge-and-the-exclusion-of-jordan-peterson.

Bliss, D. (1994). *Letters from a New Campus*. Beirut: American University of Beirut Press.

Bogelund, P. (2015). How Supervisors Perceive PhD Supervision – And How They Practice It, *International Journal of Doctoral Studies*, 10, 39–55.

Bottrell, D., and Manathunga, C. (eds.). (2019). *Resisting Neoliberalism in Higher Education Volume I: Seeing through the Cracks*. Basingstoke and New York: Palgrave Macmillan.

Bourdieu, P. (1986). The Forms of Capital (pp. 241–258). In J. G. Richardson (ed.), *Handbook of Theory and Research for the Sociology of Capital*. Westport, CT: Greenwood Press.

Brew, A. (2003). Teaching and Research: New Relationships and Their Implications for Inquiry-Based Teaching and Learning in Higher Education, *Teaching in Higher Education*, 22(1), 3–18.

Brown University (2019). Updated: Brown Statements on Gender Dysphoria Study. Accessed 6 September 2019 at: https://news.brown.edu/articles/2018/08/gender.

Bryant, A., and Charmaz, K. (2007). Grounded Theory in Historical Perspective: An Epistemological Account (pp. 31–57). In A. Bryant and K. Charmaz (eds.), *The Sage Handbook of Grounded Theory*, London: Sage.

Buckner, E. (2011). The Role of Higher Education in the Arab State and Society: Historical Legacies and Recent Reform Patterns, *Comparative & International Higher Education*, 3, 21–26.

Burawoy, M. (2011). Redefining the Public University: Global and National Contexts (pp. 27–41). In J. Holmwood (ed.), *A Manifesto for the Public University*. London: Bloomsbury Academic.

Burke, P. J. (2013). The Right to Higher Education: Neoliberalism, Gender and Professional Mis/Recognitions, *International Studies in Sociology of Education*, 23(2), 107–126. doi:10.1080/09620214.2013.790660.

Butler, J. (2015). Exercising Rights: Academic Freedom and Boycott Politics. In A. Bilgrami and J. Cole (eds.), *Who's Afraid of Academic Freedom?*. New York: Columbia University Press.

Callan, E. (2016). Education in Safe and Unsafe Spaces, *Philosophical Inquiry in Education*, 24 (1), 64–78.

Calnan, M., and Williams, S. (1992) Images of Scientific Medicine, *Sociology of Health and Illness*, 14(2), 232–254.

Campaign for the Public University. Social Science Space. Accessed 21 July 2023 at: https://www.socialsciencespace.com/author/campaignforthepublicuniversity/.

Campante, F. R., and Chor, D. (2013). The Educated Middle Class, Their Economic Prospects and the Arab Spring, *The World Financial Review*. Accessed 4 February 2013 at www.worldfinancialreview.com/?p = 2296.

Cetina, K. K. (1999). *Epistemic Cultures: How the Sciences Make Knowledge*. Cambridge, MA: Harvard University Press.

Charmaz, K. (2011). Grounded Theory Methods in Social Justice Research. In N. K. Denzin and Y. S. Lincoln (eds.), *The Sage Handbook of Qualitative Research*. Thousand Oaks, CA: Sage Publications Inc.

Chemerinsky, E., and Gillman (2017). *Free Speech on Campus*. New Haven, CT: Yale University Press.

Christian Institute (2022). Oxford's Vice-Chancellor: Free Speech and Academic Freedom Must Be Preserved. Accessed 15 October 2022 at: www.christian.org.uk/news/oxfords-vice-chancellor-free-speech-and-academic-freedom-must-be-preserved/.

Collini, S. (2012). *What Are Universities For?* London and New York: Penguin.

Collini, S. (2017). *Speaking of Universities*. London and New York: Verso.

Collyer, F. M. (2018). Global Patterns in the Publishing of Academic Knowledge: Global North, Global South, *Current Sociology*, 66(1), 56–73.

Connell, R. (2014). Rethinking Gender from the South, *Feminist Studies*, 40(3), 518–539.

Cookson Jr, P. W. (1994). The Power Discourse: Elite Narratives and Educational Policy Formation. In G. Walford (ed.), *Researching the Powerful in Education*. London: UCL Press.

Cortas, W. M. (2009). *A World I Loved: The Story of an Arab Woman*. New York: Nation Books.

Cribb, A., and Gewirtz, S. (2013). The Hollowed-Out University? A Critical Analysis of Changing Institutional and Academic Norms in UK Higher Education, *Discourse: Studies in the Cultural Politics in Education*, 34(3), 338–350.

Dallal, A. (2010). *Islam, Science, and the Challenge of History*. New Haven, CT and London, UK: Yale University Press, p. 12. ISBN 978-0-300-1591.

Darwish, M. (2010). Absent Presence, Trans. Mohammed Shaheen. London: Hesperus, cited in Lubin, A. (2016). American Studies, the Middle East and the Question of Palestine, *American Quarterly*, 68(1), 1–21.

Dascal, M. (2007). On Colonising and Decolonising Minds (pp. 308–331). In I. Kucurandi (ed.), *Papers of the 2007 World Philosophy Day*. Istanbul: Philosophical Society of Turkey.

Davies, B., and Bansel, P. (2007). Neoliberalism and Education, *International Journal of Qualitative Studies in Education*, 20(3), 247–259.

Dea, S. (2019). *A Brief History of Academic Freedom*. Accessed 15 April 2019 at www.universityaffairs.ca/opinion/dispatches-academic-freedom/a-brief-history-of-academic-freedom/.

Department for Education (2018). *Statistics: Participation Rates in Higher Education*. Accessed August 21 2019 at: www.gov.uk/government/collections/statistics-on-higher-education-initial-participation-rates.

De Tocqueville, A. (1990 [1835]). *Democracy in America*. London: Vintage Classics.

Dewey, J. (1916). *Democracy and Education: An Introduction to the Philosophy of Education*. New York: MacMillan.

Docherty, T. (2016), On Academic and Other Freedoms. In Hudson, C., and Williams, J. (eds.), *Why Academic Freedom Matters: A Response to Current Challenges*. London: Civitas.

Dorman, P. (2011). AUB and the Arab Revolt of 2011. Opening Ceremony Speech October 2011. Accessed 29 October 2015 at: www.aub.edu.lb/president/Documents/speeches/2011/opening-ceremony-2011-dorman.pdf.

Education International (2020). *Global Levels of Academic Freedom 2020*. Accessed 17 October 2022 at: www.ei-ie.org/en/item/24856:global-index-finds-most-countries-do-not-respect-academic-freedom-and-shows-signs-of-decline.

The Education Reform Act (1988). London: Her Majesty's Stationery Office (HMSO), 202 2a.

Elton, L. (2005). Scholarship and the Research and Teaching Nexus (pp. 79–91). In R. Barnett (ed.), *Reshaping the University: New Relationships between Research, Scholarship and Teaching*. Maidenhead: Open University Press, cited in Robertson, J. (2007). Beyond the 'Research/Teaching Nexus': Exploring the Complexity of Academic Experience, *Teaching in Higher Education*, 32(5), 541–566.

Faulconbridge, J. R. (2006). Stretching Tacit Knowledge beyond a Local Fix? Global Spaces of Learning in Advertising Professional Service Firms, *Journal of Economic Geography*, 6, 517–540, cited in Waters, J. L., and Leung, M. (2017). Trans-Knowledge? Geography, Mobility, and Knowledge in Transnational Education, *Mobilities of Knowledge*, 10, 269–285.

Finkin, M. W., and Post, R. C. (2009). *For the Common Good: Principles of American Academic Freedom*. New Haven, CT: Yale University Press.

Fox News (2018). Report: UAE Activist Sentenced to 10 Years for Online Posts. Accessed 19 July 2023 at: https://www.foxnews.com/world/report-uae-activist-sentenced-to-10-years-for-online-posts.

Foucault, M. (1978, orig. 1976). *The History of Sexuality 1: The Will to Knowledge*. New York and Toronto: Random House.

Foucault, M. (1991, orig. 1975). *Discipline and Punish: The Birth of the Prison*. London: Penguin Books.

Foucault, M. (2002 [1969]). *The Archaeology of Knowledge*. London and New York: Routledge.

Fransman, J., and Newman, K. (2019). Rethinking Research Partnerships: Evidence and the Politics of Participation in Research Partnerships for International Development, *Journal of International Development*, 31, 523–544. doi:10.1002/jid.3417.

Fricker, M. (2009). *Epistemic Injustice: Power and the Ethics of Knowing*. Oxford: Oxford University Press.

Fuchs, R. F. (1963). Academic Freedom – Its Basic Philosophy, Function and History, *Law and Contemporary Problems*, 28(3), 431–446.

Furedi, F. (2017). *What's Happened to the University? A Sociological Exploration of Its Infantilization*. Abingdon, UK and New York: Routledge.

Gillborn, D. (2010). The Colour of Numbers: Surveys, Statistics and Deficit – Thinking about Race and Class, *Journal of Education Policy*, 25(2), 253–276. doi:10.1080/02680930903460740.

Giroux, H. (1983). Theories of Reproduction and Resistance in the New Sociology of Education: A Critical Analysis, *Harvard Educational Review*, 53(3), 257–293.

Giroux, H. (1992). Language, Difference and Curriculum Theory: Beyond the Politics of Clarity, *Theory into Practice*, 31, 219–227.

Giroux, H. (2002). Neoliberalism, Corporate Culture, and the Promise of Higher Education: The University as a Democratic Public Sphere, *Harvard Educational Review*, 72(4), 425–464.

Goddard, J., Hazelkorn, E., Kempton, L., and Vallance, P. (eds.). (2016). *The Civic University: The Policy and Leadership Challenges*. Northampton, MA: Edward Elgar Publishing.

Goldman, A. I. (2002). *Pathways to Knowledge: Public and Private*. Oxford: Oxford University Press.

Gordon, L. R. (2014). Disciplinary Decadence and the Decolonisation of Knowledge, *Africa Development*, XXXIX(1), 81–92.

Gregg, M., and Seigworth, G. J. (2010). *The Affect Theory Reader*. Durham, NC: Duke University Press.

Grimm, J., and Saliba I (2017). Free Research in Fearful Times: Conceptualizing an Index to Monitor Academic Freedom, *Interdisciplinary Political Studies*, 3(1), 41–75.

Gross, M., and McGoey, L. (2015). *Routledge Handbook of Ignorance Studies*. London and New York: Routledge.

The Guardian (2016). Poor Little Snowflake – The Defining Insult of 2016. Accessed 22 April 2019 at: www.theguardian.com/science/2016/nov/28/snowflake-insult-disdain-young-people.

The Guardian (2018). State Control over Academic Freedom in Hungary Threatens All Universities. Accessed 16 April 2019 at: www.theguardian.com/higher-education-network/2018/sep/06/state-control-over-academic-freedom-in-hungary-threatens-all-universities.

The Guardian (2019). Cambridge University Rescinds Jordan Peterson Invitation. Accessed 13 October 2019 at: www.theguardian.com/education/2019/mar/20/cambridge-university-rescinds-jordan-peterson-invitation.

The Guardian (2021). Bristol University Sacks Professor Accused of Anti-Semitic Comments. Accessed 5 October 2022 at: www.theguardian.com/education/2021/oct/01/bristol-university-sacks-professor-accused-of-antisemitic-comments.

The Guardian (2022). Universities to Defy Government Pressure to Ditch Race Equality Group, Accessed 7 October 2022 at: www.theguardian.com/education/2022/jun/30/universities-to-defy-government-pressure-to-ditch-race-equality-group.

The Guardian (2022). US Scholars Form Academic Freedom Alliance to Defend Free Expression, *TRAFO, Blog for Transregional Research*. Accessed 15 October 2022 at: www.theguardian.com/us-news/2021/mar/08/academic-freedom-alliance-college-university-free-speech.

Guba, E. G., and Lincoln, Y. S. (1998). Competing Paradigms in Qualitative Research. In N. K. Denzin and Y. S. Lincoln (eds.), *The Landscape of Qualitative Research*. London and Thousand Oaks, CA: Sage Publications Inc.

Habermas, J. (1971). *Knowledge and Human Interests*. London: Heineman Educational Books.

Hammersley, M. (2001). On 'Systematic' Reviews of Research Literatures: A 'Narrative' Response to Evans and Benefield, *British Educational Research Journal*, 27(5), 543–554.

Hammersley, M. (2009). Against the Ethicists: On the Evils of Ethical Regulation, *International Journal of Social Research Methodology*, 12(3), 211–225.

Hanafi, S. (2010). Donor Communities and the Market of Research Production: Framing and De-Framing the Social Sciences. In M. Burawoy, M. K Chang, and F.Y. Hseih (eds.), *Facing an Unequal World: Challenges from Sociology*. Taipei: International Association of Sociology, cited in Hanafi, S., and Arvanitis, R. (2015). *Knowledge Production in the Arab World: The Impossible Promise*. London and New York: Routledge.

Hanafi, S. (2011). University Systems in the Arab East: Publish Globally and Perish Locally vs Publish Locally and Perish Globally, *Current Sociology*, 59(3), 291–309.

Hanafi, S. (2022). The Pen and the Sword: The Narrow Margin of Academic Freedom in the Arab World'. Accessed 15 October 2022 at: https://trafo.hypotheses.org/28464.

Hanafi, S., and Arvanitis, R. (2015). *Knowledge Production in the Arab World: The Impossible Promise*. London and New York: Routledge.

Harris, J., Croot, L., Thompson, J., and Springett, J. (2015). How Stakeholder Participation Can Contribute to Systematic Reviews of Complex Intervention, *Journal of Epidemiology and Community Health*, 70, 207–214.

Hedgecoe, A. (2016). Reputational Risk, Academic Freedom and Research Ethics Review, *Sociology*, 50(3), 486–501.

Herrera, L. (2007). Higher Education in the Arab World (pp. 409–421), in James J. F. Forest and P. G. Altbach (eds.), *International Handbook of Higher Education*, Springer Book Series, 18.

Herrnstein, R. J., and Murray, C. A. (1996). *The Bell Curve: Intelligence and Class Structure in American Life*. New York: Simon & Schuster.

Hess, D. (2007). *Alternative Pathways in Science and Industry: Activism, Innovation, and the Environment in an Era of Globalization*. Cambridge, MA: MIT Press.

Holmswood, J. (2010). Research Ethics Committees (RECs) and the Creaking Piers of Peer Review, *Sociological Research Online*, 15(4): 14.

Hudson, C. (2016). A Century of Academic Freedom. In C. Hudson and J. Williams (eds.), *Why Academic Freedom Matters: A Response to Current Challenges*. London: Civitas.

Humphreys, L. (1970). *Tearoom Trade: Impersonal Sex in Public Places*. Chicago: Aldine Publishing Company.

Human Rights Watch (2018). Turkey: Government Targeting Academics. Accessed 16 April 2019 at: www.hrw.org/news/2018/05/14/turkey-government-targeting-academics.

Hvidt, M. (2021). Reaching for the Stars: How and Why Do the Gulf States Aim to Transform Their Economies to 'Knowledge-Based' Economies? Accessed 15 July 2022 at: https://blogs.lse.ac.uk/mec/2021/08/19/reaching-for-the-stars-how-and-why-do-the-gulf-states-aim-to-transform-their-economies-to-knowledge-based-economies/.

IMF (2012). Youth Unemployment in the MENA Region: Determinants and Challenges. Accessed 21 August 2019 at: www.imf.org/en/News/Articles/2015/09/28/04/54/vc061312.

Independent (2017). University 'Safe Space' Policies Leave Academics in Fear of Losing Their Jobs, Claims Professor. Accessed 22 April 2019 at: www.independent.co.uk/news/education/education-news/university-safe-spaces-academics-professors-fear-lose-jobs-students-free-speech-political-correct-pc-a7815991.html.

Jaramillo, A., and Melonio, T. (2011). *Breaking Even or Breaking Through: Reaching Financial Sustainability while Providing High Quality Standards in Higher Education in the Middle East and North Africa (Arabic)*. Washington, DC: World Bank. http://documents.worldbank.org/curated/en/475761468275941860/Breaking-even-or-breaking-through-reaching-financial-sustainability-while-providing-high-quality-standards-in-higher-education-in-the-Middle-East-and-North-Africa.

Johnson, C., and Watson, L. (2015). Legitimacy, Sociology of (pp. 823–828), *International Encyclopedia of the Social & Behavioral Sciences*, 2nd edn., 13. http://dx.doi.org/10.1016/B978-0-08-097086-8.32085-2.

Jons, H., and Hoyler, M. (2013). Global Geographies of Higher Education: The Perspective of World University Rankings, *Geoforum*, 46, 45–59.

Journal of Controversial Ideas website (2023). Accessed 21 July 2023 at: https://journalofcontroversialideas.org/.

Karran, T., and Mallinson, L (2017). *Academic Freedom in the U.K.: Legal and Normative Protection in a Comparative Context, Report for the University and College Union*,

Accessed 22 April 2019 at: www.ucu.org.uk/media/8614/Academic-Freedom-in-the-UK-Legal-and-Normative-Protection-in-a-Comparative-Context-Report-for-UCU-Terence-Karran-and-Lucy-Mallinson-May-17/pdf/ucu_academicfreedomstudy_report_may17.pdf.

Kempner, J. Merz, J. F., and Bosk, C. L. (2011). Forbidden Knowledge: Public Controversy and the Production of Nonknowledge, *Sociological Forum*, 26(3), 475–500.

Kessien, B. (2022). How the Idea of a 'Transgender Contagion' Went Viral – and Caused Untold Harm, *MIT Technology Review*. Accessed 5 October 2022 at: www.technologyreview.com/2022/08/18/1057135/transgender-contagion-gender-dysphoria/.

Khalaf, S. (2012). *Protestant Missionaries in the Levant: Ungodly Puritans 1820–60*. Abingdon: Routledge.

Khouri, F. (2016). An Ambitious Agenda for the American University of Beirut, *Al-Fanar Media*. Accessed 22 February 2017 at: www.al-fanarmedia.org/2016/04/an-ambitious-agenda-for-the-american-university-of-beirut/.

Kitcher, P. (1993). *The Advancement of Science*. New York: Oxford University Press.

Kiwan, D. (2017a). Emotive Acts of Citizenship, Social Change and Knowledge Production in Lebanon, *Interface*, 9(2), 114–142.

Kiwan, D. (2017b). American Liberal Education and the Civic University: 'Citizenship' and 'Learning' at the American University of Beirut, *Geografiska Annaler: Series B*, 100, 112–130.

Kiwan, D. (2018). The Middle East (pp. 37–50). In I. Davies, L.-C. Ho, D. Kiwan, C. Peck, A. Peterson, E. Sant, and Y. Waghid (eds.), *The Palgrave Handbook of Global Citizenship and Education*. Basingstoke: Palgrave Macmillan.

Kiwan, D. (2022). Dis/Abled Decolonial Human and Citizen Futures, *Citizenship Studies*, 26 (4–5), 530–538.

Kiwan, D., and Evans, M. (2015). *Global Citizenship Education: Topics and Learning Objectives by Age*. Paris, France: UNESCO.

Klein, J. T. (2021). *Beyond Interdisciplinarity: Boundary Work, Communication and Collaboration*. New York: Oxford University Press.

Koch, N. (2016). Is Nationalism Just for Nationals? Civic Nationalism for Noncitizens and Celebrating National Day in Qatar and the UAE, *Political Geography*, 54, 43–53. doi:10.1016/j.polgeo.2015.09.006.

Kohl (2019). About Kohl. Accessed 30 September 2019 at: https://kohljournal.press/about.

Kreimer, P., and Zabala, J. P. (2008). What Knowledge for Whom? Social, Production and Social Use of Scientific Knowledge about Chagas Disease in Argentina, *Anthropology Review*, 2(3), 413–439.

Kuhn, T. S. (1970) *The Structure of Scientific Revolutions*, 2nd edn. Chicago: University of Chicago Press, cited in Stanonis, A. J. No Time for Muses: The Research Excellence Framework and the Pursuit of Mediocrity. In C. Hudson and J. Williams (eds.), *Why Academic Freedom Matters: A Response to Current Challenges*. London: Civitas.

Kvale, S. (1996). *InterViews: An Introduction to Qualitative Research Interviewing*. London and Thousand Oaks, CA: Sage Publications Inc.

Kvisito, S., and Pihlstrom, S. (2017). The Metaphors of Knowledge and Academic Impact, *Metaphilosophy*, 48(5), 780–797.

Landau, L. B. (2012). Communities of Knowledge or Tyrannies of Partnership: Reflections on North–South Research Networks and the Dual Imperative, *Journal of Refugee Studies*, 5 (4), 555–570.

Lenza, M (2004). Controversies Surrounding Laud Humphreys' Tearoom Trades? An Unsettling Example of Politics and Power in Methodological Critiques, *International Journal of Sociology and Social Policy*, 24(3/4/5), 20–31.

Lewis, Charlton T., and Short, Charles (1966) [1879]. *A Latin Dictionary*. Oxford: Clarendon Press.

Lim, M. A. (2018). The Building of Weak Expertise: The Work of Global University Rankers, *Higher Education*, 75, 415–430.

Littman, L. (2018). Parent Reports of Adolescents and Young Adults Perceived to Show Signs of a Rapid Onset of Gender Dysphoria, *PLOS One*, 13(8), 1–41.

Longino, H. (1993). Essential Tensions – Phase Two: Feminist, Philosophical, and Social Studies of Science. In L. Antony and C. Witt (eds.), *A Mind of One's Own*. Boulder, CO: Westview Press.

Lubin, A. (2016). American Studies, the Middle East, and the Question of Palestine. *American Quarterly*, 68(1), 1–21.

Lynch, K., and Ivancheva, M. (2015). Academic Freedom and the Commercialisation of Universities: A Critical Ethical Analysis, *Ethics in Science and Environmental Politics*, 15, 71–85.

MacDonald, R. (2017). Impact, Research and Slaying Zombies, *International Journal of Sociology and Social Policy*, 37(11–12), 696–710.

MacFarlane, B. (2007). Defining and Rewarding Academic Citizenship: The Implications for University Promotions Policy, *Journal of Higher Education Policy and Management*, 29(3), 261–273.

MacLure. M. (2005) Clarity Bordering on Stupidity: Where's the Quality in Systematic Review?, *Journal of Education Policy*, 20(4), 393–416. doi:10.1080/02680930500131801.

Makdisi, G. (1981). *The Rise of Colleges: Institutions of Learning in Islam and the West*. Edinburgh: Edinburgh University Press.

Makdisi, J. S. (2006). *Beirut Fragments: A War Memoir*. New York: Persea Books.

Manathunga C., and Bottrell, D. (2019). (eds.). *Resisting Neoliberalism in Higher Education Volume II: Prising Open the Cracks*. Basingstoke and New York: Palgrave Macmillan.

Masdar (2022). The City. Accessed 15 July 2022 at: https://masdar.ae/Masdar-City/the-city.

Massad, J. (2014). Academic Civility and Its Discontents, *The Electronic Intifada*. Accessed 10 September 2019 at: https://electronicintifada.net/content/academic-civility-and-its-discontents/13937.

McGreevy, P. (2018). *De-Marking the University: Hierarchy, Walls, and Critique*. ASA 2018 (unpublished paper).

Mertens, D. M. (1998). *Research Methods in Education and Psychology*. London and Thousand Oaks, CA: Sage Publications Inc.

Merton, R. K. (1973). *The Sociology of Science: Theoretical and Empirical Investigations*. Chicago, IL: Chicago University Press.

Middle East Studies Association (MESA) (2022). Middle East Scholars Vote to Endorse BDS. Accessed 15 October 2022 at: https://mesana.org/news/2022/03/23/middle-east-scholars-vote-to-endorse-bds.

Mignolo, W. (2010). Epistemic Disobedience, Independent Thought and Decolonial Freedom, *Theory, Culture and Society*, 26(7–8), 1–23.

Milgram, S. (1974). *Obedience to Authority: An Experimental View*. London: Tavistock Publications.

Miller-Idriss, G., and Banauer, E. (2011). Transnational Higher Education: Offshore Campuses in the Middle East, *Comparative Education*, 47(2), 181–207.

Mills, W.C. (1959). *The Sociological Imagination*. Oxford: Oxford University Press.

Mirza, H. (2015). Sexual Harassment: Moving from Shame to Action, or How to Make the Personal Political, *Sexual Harrassment in Higher Education (SHHE) Conference*, Goldsmiths, University of London, 2 December 2015. Accessed 10 September 2019 at: https://shhegoldsmiths.wordpress.com/shame-and-sexual-harassment/.

Morgan, K. (2004).The Exaggerated Death of Geography: Learning, Proximity and Territorial Innovation Systems, *Journal of Economic Geography*, 4, 3–21, (2017), cited in Waters, J. L., and M. Leung (2017). Trans-knowledge? Geography, Mobility, and Knowledge in Transnational Education, *Mobilities of Knowledge*, 10, 269–285. doi:10.1007/978-3-319-44654-7_14.

Moshman D., and Edler, F. (2015). Civility and Academic Freedom after Salaita, *AAUP Journal of Academic Freedom*, 6, 1–13.

Mott, C., and Cockayne, D. (2017). Citation Matters: Mobilizing the Politics of Citation toward a Practice of 'Conscientious Engagement', *Gender, Place & Culture*, 24(7), 954–973. doi:10.1080/0966369X.2017.1339022.

Nabeel, G. (2022). 80 Arab Universities are Ranked in the 2023 QS World University Rankings, *Al-Fanar Media*. Accessed 14 July 2022 at: www.al-fanarmedia.org/2022/06/80-arab-universities-are-ranked-in-the-2023-qs-world-university-rankings/.

Nandy, A. (1 July 2014). The Untamed Language of Dissent: A Few Clues to the Rebellions in the World We Have Entered, *India International Centre Quarterly*, 41(1), 1–6.

Nandy, A., and Darby, P. (2018). Challenging the Ruling Paradigms of the Global Knowledge System: Ashis Nandy in Conversation with Phillip Darby, *Postcolonial Studies*, 21(3), 278–284.

Nehring, D. (2021). How Will COVID-19 Affect Academic Freedom? *Social Science Space*. Accessed 17 October 2021 at: www.socialsciencespace.com/2021/06/how-will-covid-19-affect-academic-freedom/.

Newfield, C. (2008). *Unmaking the Public University: The Forty-Year Assault on the Middle Class*. Cambridge, MA: Harvard University Press.

Newfield, C (2016). *The Great Mistake: How We Wrecked Public Universities and How We Can Fix Them*. Baltimore, MD: Johns Hopkins University Press.

Nichols, T. (2017). *The Death of Expertise: The Campaign against Established Knowledge and Why It Matters*. New York: Oxford University Press.

Noble, M., and Ross, C. (eds.) (2019). *Reclaiming the University for the Public Good*. Basingstoke and New York: Palgrave Macmillan.

Oakley, A. (2003). Research Evidence, Knowledge Management and Educational Practice: Early Lessons from a Systematic Approach, *London Review of Education*, 1(1), 21–33.

OECD (2018). *The Education GPS: The World of Education at Your Fingertips. United States*. Accessed 21 August 2019 at: http://gpseducation.oecd.org/CountryProfile?primaryCountry=USA&treshold=10&topic=EO.

Olds, K. (2007). Global Assemblage: Singapore, Foreign Universities, and the Construction of a 'Global Education Hub', *World Development*, 35(6), 959–975.

References

Olssen, M., and Peters, M. (2005). Neoliberalism, Higher Education and the Knowledge Economy: From the Free Market to Knowledge Capitalism, *Journal of Education Policy*, 20(3), 313–345. doi:10.1080/02680930500108718.

O'Sullivan, M. (2016). *Academic Barbarism, Universities and Inequality*. Basingstoke and New York: Palgrave Macmillan.

Our World in Data (2018). *Tertiary Education*. Accessed 21 August 2019 at: https://ourworldindata.org/tertiary-education.

Paul, K. T., and Haddad, C. (2023). The Pandemic as We Know It (pp. 221–233, 2nd edn.). In M. Gross and L. McGoey (eds.), *Routledge International Handbook of Ignorance Studies*. London, UK: Routledge.

Peck, J., Theodore, N., and Brenner, N. (2009). Neoliberal Urbanism: Models, Moments, Mutations, *SAIS Review of International Affairs*, 29(1), 49–66.

Phipps, A. (2015). Sexism and Violence in the Neoliberal University, Sexual Harassment in Higher Education (SHHE) Conference, Goldsmiths, University of London, 2 December 2015. Accessed 10 September 2019 at: https://genderate.wordpress.com/2015/12/02/sexism-and-violence/.

Phipps, A. (2017). Speaking Up for What's Right: Politics, Markets and Violence in Higher Education, *Feminist Theory*, 18(3), 357–362.

Plomin, R. (2018). *How DNA Makes Us Who We Are*. Cambridge, MA: MIT Press.

Policy Exchange (2019). Academic Freedom in the UK. Accessed 15 October 2022 at: https://policyexchange.org.uk/wp-content/uploads/2019/11/Academic-freedom-in-the-UK.pdf.

Politics Today (2021). I Was Fired from the University of Bristol Despite Being Cleared of Anti-Semitism – An Interview with David Miller. Accessed 5 October 2022 at: https://politicstoday.org/i-was-fired-from-the-university-of-bristol-despite-being-cleared-of-anti-semitism-an-interview-with-david-miller/.

Popovic, M., Matel, L., and Joly, D. (2022). *Changing Understandings of Academic Freedom in the World at a Time of Pandemic*. Budapest, Hungary: Central European University: OSUN Global Observatory of Academic Freedom.

Prelec, T., Furstenberg, S., Heathershaw. J., and Thomson, C. (2022). Is Academic Freedom at Risk from Internationalisation? Results from a 2020 Survey of UK Social Scientists, *The International Journal of Human Rights*, 26(10), 1698–1722. doi:10.1080/13642987.2021.2021398.

Pring, R. (2000). *Philosophy of Educational Research*. London: Continuum.

Prior, L. (2002). Belief, Knowledge and Expertise: The Emergence of the Lay Expert in Medical Sociology, *Sociology of Health & Illness*, 25(Silver Anniversary), 41–57.

Procter, R. N. (1995). *Cancer Wars: How Politics Shapes What We Know & Do Not Know about Cancer*. New York: Basic Books.

Puar, J. (2015). Introduction. E. L. Espirito (2015). Civility, Academic Freedom and the Project of Decolonisation: A Conversation with Steven Salaita, *Qui Parle*, Fall/Winter 2015, 24(1), 63–68.

Punch, M. (1994). Politics and Ethics in Qualitative Research. In N. K. Denzin and Y. S. Lincoln (eds.), *The Landscape of Qualitative Research*. London and Thousand Oaks, CA: Sage Publications Inc.

QS World University Rankings (2022). *QS World University Rankings 2023: Top Global Universities*. Accessed 14 July 2022 at: www.topuniversities.com/university-rankings/world-university-rankings/2023.

Reay, D. (2018). Race and Elite Universities in the UK (pp. 47–66). In J. Arday and H. S. Mirza (eds.), *Dismantling Race in Higher Education: Racism, Whiteness and Decolonising the Academy*. New York: Palgrave Macmillan.

Reichman, H. (2018). Free Speech on Campus Review, *Academe*, 104(3), 45–49.

Robertson, J. (2007). Beyond the 'Research/Teaching Nexus': Exploring the Complexity of Academic Experience, *Teaching in Higher Education*, 32(5), 541–566.

Rocki, M. (2005). Statistical and Mathematical Aspects of Ranking: Lessons from Poland, *Higher Education in Europe*, 30(2), 173–181.

Sadiki, L. (2015). Towards a 'Democratic Knowledge' Turn? Knowledge Production in the Age of the Arab Spring, *The Journal of North African Studies*, 20(5), 702–721. doi:10.1080/13629387.2015.1081461.

Said, E. (1978). *Orientalism*. New York: Pantheon Books.

Salaita, S. (2015). *Uncivil Rites: Palestine and the Limits of Academic Freedom*. Chicago, IL: Haymarket Books.

Salaita, S. (2015). Steven Salaita: I Will Always Condemn Injustice, No Matter the State of My Employment, *The Nation*. Accessed 10 September 2019 at: www.thenation.com/article/steven-salaita-i-will-always-condemn-injustice-no-matter-the-state-of-my-employment/.

Salaita, S. (2019). @stevesalaita. Accessed 22 July 2023 at: https://twitter.com/stevesalaita/status/1142229344766582784.

Saliba, I. (2018). Academic Freedom in the MENA Region: Universities under Siege, IEMed Mediterranean Yearbook 2018, Accessed 15 October 2022 at: www.iemed.org/publication/academic-freedom-in-the-mena-region-universities-under-siege/.

Sayer, D. (2014) Five Reasons Why the REF Is Not Fit for Purpose, *The Guardian* 15 December 2014. Accessed 20 August 2015 at: www.theguardian.com/ higher-education-network/2014/dec/15/research-excellence- framework-five-reasons-not-fit-for-purpose. Cited in Stanonis, A. J. (2016). No Time for Muses: The Research Excellence Framework and the Pursuit of Mediocrity, in C. Hudson and J. Williams (eds.), *Why Academic Freedom Matters: A Response to Current Challenges*. London: Civitas.

Sbaiti, N. (2010). If the Devil Taught French: Strategies of Language Learning in French Mandate Beirut (pp. 59–83). In O. Abi-Nershed (ed.), *Trajectories of Education in the Arab World: Legacies and Challenges*, London: Routledge, published in association with contemporary Arab Studies, Georgetown University.

School of Advanced Study, University of London (2021). Academic Freedom and Internationalisation Working Group. Accessed 15 October 2022 at: https://hrc.sas.ac.uk/networks/academic-freedom-and-internationalisation-working-group.

Scott, J. W. (2019). *Knowledge, Power and Academic Freedom*. New York: Columbia University Press.

Shahvisi, A. (2018). From Academic Freedom to Academic Responsibility: Privileges and Responsibilities Regarding Speech on Campus: The Value and Limits of Academic Speech (1st edn.). In D. A. Downs and C. W. Surprenant (eds.), *Philosophical, Political, and Legal Perspectives*. London and New York: Routledge.

Shapin, S. (1994). *A Social History of Truth*. Chicago, IL: University of Chicago Press.

Singer, P. (1993). *Practical Ethics* (2nd edn.). Cambridge, UK: Cambridge University Press.

Spannagel, J. Kinnselbach, K., and Saliba, I. (2020). The Academic Freedom Index and Other New Indicators Relating to Academic Space: An Introduction. V Dem-Institute. Accessed 15 October 2022 at: https://v-dem.net/media/publications/users_working_paper_26.pdf.

Staeheli, L., and Hammett, D. (2013). 'For the Future of the Nation': Citizenship, Nation, and Education in South Africa, *Political Geography*, 32, 32–41.

Stanonis, A. J. (2016). No Time for Muses: The Research Excellence Framework and the Pursuit of Mediocrity. In C. Hudson and J. Williams (eds.), *Why Academic Freedom Matters: A Response to Current Challenges*. London: Civitas.

Stone, G. R. (2015). A Brief History of Academic Freedom. In A. Bilgrami and J. R. Cole (eds.), *Who's Afraid of Academic Freedom*. New York: Columbia University Press.

Telegraph (2016). Trigger Warnings at Oxford Would Threaten Academic Freedom and Infantilise Our Future Judges. Accessed 22 July 2023 at: https://www.telegraph.co.uk/news/2016/05/11/trigger-warnings-at-oxford-would-threaten-academic-freedom-and-i/.

Teti, A., and Gervasio, G. (2011). The Unbearable Lightness of Authoritarianism: Lessons from the Arab Uprisings, *Mediterranean Politics*, 16(2), 321–327. doi:10.1080/13629395.2011.583758.

Thomas, G., and Pring, R. (eds.) (2003) *Evidence-Based Practice in Education*. Buckingham: Open University Press.

Thomas, R. (2018). *Questioning the Assessment of Research Impact*. Basingstoke and New York: Palgrave Macmillan.

Times Higher Education (2022). Free Speech Champions Seen as Fix for Academic Freedom 'Crisis'. Accessed 15 October 2022 at: www.timeshighereducation.com/news/free-speech-champions-seen-fix-academic-freedom-crisis.

Turban, J. L., Dolotina, B. L., and King, D. (2022). Sex Assigned at Birth Ratio among Transgender and Gender Diverse Adolescents in the United States, *Pediatrics*, 150(3), 49–54.

Turner, D. (2008). The Worldwide Transformation of Higher Education, *International Perspectives on Education and Society*, 9, 27–61.

Tuvel, R. (2017). In Defense of Transracialism, *Hypatia*, 32(2), 263–278.

Tzanakou, C., and Pearce, R. (2019). Moderate Feminism within or against the Neoliberal University? The Example of Athena SWAN, *Gender Work Organ*, 26, 1191–1211.

UCU (2016). *Chartermarks*. Accessed 21 July 2023 at: https://www.ucu.org.uk/article/8220/Chartermarks.

UCU (2017). *UCU Statement on Academic Freedom*. Accessed 22 April 2019 at: www.ucu.org.uk/academicfreedom.

UCU (2022). UCU House of Lords Briefing on Academic Freedom. Accessed 15 October 2022 at: www.ucu.org.uk/article/12368/UCU-House-of-Lords-briefing-on-academic-freedom.

UNESCO (1997). Recommendation Concerning the Status of Higher-Education Teaching Personnel. Accessed 22 April 2019 at: http://portal.unesco.org/en/ev.php-URL_ID=13144&URL_DO=DO_TOPIC&URL_SECTION=201.html.

UNESCO (2018). *UNESCO Study Report on Financing Higher Education in Arab States*. Beirut: UNESCO.

UNESCO (2023). *Global Flow of Tertiary Level Students*. Accessed 7 March 2023 at: https://uis.unesco.org/en/uis-student-flow.

University and College Union (UCU) (2012). *Survey Shows Bullying and Harassment Far Too Common in UK Universities*. Accessed 10 September 2019 at: www.ucu.org.uk/article/6383/Survey-shows-bullying-and-harassment-far-too-common-in-UK-universities.

University Business (2022). With Academic Freedom under Attack, How Does the U.S. Stack Up vs. Other Nations? Accessed 15 October 2022 at: https://universitybusiness.com/with-academic-freedom-under-attack-how-does-the-u-s-stack-up-vs-other-nations/.

Varieties of Democracy (V-Dem) (2022). Policy and Collaborations. Accessed 17 October 2022, at: www.v-dem.net/policy_collaborations.html.

Vora, N. (2019). *Teach for Arabia: American Universities, Liberalism and Transnational Qatar*. Stanford, CA: Stanford University Press.

Walsh, A. Brugha, R., and Byrne, E. (2016). 'The Way the Country Has Been Carved Up by Researchers': Ethics and Power in North–South Public Health Research, *International Journal for Equity in Health*, 15, 204.

Wasserman, G. (2017). *The Doha Experiment: Arab Kingdom, Catholic College, Jewish Teacher*. New York: Skyhorse Publishing.

Watermeyer, R. (2016). Impact in the REF: Issues and Obstacles, *Studies in Higher Education*, 41(2), 199–214. doi:10.1080/03075079.2014.915303.

Waters, J. L. (2016). Education Unbound? Enlivening Debates with a Mobilities Perspective on Learning, *Progress in Human Geography*, 41(3), 279–298.

Waters, J. L., and Leung, M. (2017). Trans-Knowledge? Geography, Mobility, and Knowledge (pp. 269–285). In H. Jons, P. Meusburger, and M. Hefferman (eds.), *Mobilities of Knowledge*, Knowledge and Space 10. London: Springer Open.

Weber, M. (1978). *Economy and Society: An Outline of Interpretative Sociology*. Berkeley, CA: University of California Press.

Weiler, H. N. (2009). Whose Knowledge Matters? Development and the Politics of Knowledge. Accessed 17 May 2019 at: https://web.stanford.edu/~weiler/Texts09/Weiler_Molt_09.pdf.

Whittington, K. E. (2019). Academic Freedom and the Scope of Protections for Extramural Speech, *Academe*, 105(1), 20–25.

Williams, J. (2016). *Academic Freedom in an Age of Conformity*. London and New York: Palgrave Macmillan.

Williams, J. J. (2012). An Emerging Field Deconstruct Academe, *The Chronicle of Higher Education*, 19 February 2012, accessed 22 July 2023 at: https://www.chronicle.com/article/deconstructing-academe/.

World Education News and Reviews (2018). *Education System Profiles: Education in the United Arab Emirates*. Accessed 21 August 2019 at: https://wenr.wes.org/2018/08/education-in-the-united-arab-emirates.

Young, M. (1971). *Knowledge and Control: New Directions for Sociology of Education*. New York: Collier MacMillan.

INDEX

abortion. *See* bioethics
academic appraisals, 79–83
academic freedom
   a brief intellectual history, 16–19
   conditions of, 92–94
   constructions and contestations, 24, 159–163, 177–178
   historical perspective, 3
   key legal and policy statements, 20–23
   meaning of, 1, 3–4
   qualitative and quantitative measures, 8
   relationship with conceptions of knowledge, 163–166
   as under threat, 1–2
   transnational theory of, 13–14, 159
   universalised position, 39
academics' responsibility, 24–26, 106, 161
activism, and knowledge production, 46–48
affect, 34–38
American Association of University Professors (AAUP), 17–18, 20–23, 160
American studies programmes, 53–55, 60–62
anonymity, 7–8
appraisals, 79–83
arts subjects, 68–72
audit culture, 79–83

behavioural science, 57–58
bias, use of systemic reviews, 45–46
   See also Western bias
bioethics, 118–120, 132–133, 171–173
Bourdieu, P. **135**, 154
Boycott, Divestment, and Sanctions (BDS) movement
   conditions of academic freedom, 92–94
   global awareness, 2–3
   national citizenship, 31–32
   power, knowledge and morality, 26–29
branch campuses, 92
British Canon, 145–148
   See also Western bias
Butler, Judith, 31–32, 91–94, 160–161

the 'Canon', 62, 145–148, 165–166
   See also Western bias
capital, 41–42, 43, 154
Centre for American Studies and Research (CASAR), 53–55, 60–62, 78–79

Centre for Research on Race in Education (CREE), 84
the civic university, 29, 64–65, 66, 88, 162
civility, 34–38, 148–150, 163
colonialism, 18–19
'colonising the mind', 48–49
confidentiality, 7–8
constructivist grounded theory, 6–7
controversial science, 118–120, 132–133, 171–173
the corporate university, 69–70
COVID-19 pandemic, 2
critical university studies (CUS), 65, 166–169

'death of knowledge', 165–166
death threats, 37–38
decolonisation discourses, 72–74
decolonisation of knowledge, 48–51, 164
delegitimation of knowledge, 156–157, 176
democracy and academic freedom, 56
democratisation of knowledge, 13, 140–142
development
   real-world applicability of research, 44–45
   social change, 50–51
   temporal and geographical positionality, 51–56
'dignity safe', 29–32
   complementarity of freedom and diversity, 16, 160–161
   psychologisation of society, 32–33
disability rights, 118–120
disciplinarity, 26–29
'disciplinary decadence', 58–59
   See also interdisciplinary approach
disciplinary quality, 145–148
diversity
   mangerialisation of, 83
   'oversensitivity', 16
   university initiatives, 144–145, 174
   See also freedom vs. diversity/inclusion
dominance, knowledge production, 49
Douglas, Mary, 48–49

education, value of, 42–46
emotion
   and civility, 34–38
   public performance of academic debate, 36–37
   as a social and political practice, 82–83

employability, in the knowledge economy, 42–46, 68–72, 175
employment
  job security of academics, 81, 162
  liberal arts and the 'knowledge economy', 68–72
  precarity as an academic, 38
  restriction of academic freedom, 81, 175
  skills, employment, and research assessment, 151–152
enrollment rates, university, 10, 74–79, 167–168
entrepreneurship, 42–46, 151–152
epistemic violence, 137
ethics committees, at universities, 95–98, 169–170
Eurocentrism, 129–130
euthanasia, 118–120, 132–133
  See also bioethics
exceptionalism, 87–89
expertise, 24–26, 140–142, 161
extramural speech, 17–18, 25, 106
extremism, 125–129, 172–173

forbidden knowledge, 12–13, 112–113
  agentic boundary work, 129–133
  conceptualising rationales of, 113–129
  controversial science, 118–120, 132–133, 171–173
  gatekeeper mechanisms, 171–177
  publishing and dissemination, 129–133, 173
  taboo topics, 116–118
Foucault, M., 135
free speech, 161
  contested understandings, 24–26
  definition and distinction from academic freedom, 3–4
free speech champions, 2–3
'freedom to'/'freedom from', 31
freedom vs. diversity/inclusion, 1, 8–9
  complementarity of, 16, 160–161
  contextualisation and preconditions, 29–32
  irreconcilability debate, 16
funding
  legitimate knowledge, 153–155
  research, 44–45, 64–85
  'strong research', 135–145

gender
  forbidden knowledge, 121–125, 172
  intimidation and threats against female academic, 37–38
  race and, 30–31
  real-world applicability of research, 44–45
  sexual harassment, 102–106
  vulnerable academics, 81
gender dysphoria, 120–121, 146
geographical positionality, 51–56, 60–62
global neoliberalism, 11–12

Global North
  development research, 44–45
  gender and sexuality, 129–130
  international division of knowledge labour, 156–157, 176–177
  missions of universities, 31–32
  understandings of academic freedom, 31–32, 177
  See also Western bias
Global South
  development research, 44–45
  drive for internationalisation, 11, 108
  funding and international partnerships, 153–155
  gender and sexuality, 130
  impact agendas, 175–176
  international division of knowledge labour, 156–157, 176–177
  marketisation of higher education, 11
  missions of universities, 31–32
global university rankings, 155–158, 176–177
governance of universities
  contextualisation of constraints, 91
  exceptionalism and context, 87–89
  funding, 64–85
  management and audit culture, 79–83
  procedural irregularities, 98–100, 170
  role of universities, 168–169
  unions, 85–87
grievance studies, 34–36, 68

habitus, 154
Hanafi, S., 153–154, 157
harassment, 102–106, 170
hate speech, 25, 133–134, 150
hegemony of knowledge, 49, 178
hierarchy of rights, 30–31
higher education. *See* universities
historical perspective on academic freedom, 3, 16–19
human rights, 20, 159–160
humanities subjects, 68–72
Humboldtian model of higher education, 17–18, 29–32, 41–42

identity politics, 24
ignorance studies, 113–115
inclusive knowledge, 29–32
indigenous knowledge, 142–143
individualisation of society, 32–34, 162
infanticide 118–120
  See also bioethics
infantilisation of students, 32–33, 162
insecurity, job, as an academic, 37–38, 81, 162
interdisciplinary approach, 5, 56–62
international division of knowledge labour, 156–157, 176–177

internationalisation of universities, 4–5, 10, 74–79, 108, 153–155
interpretivist paradigm, 7
intersectionality, 170–178
intimidation, 37–38
Israel/Palestine debate, 52–55, 120–121, 172

job security, as an academic, 37–38, 81, 162
Journal of Controversial Ideas, 129–133
justice, epistemic violence, 137
justified true belief, 136–137

knowledge
    constructions of, 136–137, 163
    contested understandings, 26–29, 40–48, 161–162
    inclusive, 29–32
    relationship with conceptions of academic freedom, 163–166
knowledge economy, 42–46, 68–72, 175
knowledge production, 9–10
    'death of knowledge', 165–166
    decolonisation, 48–51, 164
    democratisation, 13, 140–142
    Humboldtian model, 41–42
    implications for academic freedom, 62–63
    inter/disciplinarity, 56–62
    internal and external restrictions, 91–92
    positionality, 45–48, 164–165
    quality, 174–175
    role of universities, 4–5, 10, 64–66
    temporal and geographical positionality, 51–56
    'truth' and 'public good', 66–68
    See also forbidden knowledge; legitimate knowledge

lay expertise, 142
Lebanon
    compliance with US regulations, 108–110
    methodological approach to research in, 5–8
    Palestine/Israel debate, 52–55
    universities in, 10–11, 19–20
legal context of academic freedom
    mobilities, 110
    national, 106–108
    policy statements, 20–23
    transnational, 108–110
legal status, working in UAE, 37–38
legitimacy, 136–137, 161–162
legitimate knowledge, 13, 135
    the 'Canon', 62, 145–148, 165–166
    disciplinary quality, 145–148
    discourses of civility, 148–150
    funding and international partnerships, 153–155
    global legitimating systems, 155–158
    meaning of, 138

positionality, 138–143, 174
skills, employment, and research assessment, 151–152
social context, 173–174
university diversity initiatives, 144–145
LGBT
    forbidden knowledge, 121–125, 172
    publishing difficulties, 130–132
liberal arts, 68–72
libertarian perspective, 1, 8–9

madrasas, 16–17
management of universities, 79–83
marketisation of higher education, 11, 100–102, 163–164, 169–171, 176–177
masculinity, and sexism, 54
McCarthyism, 17–18
medicalisation of society, 32–33
mission of the university, 66–72, 166–167
mobilities
    legal regulation, 110
    state and international levels, 170–178
    transnational education, 78
moral virtue, 26–29, 161–162, 163
Murray, Charles, 126–127
Muslim Brotherhood, 128

Nandy, A. 49, 51
nation-state formation, 72–74
national citizenship, 31–32
national educational systems, history of, 18–19
national identity, 128–129
national legislation, freedom of speech, 20–23, 106–108
neoliberalism, 11–12
    diversity initiatives, 144–158
    as a framing discourse, 94–95, 169–170
    marketisation of higher education, 11, 100–102, 163–164, 169–171, 176–177
    skills and employment, 42–46, 175

objective truth, 68
offshore campuses, 92
online teaching, 2
organisational culture, 79–83
'oversensitivity', 16, 32–33, 150
Oxbridge, 17–18, 29–32, 160

Palestine/Israel debate, 52–55, 120–121, 172
participation rates, university, 10, 74–79, 167–168
patriarchy
    decolonisation discourses, 72–74
    race and gender, 30–31
policy statements, academic freedom, 20–23
political economy of knowledge production, 175–176

positionality
    as academics, 38
    decolonisation of knowledge, 48–51
    forbidden knowledge, 120–121
    geographical, 51–56, 60–62
    knowledge production, 46–48, 164–165
    legitimate knowledge, 138–143, 174
    race, 139–140, 164–165
    temporal, 51–56
power, 26–29, 34–38, 161–162
precarity, 38
privilege, and responsibility, 26, 28
pro life/pro choice, 118–120
    See also bioethics
psychologisation of society, 32–34, 162
public good
    contested understandings, 25–26
    role of universities, 66–68
public knowledge, 46–48
public performance of academic debate, 36–37
publishing forbidden knowledge, 129–133, 173

qualitative measures, academic freedom, 8
qualitative research, 147
quality, knowledge production, 44–45, 174–175
quantitative measures, academic freedom, 8
quantitative research, 147

race
    decolonisation discourses, 72–74
    ethnic minority academics, 140
    forbidden knowledge, 125–129, 172–173
    funding of research, 84
    gender and, 30–31
    positionality, 139–140, 164–165
    real-world applicability of research, 44–45
    transracialism, 117
    white researchers, 51, 139–140
rape threats, 37–38
rationality
    civility, 34–38
    knowledge production, 46–48
real-world applicability of research, 44–45
religion, 125–129, 172–173
remote learning, 2
research
    fear of the mis/application of research findings, 113–115
    funding, 44–45, 64–85
    methodological approach, 5–8
    role of universities, 168–169
    skills, employment, and research assessment, 151–152
    'strong research', 135–145
Research Evaluation Framework (REF), 152, 170–178
research funding councils, 92

responsibility, 24–26, 106, 161
retirement, taking early retirement, 82
right to life, 118–120
    See also bioethics

safe spaces, 32–33
Said, Edward, 140
Salaita, Stephen, 149
scholars. *See* academics' responsibility
sciences, technology, engineering, maths and medicine (STEMM), 144–145
Scientific Women's Academic Network (SWAN), 144–158
security, 125–129, 172–173
self-censorship
    ethnic minority academics, 140
    forbidden knowledge, 123–125
    hostile environments, 102–106, 170
    literature on academic freedom, 24
    students, 100–102, 170
    vulnerabilities, 170
seniority of academics, 81, 162
sexism, and masculinity, 54
sexual harassment, 102–106, 170
sexuality
    forbidden knowledge, 121–125, 172
    and transracialism, 117
Singer, Peter, 129–133
skills and employment, 42–46, 175
'snowflakes', 32–33, 150
social change, 50–51
social justice, 34–36
social media, 82
social science subjects, 68–72
state-imposed constraints on research, 92
'strong research', 135–145
students
    infantilisation of, 32–33, 162
    self-censorship, 100–102, 170
    as university customers, 100–102, 170
systemic reviews (SRs), 45–46

taboo topics, 116–118
    See also forbidden knowledge
temporal positionality, 51–56
tenure, job security of academics, 81, 162
therapeutic turn in higher education, 32–33
transnational production of knowledge
    legitimate knowledge, 155–158
    methodological approach, 5–8
    role of the university, 166–169
    shifting conceptions of academic freedom, 159–163
transnational theory of academic freedom, 13–14, 159
transracialism, 117
transsexual, 120–121

Index

truth
  contested understandings, 25
  Humboldtian model, 41–42
  interdisciplinary approach, 56–62
  as justified true belief, 136–137
  legitimate knowledge, 138
  positionality, 161–162
  role of universities, 66–68

UAE
  forbidden knowledge, 12–13
  legal status of academics in, 37–38
  methodological approach to research in, 5–8
  mobility restrictions, 170–178
  transition to knowledge-based economy, 42–46, 64–66
  universities in, 10–11, 19–20
UK
  conception of academic freedom, 160
  methodological approach to research in, 5–8
  national legislation, 106–108
  Research Evaluation Framework (REF), 152, 170–178
  systemic reviews, 45–46
  temporal and geographical positionality, 51–56
  universities in, 17–18
uncertainty, knowledge production, 41–42
unions, at universities, 85–87
universities
  a brief intellectual history, 16–19
  the civic university, 29, 64–65, 66, 88, 162
  contextualisation and preconditions, 29–32
  diversity initiatives, 144–145, 174
  global university rankings, 155–158
  internationalisation of, 4–5, 10, 74–79, 153–155
  participation rates, 10, 74–79, 167–168
  public sphere for debate, 11

universities, role of
  contextualising academic freedom, 166–169
  (de-)constructing the nation, 72–74
  exceptionalism and context, 87–89
  governance and funding, 79–87
  knowledge production, 4–5, 10, 65
  liberal arts and the 'knowledge economy', 68–72
  mission of the university, 66–72, 166–167
  transnational production of knowledge, 166–169
  'truth' and 'public good', 66–68
University and College Union (UCU), 22–23
university enrolment rates, 167–168
university ethics committees, 95–98, 169–170
university procedures, 12
US
  American studies programmes, 60–62
  conception of academic freedom, 160
  global compliance with US regulations, 108–110
  literature on academic freedom, 24
  methodological approach to research in, 5–8
  temporal and geographical positionality, 56

value of education, 42–46
'virtues', discourse, 36, 163
vulnerable academics, 81, 162

Western bias
  the 'Canon', 62, 145–148, 165–166
  disciplinary quality, 145–148
  geographical positionality, 51–56
  international division of knowledge labour, 156–157
  knowledge production, 62
  publishing forbidden knowledge, 129–130
  See also Global North
'woke', 36, 150
women's history, 57

Milton Keynes UK
Ingram Content Group UK Ltd.
UKHW050806250124
436659UK00007B/15